The Light

The Light Has Come

An Exposition
of the Fourth Gospel

Lesslie Newbigin

William B. Eerdmans Publishing Company
Grand Rapids, Michigan

Handsel Press Ltd, Edinburgh

Published by

Wm. B. Eerdmans Publishing Co.

255 Jefferson Ave. S.E., Grand Rapids, Michigan 49503

and

The Handsel Press Limited

The Stables, Carberry, EH21 8PY, Scotland

Printed in the United States of America

00 99 98 97   7 6 5 4 3

Library of Congress Cataloging-in-Publication Data

Newbigin, Lesslie.

The light has come.

Includes indexes.

1. Bible. N.T. John — Commentaries.   I. Title.

BS2615.3.N48   226'.5077   82-2449

ISBN 0-8028-1895-1   AACR2

British Library Cataloguing in Publication Data

A Catalogue Record for this publication is available from the British Library.

ISBN 1-871828-31-7

CONTENTS

Preface   vii
1. Overture (1:1-18)   1
2. The First Disciples (1:19-51)   12
3. The First Signs (2:1-22)   24
4. Nicodemus (2:23–3:21)   35
5. Jesus and John (3:22-36)   45
6. Samaria and Galilee (4:1-54)   49
7. The Son and the Father (5:1-62)   61
8. Bread from Heaven (6:1-71)   73
9. Light and Darkness (7:1–8:59)   91
10. Sight and Blindness (9:1-41)   117
11. The Good Shepherd (10:1-42)   125
12. Lazarus (11:1-57)   138
13. Prelude to the Passion (12:1-50)   149
14. The Supper (13:1-30)   166
15. Jesus and His Disciples (13:31–14:31)   175
16. Jesus, the Disciples, and the World (15:1–16:33)   195
17. The Consecration (17:1-26)   223
18. The Victorious Passion (18:1–19:42)   237
19. Reunion in Jerusalem (20:1-31)   261
20. Reunion in Galilee (21:1-25)   274

PREFACE

THERE IS A CONSTANTLY GROWING CATARACT OF LITER-
ature about the Fourth Gospel. More than any other book of the
Bible it fascinates and perplexes people who come to it from
every angle. The reader may therefore ask what justification there
can be for yet another exposition—especially by one who is no
expert in the field. The writer must attempt a brief *apologia*, even
if only to save the reader from mistaken expectations.

When I was made a bishop in the Church of South India I
was required to give affirmative answers to the following
questions:

Do you accept the Holy Scriptures as containing all things
necessary for salvation, and as the supreme and decisive standard of faith?

Will you be diligent in the study of the Holy Scriptures,
praying for a true understanding of them, that you may be
able to feed your people with the bread of life, to lead them
in accordance with God's will, and to withstand and convince false teachers?

The present book is simply a part of what has grown in the
course of trying to be faithful to those commitments.

It is of course perfectly possible and legitimate to study the
text from the standpoints offered by other commitments. During
my early years in India I shared with the monks of the Rama-
krishna Mission in the town where I lived in a weekly study group
on St. John's Gospel and the Svetasvara Upanishad, and I heard
the Gospel being interpreted through the categories of the Vedanta. It is also possible, and normal in the modern university,
to read the Gospel from the point of view afforded by commit-

ment to the methods, models, and axioms of post-Enlightenment historical science. The text is examined "objectively" in the sense that the student has no commitment to believe what it says, but studies it with the critical tools of modern science to discover how it was formed, what influences and interests shaped its formation at various stages, what were the original intentions of the writers and editors, and how it is to be related to other evidence from the time and place of its origin. This "objectivity" involves the absence of prior commitment to the truth of the text, but the presence of a prior commitment to the validity of the scientific method.

What is also possible is that the same scholar has commitments in both directions. If he is both a member of the community of a modern university and a Christian believer, he may have two pairs of spectacles, reading the text with one pair when he is at his prayers and with another when he is in his study or lecture room. Even the best bifocals do not altogether eliminate eyestrain. What is, of course, clear is that no one reads and understands any text except from within the commitments which are implied in his worldview. "Critical study" is never a value-free enterprise. No critical activity is possible except on the basis of assumptions which are—for the moment—uncriticized. The study of a text involves the interaction between the prior commitment of the student to the models by means of which he has hitherto grasped his experience, and the new commitments to which the text summons him by its opening up of new visions of reality.

It is therefore necessary that the prior commitments of the expositor be openly exposed so that the reader may know how to judge what the expositor is making of the text. I am a Christian believer, and I read the text of the Fourth Gospel as witness to Jesus Christ, the presence of God in human history and therefore the source of truth and life. By "the text" I mean the text as it stands, whatever conclusions I may reach about the way by which and the writers and editors by whom it was brought to its present form. And by "reading it as witness" I mean that through the study of the text I am brought under the power of the truth who is Jesus Christ and that in this way the stated purpose of the book is realized—namely, that I may believe and receive the gift of life in the name of Jesus (20:31).

But I am also a twentieth-century European with a university education and a long involvement with the world of Hinduism.

There are very large gaps between the cultural world in which the Gospel was written and both of these two worlds in which I have lived and now live. I have been trained in "modern" methods of critical study, and I feel the enormous power and rationality of the post-Enlightenment European culture of which I am a part. I have lived most of my life in India and feel the immense power and rationality of the Vedantin's vision of reality—in many ways much more powerful and rational than the "modern" world view. I cannot fail to be aware of the critical questions which are put to the text of the Gospel from both of these standpoints—very different questions in each case. I am also aware—as a Christian missionary—of the counterquestions which the text puts to both. In the present work I am concerned with the first of these two worlds: I am writing in the context of the "modern" Western world, as one who belongs to it, but who is also a Christian believer with commitments to the ecumenical fellowship of Christian believers in all cultures (including some for whom the "modern" world view is a bundle of strange myths). My task is to make clear to myself and (if possible) to others the word which is spoken in the Gospel in such a way that it may be heard in the language of this culture of which I am a part with all its power to question that culture.

This enterprise is possible only because of the promise recorded in the Fourth Gospel, a promise of which the Gospel itself is one of the firstfruits, that the Holy Spirit would—after the victory of Jesus over the ruler of this world—bring the words of Jesus to the remembrance of his disciples (14:25f.), bear witness to Jesus (15:26), expose the fundamental errors of the world (16:8-11), and guide the disciples into the truth about him and about the world (16:12-15). These promises are part of the preparation of the Church for its missionary encounter with all the varied communities and cultures of the world. These are real encounters by which both the world and the Church are changed. The attempt to expound the words and works of Jesus in the context of twentieth-century Western culture is part of the encounter. It involves listening to the questions which the "modern" world puts to the text and to the questions which the text puts to the world. The promise upon which this enterprise rests is made to the Church as a whole. The enterprise, therefore, has to be conducted in and with the Church and at its service, depending upon the faithfulness of God toward those whom the Church calls to this ministry of study and teaching.

These studies in the Fourth Gospel have developed over a period of thirty years in the course of which I have been asked to lead Bible studies—mostly in the context of the Church of South India. In preparing the present volume I have chiefly relied upon the following studies.

C. K. Barrett: *The Gospel according to St. John* (2nd ed.), 1978

Raymond E. Brown: *The Gospel according to John* (2 vols.), 1966

Rudolf Bultmann: *The Gospel of John*, 1964, E.T. 1971

Oscar Cullmann: *The Johannine Circle*, 1975 E.T. 1976

C. H. Dodd: *The Interpretation of the Fourth Gospel*, 1953

C. H. Dodd: *Historical Tradition in the Fourth Gospel*, 1963

E. C. Hoskyns (ed. F. N. Davey): *The Fourth Gospel*, 1940

R. H. Lightfoot (ed. C. F. Evans): *St. John's Gospel*, 1956

Barnabas Lindars: *The Gospel of John*, 1972

B. F. Westcott: *The Gospel according to St. John* (2 vols.), 1908

This minute fraction of the contemporary literature on the Gospel comprises well over 6,000 pages of print. There is hardly a verse on which critical questions—textual, grammatical, historical, exegetical—do not arise. Fortunately most of these do not seriously affect the meaning, though many do. Among scholars there is an enormous variety of opinions, and greatly respected scholars reach diametrically opposed conclusions at many points. There are very few "agreed results," for it is of the essence of the critical approach that it devours its products. But the critical questions must be honestly faced; to refuse to do so would be—in Johannine language—to walk in the darkness. On the other hand it is, I think, impossible to accept the assumption which often seems to be present in this enterprise, that "modern" scholarship is necessarily in a position to understand better than the original writer what really happened and what Jesus really intended. One is not impressed by the commentator who (having perhaps forgotten which pair of spectacles he is wearing) appears to treat the text as though it were an undergraduate's essay and reluctantly awards St. John a passing grade. What is necessary above all is to expose the presuppositions behind the questions so that there may be an open encounter between the ultimate commitments on both sides, between the word and the world.

If this were a critical commentary in the proper sense, and

if I were competent for such an undertaking, I would have set out at each point the various views, discussed them, and given reasons for my conclusions. The disadvantage of this (leaving aside the problem of sheer size) is that in the clash of rival opinions *about* the text, the reader fails to hear himself being personally addressed by the text itself. My purpose has been to hear for myself and to help the reader to hear the original word spoken today to the mind and conscience of the "modern" student. I have tried to weigh carefully all the arguments at each point and to reach the best conclusion I could. Having done so, I have put the arguments behind me and simply tried to state the meaning of the text as clearly as I could in the language of the world that I inhabit. The reader is, of course, entirely free to disagree with my conclusions and to go to the scientific commentaries in order to reach his own. The present attempt to expound the Gospel will fulfil its purpose if it helps to fulfil the purpose for which the Gospel itself was written (20:31). I have been told (by Bishop Stephen Neill) of his finding a copy of Barth's *Commentary on Romans* in which a student had scribbled on the last page: "Nun kann ich wieder predigen" ("Now I can preach again"). With no comment on that particular commentary I would be satisfied if one person was moved to say the same at the end of this one.

The English text which I have followed is that of the Revised Standard Version (1952). In a very few cases I have followed the margin. In one place (16:8) I have followed the marginal reading of the RSV (1971). None of the many proposed rearrangements of the text (apart from the omission of the story of the woman taken in adultery) has support in the early manuscripts, and none has won general approval. I have ignored them and taken the text as it stands.

As regards paragraphing, the circular, cumulative style of John's discourses makes it hard to decide where divisions should be made. I have taken the simple course and adopted the paragraphing of the RSV.

The frequent references to other parts of the Bible are an integral part of the exposition; I plead that they will not be bypassed. Citations from other books of the Bible are made in the ordinary way, those from other parts of the Gospel by chapter and verse only (e.g., 15:5), and those of other parts of the chapter under review by verse only (e.g., v. 5).

Phrases such as "the Evangelist," "St. John," "the writer,"

etc. are used indiscriminately to designate the person responsible for the text under review and carry no implications as to who that person was, and whether he was author or redactor. The question of the authorship of the Gospel is one on which the argument is voluminous, fascinating, and inconclusive. I have no competence to contribute to the discussion. As already stated, I have taken the text as it stands. But—without claiming for this position anything more than that it is possible and seems reasonable to me—I should perhaps state the belief about the matter which I now hold.

It is evident that behind all the four Gospels there is a quantity of traditional material based upon the memories of the original eyewitnesses and embodied in oral and written traditions which took shape and developed in different ways in the various centers of Christian life and teaching. The Fourth Gospel obviously draws upon this material and includes many sayings and incidents which also appear—in more or less similar forms—in the first three. Modern scholars seem to be moving to the view that the fourth evangelist did not have the present text of any of the first three Gospels before him, but relied on a version of the common tradition distinct from but not less trustworthy than those upon which the synoptists depended. The fourth evangelist gives evidence of accurate knowledge of conditions in Palestine in the time of Jesus, and his accuracy about matters of local detail has not been disproved. While he is more concerned to draw out the theological meaning of the things he records than to place them in chronological order, there is no reason to disbelieve the historicity of the things he records. If his purpose is avowedly theological (20:31), the heart of his theology is that the word became flesh—that is to say, became part of history.

However, the Gospel as we have it is not a mere collation of traditional material. It is the work of a powerful mind which has shaped the material into an intricately wrought and massively coherent pattern. Whose was this mind? The Gospel itself claims to rest upon the witness of one who was a close companion of Jesus, the "beloved disciple." In the final chapter (21), which seems to be an addition to the main body of the book, but to bear the imprint of the same mind or at least of the same school of thought, the writer uses the first person plural ("we know") to affirm on behalf of the community he represents that it is the beloved disciple who wrote—or caused to be written—what goes before (21:24). It seems reasonable to suppose that over a period of time, through many years of reflection, teaching, and preaching (to Jews, Greeks, believers, and inquirers), the witness of the beloved disciple has been developed and matured in the company of his friends and disciples; that the different units of teaching have developed to meet the needs of different teaching occasions; and that one of the company has been responsible for bringing the whole (or most) of chapters 1 to 20 into their present form; and that at a somewhat later date chapter 21 was added (either by the same writer or by another member of the company) from the same body of material. This addition must have been made sometime after the death of St. Peter—that is, after A.D. 65.

Who, then, was the "beloved disciple"? In view of the massive consistency with which the writer protects the anonymity of this witness, this is a question which a faithful expositor should perhaps decline even to ask. Among the various names which have been suggested, that of John the son of Zebedee still seems the most probable. But this is not the important matter. One should rather ask what is the purpose for which the evangelist both brings this witness before us and refuses to identify him by more than the repeated statement that Jesus loved him. (The suggestion that the beloved disciple is a figment of the writer's imagination does not stand up to serious examination.) The point, surely, is this: the one who wrote the words just quoted (21:24), affirming that his whole record rests upon the testimony of this disciple, also maintains a firm and consistent silence about his identity. The question to be pressed is not: "Who is the beloved disciple?" but "What is the purpose of this silence?", and the answer—in the light of the Gospel as a whole—is not far to seek. The silence is there precisely to invite us to listen to the word: "We know that his testimony is true." Like the other John at the very beginning of the Gospel, the first witness to Jesus, he is only a voice. The identity of the speaker does not matter: what matters is the witness he gives. "It is notorious," remarks Raymond Brown, "that many biblical scholars are also passionate readers of detective stories. The two interests come together in the quest for the identity of the author of the fourth Gospel" *The Gospel according to John*, p. lxxxvii). No doubt they do. But the Gospel was not written with this interest in mind. We are solemnly warned at the beginning and at the end of the Gospel that it has only one purpose—namely, that the reader should be confronted by the truth which is the presence of God himself in the "flesh" of Jesus. We are not intended to direct our curiosity toward the person of the witness, but simply to allow that of which he bears witness to be heard and believed. For his witness is true—the truth of God which is also the life of God.

An exposition of the Fourth Gospel must be judged by whether or not it enables that to happen.

It only remains for me to add that I am deeply grateful to my friend Verleigh Cant who, as a labor of love, converted my illegible manuscript into lucid type. I am much in her debt.

LESSLIE NEWBIGIN

1

OVERTURE
(1:1-18)

THE FIRST EIGHTEEN VERSES OF THE GOSPEL ARE USUALLY referred to as the "Prologue," but it would be more accurate to describe them as an overture. Like the overture to an opera they announce in brief form the great themes which will be developed as the story unfolds. Most scholars believe that these verses were added after the main body of the Gospel was formed. Certainly they can only be understood in the light of the later development of the themes which they announce—life, light and darkness, truth, glory. Yet no reader can fail to note how completely the prologue is integrated into the ensuing narrative by the central place given to the witness of John. There is no break, in the Gospel as it now stands, between verses 18 and 19.

1:1-5

In the beginning was the Word, and the Word was with God, and the Word was God. He was in the beginning with God; all things were made through him, and without him was not anything made that was made. In him was life, and the life was the light of men. The light shines in the darkness, and the darkness has not overcome it.

The gospel is news about a man called Jesus, and there were witnesses who had known him, seen him, heard him speak, and touched him (I John 1:1). These witnesses had gone everywhere telling the story of Jesus. But when the hearers—Jews, Greeks, sophisticated students of religion, and illiterate slaves—began to ask "But who is Jesus?", how could one begin to answer the question? That is the inescapable problem of the missionary. Ob-

1

viously the missionary can only begin by using words which have some meaning for his hearers. He has to begin by assuming a common framework of language, of experience, of inherited tradition, of axioms and assumptions embodied in the forms of speech. He can only introduce what is new by provisionally accepting what is already there in the minds of his hearers.

But what if the new thing which he wants to introduce is so radically new that it calls in question all previous axioms and assumptions, all inherited tradition and all human experience, so that even language itself cannot serve to communicate it? What if the new thing is in fact the primal truth by which all else has to be confronted and questioned? How do you begin to explain that which must in the end be accepted as the beginning of all explanation? That is the problem of the evangelist.

When we look at the four "gospels" we see that all take the ministry of John the Baptist as the historical starting point for the public ministry of Jesus. Mark does so abruptly, mentioning only that this was foreshadowed in the words of the ancient prophets. "The beginning of the gospel of Jesus Christ, the Son of God [as foretold by the prophet] . . . John the baptizer appeared . . ." (Mark 1:1-4). Matthew begins the story with Abraham, and Luke starts even farther back with Adam. John sees that even this is not enough to begin to say who Jesus is. Before Abraham was, before Adam was, before time was, God was. It was by God's word that all things came to be. All that is, is by God's word— for his word is not other than his deed. He spoke and all things were created, and by his word they exist. If we ask the fundamental question of the philosopher "Why is there not nothing?" the answer is that "in the beginning was the Word." The fact that there is "something" is not an afterthought or an accident. God's creative word, which is also his revealing word, was with him before time was. The creative word of God is God, for none but God can create. The revealing word is none other than God, for none but God can reveal God. But this revealing word is not an abstraction of the inquiring philosopher. The word is "He," Jesus, of whom we are about to speak. He, Jesus, is the one who is God's word, who is God, and who was with God from before time was. This is the one about whom we are to tell.

Only when the whole story has been told will the reader be able to understand what these words mean. But at the outset of the telling he must be alerted to understand that although the

2

story is about a man among men, occupying one place and time in the created order of time and space, the subject of the story is the one who stands beyond all time and space, the author of the creation of which he has become a part. To call him "the Word" does not by itself say all this. That title could evoke in the mind of the reader many different images: the creative word of Genesis, the word of God in the mouth of prophets and evangelists, the *logos* of the Stoic philosopher and of the various schools of thought which sought to use that word as a point of fusion between Greek and Hebrew thinking. Only when the reader has come to know Jesus himself will he be able to understand that it is Jesus who is the word, that in him all things were created and in him all things hold together (Col. 1:16f.), that he is himself the gospel which is preached, and that it is in his name "that there is life" (20:31). The opening words of the Gospel cannot by themselves say all this, but they can alert the reader to the fact that the story he is going to read has a meaning which will radically redefine even his most fundamental terms. Above all it will mean that the most fundamental of all words, the word "God," has to be redefined. It will have to be redefined in view of the fact that he—Jesus— was in the beginning with God and was from the beginning God, and that he is himself the word of God, a word which is not merely declaratory but creative and life-giving.

"All things were made through him, and without him was not anything made that was made." Jesus is the clue for understanding all that is, for "in him all things were created, in heaven and on earth, visible and invisible . . . all things were created through him and for him" (Col. 1:16). The dichotomies which dominated the world to which the Gospel came, and which still dominate much of the world's thought, are eliminated. There is no ultimate division of things into "material" and "spiritual." All that is has its unity of origin and purpose in Jesus.

"In him was life, and the life was the light of men." Because Jesus is the word of God, God in his self-revealing action, he is the bearer of the life of God. "For as the Father has life in himself, so he has granted the Son also to have life in himself" (5:26). But this life is not for himself but "for the life of the world," for Jesus has come to give "eternal life," "life in his name," to those whom the Father gives him. But this life is also light for the world. The coming of Jesus is the coming of "light into the world" (3:19; 12:46). The life of God given to men in Jesus—in his life, death, and resurrection and in the coming of the Spirit—is at the same time understanding of how things truly are. It is participation in the truth. These cannot be separated. The first act of God's creation was in the words "Let there be light," and when St. Paul describes what the coming of Jesus means, he says that the God who said "let light shine out of darkness" has shone in our heart to give the light of the knowledge of the glory of God in the face of Jesus Christ (II Cor. 4:6). The coming of Jesus is not an event which has to be subsequently interpreted. He is the bearer both of life and of light, and the two are not to be separated, for the life of God is also the light of truth.

But human life is not just the story of life and light. There is also death and darkness. This is a fact. If we ask "Why is there darkness?" we do not receive an answer. God did not say in the beginning, "Let there be darkness." He said, "Let there be light," and he "separated the light from the darkness" (Gen. 1:3f.). The darkness cannot be as such a subject for research; it is simply darkness. It is what confronts one who turns away from the true source of his being, tries to find its meaning elsewhere, and is thereby plunged into meaninglessness. But the light shines in the darkness. We know that there is darkness only when we look away from the light. The light does not eliminate the darkness, but it goes on shining. There is no peaceful coexistence of light and darkness. The business of light is to banish darkness, and darkness remains the background to the story which John will tell—up to the moment when Judas walks out of the light of the Upper Room into the darkness of the night (13:30), and right up to the final words of Jesus' consecration prayer: "The world has not known thee, but I have known thee; and these know that thou hast sent me. I have made known to them thy name, and I will make it known . . ." (17:25f.). The darkness does not comprehend the light, but also does not overwhelm it. The word has both meanings, and both are intended. The light which shone in Jesus, and which shines on as the name of Jesus is proclaimed throughout the world, is none other than the light of God himself, his first creation, the light that enlightens every human being (v. 9).

1:6-8

There was a man sent from God, whose name was John. He came for testimony, to bear witness to the light, that all might believe through him. He was not the light, but came to bear witness to the light.

We have been speaking of realities beyond the created world of time and space. We might almost be in the timeless world of the Upanishads. And suddenly we are hearing a very ordinary, matter-of-fact piece of human story. The words remind us of the opening words of a story in the Old Testament (e.g., I Sam. 1:1; Job 1:1). Indeed some scholars think that these were the opening words of the Gospel as it was before the material of the Prologue was added, an opening almost exactly the same as that of Mark. If this be so, it is an excellent example of something which is central to the whole purpose of the fourth evangelist. The timeless sayings of the Prologue are deliberately not separated from but intertwined with plain narration of history, because it is in this history that the eternal reality of God is present, active, and manifest. We are not dealing with an idealist philosophy for which actual happenings can be at best only illustrative; we are dealing with events of history, and therefore events belonging to a particular place and time, in which that which is before and beyond all time and place is present as the life and light of God himself.

The other three Gospels speak in some detail of John's ministry of preaching and baptism—a ministry which provided the context and starting point for the public ministry of Jesus. The fourth evangelist portrays John simply as a witness to Jesus. Jesus is the light itself; John is a reflection of the light. The prophets and psalmists of Israel constituted a long line of such reflectors, and their testimony will be referred to as the story of Jesus is unfolded. John is the last of this line. He points his hearers to Jesus (e.g., 1:29ff., 36ff.; 3:27ff.); Jesus draws his hearers to himself. But these hearers will in turn become witnesses through whom others may believe (15:27; 17:20; 20:31), for the purpose is that not some but all men may come to faith. This book in its final form is based upon the testimony of one of these witnesses (21:24), and its purpose is that its readers may believe that Jesus is the Christ, the Son of God, and believing may have life in his name (20:31).

1:9-11

The true light that enlightens every man was coming into the world. He was in the world, and the world was made through him, yet the world knew him not. He came to his own home, and his own people received him not.

5

John was a light, but only a reflected light. The true, the authentic, the real light was coming into the world. It is of this coming that the evangelist will write. He has already spoken of the one who is coming as possessing the life which is the light of men (v. 4). Now this is repeated with more precision: this light is the light which enlightens everyone. In what sense? There is a long tradition which understands this enlightenment as the inner illumination of reason and conscience, thus bringing it into line with Stoic ideas about the *logos* as something which indwells every human being, a seed within each one capable of developing into full understanding. More strangely still, it has often been assumed that this inner illumination is to be identified with the various religions of mankind. Nothing in the text suggests this. The text must be interpreted in line with the consistent usage of the evangelist throughout the Gospel. A study of all the texts where the word "light" occurs will show what this is (see 3:19-21; 8:12; 9:5; 11:9f.; 12:35f., 46). With the coming of Jesus "light has come into the world" (3:19). The coming of the light means judgment, because it reveals the fact that men love darkness rather than light (3:20). Apart from the light, men stumble, because they do not have the light in themselves (11:9f.) and do not know where they are going (12:35). Yet the purpose of this coming is not to bring judgment, but to create faith (12:46) and so to bring salvation to the world (3:17).

The presupposition of all this is that in fact Jesus is "the true light" and therefore the light which shines on every human being. There is no other light. There are not different varieties of light. There is only one light, namely, that which enables us to see things as they really are. And things really are as they are shown to be in the light of Jesus, because he is the word through whom they all came to be. It follows that all men, whether they believe or not, live under the light just as they live by the creative word of God. And thus it follows that when a person turns in faith to Jesus Christ he meets not a stranger but one whom he recognizes as the one in whom he was loved and chosen before the foundation of the world (Eph. 1:4).

Yet the incomprehensible fact of darkness still surrounds those who have turned to the light. The light shines in the darkness. He came into the world, and John was the herald of his coming. The world—not the created universe ("all things") of verse 3, but the whole human race which ought to have recognized the

6

light by which alone it lives—did not acknowledge him. And the darkness becomes still deeper when we remember that although all the world belongs to him who is its creator, yet one people had been chosen from among all the peoples to be his special possession (e.g., Ex. 19:5) and one place on earth had been chosen to be his special heritage, his holy land (e.g., Lev. 25:23; Jer. 2:7, 16-18; Zech. 2:12). The one true light came not merely "into the world," but to this place and this people specially chosen to be his own home and his own people. In this place and by this people he was rejected. Here the terrible paradox of human existence is seen in its most piercing reality. "Religion" in its purest and loftiest form is found to belong to the area of darkness. Not those who are blind, but those who confidently say "We see" are found to be in the realm of darkness (9:41).

And yet, as we shall immediately see, the light still shines and the darkness has not overwhelmed it.

1:12-13

But to all who received him, who believed in his name, he gave power to become children of God; who were born, not of blood nor of the will of the flesh nor of the will of man, but of God.

Rejection is not the last word. The first part of the Gospel (up to ch. 12) will record the rejection of the light by those who claimed to see (12:35-43). It will be followed by a section in which Jesus is alone with those who have come to the light (chs. 13–17). Darkness cannot have the last word because it is God who has said "Let there be light" and has put the darkness behind him. The word of God which is both light and life, both understanding and power, is the word of *God* and therefore not without effect. There are those who have received the word and who now believe in the name of Jesus. (There is a present tense at v. 12—"believe.") This believing "in the name," which perhaps echoes the language of baptism "in the name of Jesus," implies not only the assent of the mind but the allegiance of the whole person. Henceforth the life of those who believe is "life in his name" (20:37). It is God's gift to them that they become children of God. This is in no way an achievement of theirs. "Flesh and blood" cannot receive the word by its own wisdom or power (cf. Matt. 16:17). It can only be by an act of God himself, a new birth "from

7

above." As Jesus will tell Nicodemus, "That which is born of the flesh is flesh, and that which is born of the Spirit is spirit" (3:6). There is a fresh creative act when, in a world that is in darkness because men have turned away from the one true light, the *fiat lux* is spoken again, and men turn to the light and become children of the light. The coming of Jesus into the world of "flesh and blood" was the fresh creative act of God himself, and it has as its result the existence of a company of men and women whose life is a kind of extension of his, a new life which is no achievement of human desire or human power, but a sheer gift of God.

1:14

And the Word became flesh and dwelt among us, full of grace and truth; we have beheld his glory, glory as of the only Son from the Father.

"And the Word became flesh." In these five short words the central mystery which John will unfold is stated with absolute simplicity. It lies wholly beyond the power of flesh and blood, of the will of man, to pass from darkness to light, to lay hold of the life of God. But what is impossible has become a fact by a movement in the opposite direction. God himself in his creative and revealing being has become man and "pitched his tent" among us. The word used has profound reverberations in the Old Testament. The consonants of the Greek word are those of the Hebrew word *(shekinah)* which denotes the presence and glory of God. The "tent of meeting" was where God dwelt with his people and where his glory was seen (Ex. 40:34-38). The same glory had filled the temple of Solomon (I Kings 8:10f.). Ezekiel had seen the glory depart from the Temple (Ezek. 11:22f.), but Israel had lived by faith in the promise: "I come and I will dwell in the midst of you, says the Lord" (Zech. 2:10). Now those who have been given the gift of new life from God (v. 13) bear witness that they have seen the promise fulfilled. They have seen the glory of God tabernacling among men. In the synoptic Gospels this vision of glory is concentrated in the story of the transfiguration and the disciples foolishly propose to erect tents on the spot (Matt. 17:4; Luke 9:33). The fourth evangelist sees the whole ministry as a "tabernacling" in which the disciples again and again had glimpses of his glory (2:11; 11:40).

But this glory was "glory as of the only Son from the Fa-

8

ther." It was in no way the kind of glory which the unconverted "flesh" expects to witness in a manifestation of the divine. Jesus does not receive glory from men (5:41). He does not seek his own glory, but only the glory of his Father, and it is from the Father that he receives glory (5:44; 7:18; 8:49f.). It is not by a masterful exercise of power to control the world's affairs but by the humble obedience of a son, even to the point of death, that Jesus glorifies God and is glorified by God (12:27-33; 13:31f.; 17:1, 4f.). In this manifestation of the true glory, all the pagan conceptions of glory are eliminated. The true glory of God will be seen in the figure of a slave humbly washing the feet of his disciples, and finally offering up life itself in obedience to his Father's will. The glory is not his own; it is given by the Father to whom alone he gives glory. Not the self-glorification of a supreme monad which egocentric man fashions in his own image, a celestial reflection of man's own self-glorification, but the ceaseless and limitless giving of love and honor to the other within the being of the one God—this alone is the true glory.

And "we"—those who have been born anew by the power of God—have seen this, "full of grace and truth." Over and over again the saints of Israel had testified that the Lord is "abounding in steadfast love and faithfulness" (Ex. 34:6); and the community of the new birth echoes these words as it seeks to bear witness to what it has seen. "Grace" is a very precious word to St. Paul, but in the Fourth Gospel it appears only in these verses. When Jesus speaks in this Gospel, he speaks of "life," but for the grateful believer this life of God is grace. This life, we have learned, is also light, and "grace and truth" are perhaps "life and light" seen from the point of view of the believer. But "truth" in the Fourth Gospel and in the Old Testament is more than the correspondence of words with facts. In the Old Testament the primary reference is to God's faithfulness, so that "grace and truth" means God's faithfulness to his covenant of mercy. In St. John "truth" carries over something of this Old Testament meaning, but has also the meaning of "real" and "authentic," as opposed to that which is only the shadow. None of these shades of meaning can be excluded from this very compressed statement. In Jesus believers have seen that which Moses longed to see but could not see face to face (Ex. 33:18-23), have seen what Moses could only hear proclaimed (34:6), the true glory of God who is alone the fullness of steadfast love and faithfulness.

This, then, the "flesh" of Jesus, the concrete humanity of a man of a certain time and place, is the actual presence of the word through whom all things were made, who was from the beginning with God, and who was and is God. This is the story which is to be told, and these are the witnesses who can testify that they have seen in flesh and blood what flesh and blood cannot see.

1:15-18

(John bore witness to him, and cried, "This was he of whom I said, 'He who comes after me ranks before me, for he was before me.' ") And from his fulness have we all received, grace upon grace. For the law was given through Moses; grace and truth came through Jesus Christ. No one has ever seen God; the only Son, who is in the bosom of the Father, he has made him known.

Once again we are reminded that the first of the witnesses is John the Baptist. His loudly proclaimed testimony, which will later be recorded (v. 30), is here referred to in the past tense because the Prologue is an overture to the whole story. This reference is parallel to the reference in the Epilogue to the witness of the beloved disciple (21:24). These two, both—perhaps—named John, stand at the beginning and end of the story as representatives of the whole body of witnesses who are referred to in verses 14 and 16. On the plane of history Jesus comes after John, and was in fact one of those who received John's baptism. But in reality he is the one who was with God in the beginning. This verse is not an interpolation but an essential part of the construction of the Prologue designed to show that the story to be told is both part of the story of God's dealing with Israel and the story of the unveiling of God's eternal being and will from before and beyond all time and place.

The incarnation of the word is part of history, and therefore there is a before and an after. John the Baptist is the last link in the chain of prophecy that stretches back to Moses. These were all witnesses to Christ in that they were true children of Abraham who were not content with the world as they found it, but looked for the revealing of God's righteous rule in the midst of history (Heb. 11:10). Now—after the coming of the word made flesh— there are witnesses of another kind. These ("we all") bear witness that what the prophets longed for has happened. God's glory has

been revealed, full of grace and truth—so full, indeed, that the whole community of believers is caught up in a chain-reaction of grace, grace becoming the opportunity for more grace so that they are together "filled with all the fulness of God" (Eph. 3:19).

This was something that the law—good gift as it was—could not accomplish. Once again there is a contrast between before and after. Moses had asked to see God, and God had given him the Torah—the gracious and true teaching that was to guard and guide Israel. This was a good gift, but it was not the life of God himself. It had "but a shadow of the good things to come," not the substance (Heb. 10:1; Col. 2:17). It was a "custodian until Christ came" (Gal. 3:24). It promised life (Deut. 30:16) but it could not give life (Rom. 7:10). Only God himself who is life and light can give life and light. "We all"—the whole community which has been enabled by the new birth from above to receive him—bear witness that the life and light of God himself, God who is "abounding in steadfast love and faithfulness," has come through Jesus Christ. And so, for the first time, the full name and title of him who is the word made flesh is given in solemn continuation and contrast with the name of Moses.

Moses had longed for the vision of God, but was told that he could see only God's back as he passed by, "for man shall not see me and live" (Ex. 33:18-23). Jesus, who "was in the beginning with God," is in the bosom of the Father. He therefore, and he alone, is able to make God known. Jesus himself will reaffirm this in his dialogue with the Jews (6:46), and when his disciple pleads "Show us the Father and we shall be satisfied," will answer "He who has seen me has seen the Father" (14:8f.). The Prologue thus ends with what is in effect a restatement of its opening. Jesus *is* God's word. There is, therefore, only one way to know God, and that is to attend to his word. All men share the longing to know the ultimate secret of their life. Without this they are in darkness. The "good news" which John is about to tell is that the light, the only light there is, has come into the world, that the word of God has become flesh in the man Jesus Christ, and that here, therefore, in this life, God has made himself fully known. For the beloved Son, who is the word of God, is God, and only God can make God known.

11

2

THE FIRST DISCIPLES
(1:19-51)

1:19-23

And this is the testimony of John, when the Jews sent priests and Levites from Jerusalem to ask him, "Who are you?" He confessed, he did not deny, but confessed, "I am not the Christ." And they asked him, "What then? Are you Elijah?" He said, "I am not." "Are you the prophet?" And he answered, "No." They said to him then, "Who are you? Let us have an answer for those who sent us. What do you say about yourself?" He said, "I am the voice of one crying in the wilderness, 'Make straight the way of the Lord,' as the prophet Isaiah said."

The gospel is—by definition—news. It is something new. When we are confronted by something new we can only grasp it by trying to relate it to what we already know. This may be less or more difficult. Some "news" is quickly seen to be not so new after all; it is a foreseeable development of the existing situation. Some news is more startling. We could not have expected it. But now that it has happened we set to work to integrate it into what we already know, so that it does not totally upset our previous way of understanding things.

So "the gospel" has to be integrated into the general experience, particularly the religious experience, of mankind. We have to show that it has a place in the whole seamless fabric of human experience. We try to make our theology "contextual." In our evangelism we try to "begin where people are." We look for "points of contact." And to question this seems preverse—unless the newness of the gospel is so radical that it calls for a total reconstruction of belief.

John, like the synoptics and Acts (e.g., Acts 1:22; 10:37;

13:24), sees the mission of John the Baptist as "the beginning of the gospel" (Mark 1:1). He therefore begins with an exposition of the witness of John to Jesus which raises at the outset the problem of the "point of contact."

In the Fourth Gospel "the Jews" represent the world, and especially the religious world, organized and established apart from faith in Jesus. In the drama of the Gospel they represent the fact that "religion is unbelief" (Barth). (It is an appalling illustration of the demonic power of religion as unbelief that for so many centuries the treatment of the Jews in the Fourth Gospel has been taken as an excuse for anti-Semitism. In fact, of course, the Church should have recognized and must recognize today in the portrait of the Jews a portrait of itself.) "The Jews," then, exercising their proper responsibilities as guarantors of the tradition, send qualified persons to ask the Baptist "Who are you?" There are already in the revealed traditions categories by which John's mission could be understood. This "understanding" would thus be a "grasping" because it would put John's mission in a place where the guardians of the tradition would know how to handle it.

John disclaims totally all the three places suggested. He is not the promised Messiah. He is not Elijah who was to herald the dread Day of the Lord (Mal. 4:5). He is not the prophet like Moses who would speak God's word to the people (Deut. 18: 15-18). There are no slots prepared for him in God's ordering of the world as they understand it. So "Who are you? Let us have our answer for those who sent us." The question is not academic: it is urgent and practical. One must know how to act.

"I am the voice of one crying in the wilderness, 'Make straight the way of the Lord.' " He is only a voice; it is futile to try to get hold of the person behind the voice and fix him in a place in your scheme of things. There is nothing there for you to get hold of. The speaker has no importance. He is not one of the *dramatis personae*. You must just listen to the voice.

When you do you will find that the words do not enable you to fix the speaker in his context. His voice is the voice of scripture—of scripture as the promise of God. It speaks (or sings) of the still awaited presence of the Lord. It forbids you to try to file the word away in one of your already well-organized categories. It requires you to look up, listen, wait for the one who is coming.

Because we are concerned with the gospel, with something

13

radically new, this is the only possible attitude. The proper word is "witness." John is the first witness, and "witness" is the proper word because the function of a witness is not to develop conclusions out of already known data, but simply to point to, report, affirm that which cannot come into the argument at all except simply as a new datum, a reality which is attested by a witness.

1:24-28

Now they had been sent from the Pharisees. They asked him, "Then why are you baptizing, if you are neither the Christ, nor Elijah, nor the prophet?" John answered them, "I baptize with water; but among you stands one whom you do not know, even he who comes after me, the thong of whose sandal I am not worthy to untie." This took place in Bethany beyond the Jordan, where John was baptizing.

John's reply to the inquiry provokes a further question from the deputation. John has denied any independent significance to his person, and described himself simply as a voice. But he is not only a voice; there is the action of baptism. How is this to be explained?

Washing in water is a very ancient and widespread symbol of spiritual cleansing. It formed part of the regular ritual of the Jews as it does in many religions. But the Old Testament also contains promises of something to come which is more than recurrent ritual. The eschatological promises of Ezekiel 36 and Zechariah 13 link washing with water to the bestowal of the Spirit. John's baptisms in the Jordan are clearly outside the normal ritual of the law. They would seem, therefore, to suggest a link with these eschatological promises. But the Baptist disclaims all the possible eschatological roles. Why, then, the baptisms? It is a reasonable question.

John's answer once again opens the gap—the communication gap—between the well-mapped world of religion and the radically new reality which is breaking into the world. Symbolism is not identity. The sign does not guarantee the presence of the thing signified even though no communication is possible without signs. What is the relation between baptism in water and baptism in the Spirit? In the four Gospels and Acts this is a sharply posed question. The synoptics represent John as making the contrast from the beginning between his own baptism—in water—

and the baptism which is to come in the Spirit and in fire. They also show the closing of the gap when Jesus, in the act of accepting baptism in water, receives the baptism of the Spirit. The gap is closed by the concrete action of Jesus.

In the Fourth Gospel the same theme is developed in a slightly different way. The present saying simply states the fact of the gap. This baptism is simply baptism in water. It is a sign. The reality to which it points is still hidden. It cannot be searched out. It will (as the next paragraph shows) be revealed. Meanwhile, all that can be said of the reality is that it is immeasurably greater than the sign. The sign is only the humblest possible servant of that reality. But that is its service. It points away from itself to the one who is coming.

1:29-34

The next day he saw Jesus coming toward him, and said, "Behold, the Lamb of God, who takes away the sin of the world! This is he of whom I said, 'After me comes a man who ranks before me, for he was before me.' I myself did not know him; but for this I came baptizing with water, that he might be revealed to Israel." And John bore witness, "I saw the Spirit descend as a dove from heaven, and it remained on him. I myself did not know him; but he who sent me to baptize with water said to me, 'He on whom you see the Spirit descend and remain, this is he who baptizes with the Holy Spirit.' And I have seen and have borne witness that this is the Son of God."

From the negative we move to the positive. Neither John's person nor his action in baptizing is anything in itself. He is a voice. It is a sign. Both direct attention away from themselves to the one who is to come. John "was not the light." He came "to bear witness to the light."

This witness is now positively stated, solemnly concluded with the words: "I have seen and have borne witness. . . ." The man Jesus, whom John sees "coming toward him," is revealed as the one who is to come. This is strictly defined as revelation. It is not the result of a human act of recognition. "I myself knew him not" is twice repeated in contrast to the central affirmation of divine revelation: "He who sent me said to me. . . ."

In the synoptics there is ambiguity about John's knowledge of Jesus. Luke emphasizes that the two were related and Matthew describes John as recognizing Jesus and protesting at the impropriety of his submitting to baptism. But both also report that John sent from prison to ask whether or not Jesus was the coming one (Matt. 11:2-6; Luke 7:13-23). In the Fourth Gospel this ambiguity is replaced by a firm theological interpretation: John did not know, but it was revealed to him. To know that the carpenter's son from Nazareth is the Son of God is not something of which "flesh and blood" is capable. It can only be "given by my Father" (cf. Matt. 16:17). This knowledge can only be a gift, never an achievement. Without this gift the person of Jesus can only be a cause of scandal—as is made clear in the "punch line" of Jesus' reply to John in the synoptic record (Matt. 11:6; Luke 7:23).

This gift of revelation is a free work of the Spirit. And John has received the revelation by the manifest work of the Spirit in the baptism of Jesus. According to all the four Gospels and Acts (e.g., Acts 1:22 and 10:37) the baptism of Jesus by John marked the beginning of his ministry. John's teaching and baptism looked forward to the coming eschatological gift of the Spirit. His baptism in water was a sign pointing away from itself to that. Jesus accepted the sign. As a son of Israel, "looking for the consolation of Israel," he heard the message of John as a call from the one whom he knew in the profoundest intimacy as "Father." But this unique intimacy in no way removed him from solidarity with his people. As one who took as his own the sin of his people, as one of a multitude turning to God in repentance and hope, Jesus presented himself before John to receive the baptism which was a sign of that cleansing from sin which was promised by the power of the Spirit. He accepted the sign. And in that act the sign and the thing signified met. Jesus was anointed by the Spirit. He heard in his ears words that echoed the word of the Lord: "Behold my servant, whom I uphold, my chosen, in whom my soul delights. I have put my Spirit upon him, he will bring forth justice to the nations" (Isa. 42:1)

What happened is described with the visual image of the dove. Mark and Matthew say that Jesus saw the dove. Luke is silent as to who was the witness. In the Fourth Gospel the Baptist says: "I saw." John's position as the first witness is thus affirmed. Only the action of the Spirit can reveal who Jesus is. In the most fundamental sense it is the Spirit who is the witness (cf. 15:26). But through the action of the Spirit there are those who became "also" witnesses (15:27), and among those John the Baptist is the first. Because of the manifest action of the Spirit he can and must bear witness that Jesus is the Son of God and that he is the one who will fulfil the eschatological promise of baptism not just with water but "with the Holy Spirit."

Human wisdom is incapable of arriving at this knowledge because all human wisdom is in the grip of "the sin of the world." This single complex and yet terribly monolithic reality (not sins but sin) makes it impossible that we should be able to extrapolate from our human wisdom so as to arrive at the true knowledge of God. If we are to know God as he truly is, know him in the intimacy of personal communion, know him with the intimacy with which Jesus knew the Father, then the "sin of the world" has somehow to be taken away.

To take away sin is, of course, the purpose of the whole vast apparatus of ritual sacrifice. At the very heart of the religion of Israel was the ritual slaying of a lamb whose blood, smeared on the doorpost, would deliver the household from the destroying evil (Ex. 12) In Jesus' time the slaying of the paschal lamb had acquired a sacrifical significance, and Jesus himself associated his death with the Passover. The lambs slain year by year could at best take away the sins of the worshipper, of the house of Israel. Jesus is the lamb who takes away the sin of the world in its single and fearful totality.

It can only be by revelation that God makes himself known, and there can be no revelation apart from reconciliation, for "the sin of the world" so shapes all human existence that a "god" extrapolated from unredeemed human experience is not God. But there is a real and reliable knowledge of God which depends upon an action of the Holy Spirit, by whom it is made possible to acknowledge that the man, Jesus of Nazareth, is himself the Son of God and the one who takes away the sin of the world. This is a true knowledge which bridges the "communication gap"— from the other side!

By the power of the Spirit God thus reveals himself in Jesus. But if it is God himself who is revealed, the revealer and the revealed are one, not two. Then we must say of Jesus that though he comes after John the Baptist, yet he was before him. The one in whom the eschatological promise is fulfilled can only be the one who was before all things and through whom all things were made. The word which is both revelation and reconciliation "was in the beginning."

The revelation is "to Israel" (v. 31). Israel was and is the original bearer of the revelation. The "blessing" which is both revelation and reconciliation is first of all for Israel. Nothing can alter that. Nothing that John will have to say about "the Jews" can alter that. "The gifts and the calling of God are irrevocable" (Rom. 11:29).

But it is "to Israel" for the world. The Lamb of God is to take away not just the sins of Israel but "the sin of the world." And so in spite of the curiosity of "the Greeks," the Son of man must be "lifted up" before he can draw "all men" to himself (12:20-32).

1:35-42

The next day again John was standing with two of his disciples; and he looked at Jesus as he walked, and said, "Behold, the Lamb of God!" The two disciples heard him say this, and they followed Jesus. Jesus turned, and saw them following, and said to them, "What do you seek?" And they said to him, "Rabbi (which means Teacher), where are you staying?" He said to them, "Come and see." They came and saw where he was staying; and they stayed with him that day, for it was about the tenth hour. One of the two who heard John speak, and followed him, was Andrew, Simon Peter's brother. He first found his brother Simon, and said to him, "We have found the Messiah" (which means Christ). He brought him to Jesus. Jesus looked at him, and said, "So you are Simon the son of John? You shall be called Cephas" (which means Peter).

John was not the light. He came to bear witness to the light. And the purpose of the witness was "that all might believe through him" (1:7). Whereas John's denials in verses 19-28 are directly addressed to "the Jews" his positive affirmations in verses 29-34 are without a specific addressee. They are simply "witness" addressed to any who will hear.

But this witness cannot remain a disembodied voice. The word of God does not return to him void (Isa. 55:10f.). Two of John's disciples hear and respond. We are introduced to the story of the beginnings of the Church.

The historical details as given here are not compatible with those given in the synoptics, and seem to rest on independent tradition. But the names are familiar—Andrew and his brother and Philip. And there is that "other disciple" who is unnamed but whom—in the light of the Fourth Gospel as a whole—we may perhaps identify with John. Perhaps—although this is far from certain—there is a suggestion that this unnamed disciple also brought his brother James. In that case we would have here the four disciples frequently identified in the synoptics as the inner core of Jesus' company.

The first response of the two disciples is to "follow Jesus." Here we are introduced to one of the fundamental words of Christianity. We shall see how this word, which—to begin with—seems to mean only a simple movement, is shown to have more and more profound levels of meaning until at the end Peter—who has been told "You cannot follow me now"—comes to learn what "following" really means and receives the definite summons "Follow me" (21:19). And at this final point, too, the same unnamed disciple is beside him (21:22). One could, in fact, describe the whole book as an exposition of what it will mean to "follow Jesus."

But that exposition is still in the future. It is hidden from the disciples and will be until after Jesus has completed his work and the Spirit "rests upon" the disciples as it did on Jesus. So Jesus' first word is a question: "What do you seek?"

How can we know what we seek until we have found it? Only if God has so made us that we have the sense of it and the longing for it before we have the possession of it. Only if, in truth, "all things were made through him" so that when he comes to us—even if we do not know him—he is "coming to his own."

It is the witness of John which directs the gaze of these disciples to Jesus, and his witness was itself the outflow of an action of the Spirit (vv. 32f.). God's initiative procedes and evokes our search. "You did not choose me, but I chose you" (15:16). But this does not mean that ours is a passive role. On the contrary we are questioned, challenged, called upon to take responsibility for the direction of our seeking. In all the accounts of Jesus' teaching and practice, this element of probing and questioning is prominent. "What do you think?" "What do you want me to do for you?" And so here at the very beginning the first recorded saying of Jesus is such a question. "What are you looking for?" It is a question put to everyone. At some point one has to answer it.

The answer of the disciples introduces us to another of the fundamental words of the Gospel. "Where are you staying?" is—at this stage—merely the request for an address. But we shall learn as we go on that the goal of all human seeking is that place where Jesus "abides" in the Father and the disciples "abide" in him (chs. 14 and 15). But this, too, is still beyond the horizon. Jesus is only "Rabbi"—one who can perhaps teach the way of God, not himself the one who *is* the Way.

Jesus answers, "Come and see." The knowledge of that true "abiding" which is the goal of the human journey can never come simply as a matter of theory. There is a vision *(theoria)*, but it depends upon first "coming." The challenge to faith has to be accepted. Faith is not a second-class substitute for knowledge: it is the indispensable precondition for knowledge. This is true in every sphere but supremely true when we are thinking of the knowledge of God. There is a personal invitation which has to be accepted on trust if we are to have the possibility of vision. The common idea in our secular culture that this "personal knowledge" is of an inferior validity to that which depends upon pure induction from the data of the senses, or upon extrapolation from the requirements of a logical system, has no foundation.

The two disciples accept the invitation and have their first experience of "abiding" with Jesus. What does "that day" mean, when the writer goes on to say that it was already 4 p.m. when they arrived? The Jewish day began at sundown: was it—perhaps—the eve of the Sabbath (4 p.m. on Friday), and was "that day" the following Sabbath during which it would have been forbidden to make the journey home?"

However it may have been, that first day of "abiding" with Jesus makes Andrew into a witness to Jesus. It is no longer a secondhand witness, dependent on that of John; it is based on personal experience: "We have found." But like so much that is based on personal experience it is defective. The one whom they have found is no longer merely a teacher. Nor have they yet seen "the angels of God ascending and descending on the Son of man" (v. 51). They report him as "Messiah"—the anointed King of Israel.

As the sequel will show, it is defective testimony. But it is not therefore ineffectual—quite the contrary. It brings to Jesus the one who is to become "the Rock" on which he will build his Church. Witness may be defective—indeed human witness to Jesus will always be defective. For how can any human word, however orthodox, convey the full reality of him "through whom all things were made"? But if it is witness to *Jesus*, then it is not without fruit. The promise that the word of God will not return empty is valid. For in fact it is God himself who calls these disciples and gives them to Jesus as his gift (see 17:6).

1:43-51

The next day Jesus decided to go to Galilee. And he found Philip and said to him, "Follow me." Now Philip was from Beth-saida, the city of Andrew and Peter. Philip found Nathanael, and said to him, "We have found him of whom Moses in the law and also the prophets wrote, Jesus of Nazareth, the son of Joseph." Nathanael said to him, "Can anything good come out of Nazareth?" Philip said to him, "Come and see." Jesus saw Nathanael coming to him, and said of him, "Behold, an Israelite indeed, in whom is no guile!" Nathanael said to him, "How do you know me?" Jesus answered him, "Before Philip called you, when you were under the fig tree, I saw you." Nathanael answered him, "Rabbi, you are the Son of God! You are the King of Israel!" Jesus answered him, "Because I said to you, I saw you under the fig tree, do you believe? You shall see greater things than these." And he said to him, "Truly, truly, I say to you, you will see heaven opened, and the angels of God ascending and descending upon the Son of man."

The first disciples have been drawn to Jesus not by his explicit recruitment but rather by a kind of inner necessity. In fact it is God himself who sends them, for "no man can come to me unless the Father who sent me draws him" (6:44). They are the Father's gift. The name "Nathanael" ("gift of God") is not found in the synoptic Gospels, but it properly applies to all of them. They all have this in common, but the ways by which they come are all different. Every true conversion is always an act of God, a miracle, something unique about which—when we look back— we can only express wonder at the ways of God.

Now, however, we see Jesus himself directly calling Philip, as the first disciples are said in the synoptic Gospels to have been called, and as Peter will—in the end—be decisively called (21:22). Philip obeys—and at once becomes a witness. As yet he knows Jesus only as the one of whom Moses and the prophets wrote. He has not yet "seen his glory" (1:14; 2:11). But because his witness—though inadequate—is witness to Jesus it bears fruit.

Nathanael is sceptical—like Thomas later. Intelligent scepticism is not condemned, for it is the necessary balance which preserves the distinction between genuine faith and foolish credulity. It is part of what it means to "walk in the light." There is always tension and conflict between the radical newness of the gospel and the necessary conservatism by which any human culture maintains its integrity. This is always a central issue in genuine missionary communication. The new is only received if it becomes part of the intellectual and cultural world of those who hear; yet it is not received unless that world is radically questioned. So scepticism is a legitimate starting point.

But it cannot have the last word, or nothing new will be learned. Philip's answer to Nathanael's scepticism is an echo of the earlier words of Jesus, "Come and see." The sceptic must suspend his scepticism if he is to have the opportunity to learn. The fact that Nathanael does so proves that he is not—like Jacob—a man of cunning and deceit, but a true son of Israel without guile. He is willing to "come to the light." His scepticism is not carried to the point where the light that he has is put under a bushel so that the light becomes darkness. He is willing to take the risk of faith and open himself even to a man from Galilee— the source of so many bogus messiahs.

So another of those whom the Father gives to Jesus comes to him. And the good shepherd knows his own, and calls them by name—the new name which corresponds to the reality. Here is a true son of Israel who is without guile. The foreknowledge of Jesus, who "knew what was in man" (2:24), has already recognized in Nathanael an example of the true Israelite (which seems to be the implication of "under the fig tree"), and this knowledge pierces the scepticism of Nathanael, who forthwith hails Jesus with the highest title which his Judaic faith could bestow.

Yet none of the titles so far given by these first disciples has grasped the full reality. With the deepest solemnity Jesus affirms that there are yet greater things which they will see. The use of the word *Amen* (verily) at the opening of an especially important saying seems to have been uniquely characteristic of Jesus. In the Fourth Gospel it is always repeated twice—"Amen, Amen." This Aramaic word, and the equally characteristic *Abba*, open for us a window into his deepest consciousness. He is the Son, and he is the one in whom the utterly reliable *Amen* of the Father is spoken.

At this climactic point all the titles so far offered by the first disciples are displaced by the one which Jesus seems to have used most consistently to describe himself—the title "Son of man." In its simplest sense this means a human being. But it has resonances given to it by the Psalm (8:5) which speaks of the son of man

22

being "crowned with glory and honor," and by the prophecy of
Daniel (7:1-14) which promises that universal dominion will be
given to "one like a son of man." The titles given to Jesus by
others—Lamb of God, Messiah, fulfiller of law and prophets,
Son of God—are neither accepted nor denied. They are quietly
displaced by this utterly simple, yet deeply mysterious self-
designation of Jesus as "Son of man." It is a self-designation
which challenges the hearer with the implied question: Who do
you say that I am?

This is a question put to all, and so the language changes
from the conversation with Nathanael to the solemn affirmation
that "You [plural] will see heaven opened, and the angels of God
ascending and descending upon the Son of man." Jacob—full
of guile as he was—had learned in a dream that the place where
he had camped for the night was in fact Beth-el, the place of
God's dwelling, the place where God is no longer hidden behind
the vault of heaven, but where there is actual revelation, actual
traffic between the world of men and the life of God. But that
was only a dream. Those who will come—like the first disciples—with their varied and stumbling efforts to say who Jesus
is, will see precisely in the Son of man, in his flesh, in his concrete
human being, the presence and the glory of God. This is to be
the theme of the Gospel—"the Word was made flesh, and we
beheld his glory." In these concrete events, which are to be nar-
rated and which happened in Judea and Samaria and Galilee in the
days of Pontius Pilate, they will witness the unveiling of the
hidden glory of God. The "Jesus of history" is the "Christ of
faith." This is the gospel of which these men are to be the first
witnesses because the Father has drawn them and given them to
Jesus for this purpose.

3

THE FIRST SIGNS
(2:1-22)

IT HAS JUST BEEN PROMISED TO THE DISCIPLES THAT they shall see "greater things." Now the fulfilling of that promise is to begin, though the full manifestation of the glory of God in Jesus is still in the future—at "the hour" which the Father will appoint. But even now Jesus will begin to unveil the glory which is promised. Jesus will do "the first of his signs."

Any unprejudiced reader of the four Gospels will be struck by the very large place given to what we usually call "miracle." Over half of Mark's Gospel consists of accounts of Jesus' "miracles." What we make of this will depend upon our whole understanding of the gospel. Contemporary Western Christianity has attempted a "spiritualization" of the gospel which is the corollary of the privatization of religion in post-Enlightenment culture. The gospel is understood to be concerned with realities which operate only within the mental world—the interior world of human thinking, feeling, and willing. From this point of view the idea that spiritual powers could operate directly to change the "material" world is excluded. Jesus could perhaps cure mental disorders but could not calm a storm or turn water into wine.

The biblical writers operate in a different world of ideas. For them this dichotomy does not exist. God is the creator and lord of all things visible and invisible without distinction. The gospel is about the manifestation of the sovereign rule of God in the life of the world, and it looks to the ultimate completion of God's total work—the creation of "new heavens and a new earth." The effective signs of the presence of this sovereign power in the ministry of Jesus form—therefore—a large part of the story which the evangelists have to tell. Without these it would simply not be the story they are telling—the gospel.

These happenings are "effective signs." They effect what they signify, and they signify what they effect—namely, the present reality of the gracious rule of God. They are thus the foundation upon which the sacramental life of the Church rests: the sacraments of the Church derive their character as effective signs from the ministry of Jesus in whom the rule of God was effectively present.

Of the two sides of the single reality—effectiveness and signification—the synoptic Gospels emphasize the first, and John the second, though neither to the exclusion of the other. In the synoptics the characteristic word for these happenings is *dynameis*—"powers," "mighty works." The emphasis is on their character as manifestations of effective power, though those who witness them are expected to penetrate behind this to an understanding of their meaning (e.g., Mark 8:14-21). In the Fourth Gospel the characteristic word is *sēmeia*—"signs." There is little emphasis upon their quality as miraculous, and the reader is directed rather to ask about what they signify.

In accordance with this emphasis John has selected out of the great store of the Church's memory seven "signs" which together illustrate the great themes of the gospel. But although these are described as "signs," there is no attempt to "spiritualize" them by filtering out the concrete details. On the contrary there is a meticulous insistence on the factuality of the story which is told, with all its details of exact time and place, quantity, and duration. The "spiritual" and the "material" are in no way help apart. John is writing about real things—water, wine, hunger and bread, blindness and sight, being dead and being alive; but in writing about these things he is writing about the presence of the living God in might and mercy. The detailed texture of these stories— in other words—is in strict correspondence with the total purpose of the book, which is to bear witness that the word has been made flesh, that this human life *is* the living word of God in action, that Jesus *is* "God's presence and his very self." These stories do not merely illustrate or symbolize divine actions. They are the record of divine action itself—a record on which we depend for knowing what divine action is.

In this perspective, therefore, true speech about God is narrative in form. Theology is history. A divorce between "the

Christ of faith" and the "Jesus of history" only arises if faith and history have first been separated. Christian theology has been so much dominated by pagan Greek metaphysics that it has lost the narrative character. The theology of the Gospels is typically in the form of parable—stories of concrete mundane realities in which the nature of God's rule may be grasped by faith. The main tradition of Western theology has seen this as something merely illustrative of truth which must be properly stated in abstract and timeless propositions. It may be the great service of the churches of Africa and Asia to help liberate Western theology from its captivity to Greek philosophy at this point.

Though witnessing the first of his "signs" the disciples "believed in him." This does not necessarily happen. Even the greatest of Jesus' miracles may lead to total rejection (e.g., 11:45ff.), or to an enthusiasm which fails altogether to grasp the meaning of the sign (e.g., 6:14f., 26). It is of God's gift to them that the disciples, those whom Jesus has called, are enabled through the signs to see his glory and to become believers.

2:1-11

On the third day there was a marriage at Cana in Galilee, and the mother of Jesus was there; Jesus also was invited to the marriage, with his disciples. When the wine failed, the mother of Jesus said to him, "They have no wine." And Jesus said to her, "O woman, what have you to do with me? My hour has not yet come." His mother said to the servants, "Do whatever he tells you." Now six stone jars were standing there, for the Jewish rites of purification, each holding twenty or thrity gallons. Jesus said to them, "Fill the jars with water." And they filled them up to the brim. He said to them, "Now draw some out and take it to the steward of the feast." So they took it. When the steward of the feast tasted the water now become wine, and did not know where it came from (though the servants who had drawn the water knew), the steward of the feast called the bridegroom and said to him, "Every man serves the good wine first; and when men have drunk freely, then the poor wine; but you have kept the good wine until now." This, the first of his signs, Jesus did at Cana in Galilee, and manifested his glory; and his disciples believed in him.

The first of the seven signs is the only one which has no parallel among the miracle stories of the synoptics. But it is entirely in the spirit of their record that Jesus is introduced at the outset of the story as one who shared in the joyful conviviality of a wedding feast. The wedding feast was an accepted symbol of the joy of God's reign. Jesus had likened himself and his disciples, in contrast to the ascetic followers of John the Baptist, to the guests at a marriage feast (Mark 2:18ff.), and he had likened the kingdom of God to a marriage banquet (Matt. 22:1ff.).

The guests, naturally, are drinking wine—"wine that makes glad the heart of man" (Ps. 104:15). Before the evangelist has completed his story we shall hear (what his readers already know) that wine has a sacramental meaning beyond its simple use in "gladdening the heart." We shall learn that Jesus himself is the true vine and that the wine of joy is in fact the blood of Jesus— the blood of the new covenant poured out for the life of the world. It is that alone which can provide joy in its fullness (15:11).

For—in fact—like every natural joy, "the wine failed." The natural joys of life which—truly understood and received—are a parable of the joy of God's kingdom, all come to an end. They do not themselves lead out into joy in its fullness. They fail.

In this crisis "the mother of Jesus" turns to her Son. Like the "beloved disciple," the mother of Jesus is never named in the Fourth Gospel. At the end, when his "hour is come," they will be united by his loving word from the cross (19:25ff.). But now the hour has not yet come. Jesus must look only to the Father whose will he serves; he cannot be at the service of his mother, though she is the closest to him in human terms. Until the hour when the blood of the true vine will be shed for the life of the world Jesus cannot become the instrument of any human purpose. His word to his mother is courteous but decisive.

Her response is the authentic response of faith. Her will is wholly subservient to his. "Do whatever he tells you." This is not apathetic resignation; it is expectant faith.

We are in the midst of an event which is under the law. Six great stone jars holding twenty to thirty gallons of water each stand there as a reminder of this fact. The water is for the rites of purification required by the law—part of the whole ritual apparatus which is provided to keep Israel a nation consecrated for the Lord in the midst of a world which is defiled by sin. Purification is a negative action. The water removes uncleanness but does not give the fullness of joy. What the law cannot supply Jesus will give—in superabundance. The action of Jesus is free, sovereign, and surpassing any mere rectification of a defect. It is the coming into experience of that which is really new—the "new wine" of the kingdom of God (Mark 2:22). It is an act of the overflowing majesty of the Creator.

The guests know nothing of the crisis and its solution. They only know that, contrary to the accepted pessimism of the worldly-wise, the best wine has come at the end. Only the servants who obeyed the strange command of Jesus know the secret—only they and Jesus' disciples. For them it was a first unveiling of the glory that would be finally revealed when "his hour" had come. "From his fulness we have all received, grace upon grace. For the law was given through Moses; grace and truth came through Jesus Christ."

One feature of the story calls for further comment because we shall meet with parallels to it as we go through the Gospel. Jesus is asked to perform a miraculous work, apparently refuses, but then proceeds to do it. He repels the temptation to turn stones into bread, but feeds the hungry in the desert. He repels the entreaty of the nobleman from Cana (4:46ff.) and of the Syro-phoenician woman (Mark 7:24-30) but proceeds to heal his son and her daughter. So in this story he repels the intervention of his mother, yet proceeds to act. He will not become the instrument of any purpose save that of his Father; but in sovereign independence and in his own time and way he will give signs which his disciples will recognize and which will enable them to believe. They will not find their petitions immediately granted, but as they go humbly and believingly along the path of obedience they are again and again "surprised by joy." Things happen which authenticate themselves as signs of Jesus' love and power. They have his signature. They manifest his glory. Those who are not in the secret do not know: they only know that the good wine has come at the end. But those who have put themselves under Jesus' orders know the secret, and they are enabled to believe and so go on following.

2:12-22

After this he went down to Caperna-um, with his mother and his brothers and his disciples; and there they stayed for a few days.

The Passover of the Jews was at hand, and Jesus went up to Jerusalem. In the temple he found those who were selling oxen and sheep and pigeons, and the money-changers at their business. And making a whip of cords, he drove them all, with the sheep and oxen, out of the temple; and

*he poured out the coins of the money-changers and overturned their tables.
And he told those who sold the pigeons, "Take these things away; you
shall not make my Father's house a house of trade." His disciples remembered that it was written, "Zeal for thy house will consume me."
The Jews then said to him, "What sign have you to show us for doing
this?" Jesus answered them, "Destroy this temple, and in three days I
will raise it up." The Jews then said, "It has taken forty-six years to
build this temple, and will you raise it up in three days?" But he spoke
of the temple of his body. When therefore he was raised from the dead,
his disciples remembered that he had said this; and they believed the
scripture and the word which Jesus had spoken.*

The happening now to be considered, unlike the previous
one, is recorded in all the three synoptic Gospels. However, there
are important differences between John and the synoptics at this
point. We may list six of the more obvious:

(i) In the synoptics the cleansing of the Temple occurs in the
last week of Jesus' ministry; in John it is the launching of the
public ministry.

(ii) John does not give the quotation from Jeremiah about
"a den of thieves"; he does not imply that there is a moral question
involved, i.e., that the traders are dishonest.

(iii) In the synoptics Jesus drives out the traders; in John it
is emphasized that he drove out the animals—except in the case
of the pigeons which, being presumably caged, he ordered to be
carried out.

(iv) In John Jesus is immediately challenged to "show a sign"
for his action; in the synoptics the demand for his "authority for
doing these things" is made but this demand is not directly con-
nected to this particular action.

(v) John brings into this context the saying about destroying
and restoring the Temple which in the synoptics occurs in other
contexts.

(vi) John makes a careful distinction at this point between
how the disciples understood Jesus' action at the time, and how
they understood it after the resurrection.

To bear these points in mind will help to sharpen our perception of how John understands this event. We shall return at
the end to the final point, which has relevance to our understanding of the whole book.

Since there is no reason to believe that Jesus twice drove the
traders out of the Temple, we have to conclude that John and the
synoptics cannot both be right about the placing of the event in

Jesus' ministry. We have to conclude, I think, that at this point—
as throughout the Gospel—John is organizing the material which
comes to him from the common tradition in such a way as to
bring out the meaning of the total "fact of Christ." In the synoptics the cleansing of the Temple is part of the final crisis in
which Jesus carries his challenge right into the heart of Jerusalem
at the Passover season. It leads on (in Mark) to the "cursing of
the fig tree" and to the parable of the Wicked Husbandman with
its closing sentence of doom: "He will come and destroy the
tenants, and give the vineyard to others" (Mark 12:1-12) John
sees this note of judgment as being present from the beginning.
From the beginning Jesus' coming is the coming of light into
darkness, of the Lord to his own who know him not. This note
is struck at the very beginning and is never absent as the story
unfolds.

We shall consider the story in the place and in the form in
which John tells it. As we do so, we shall find that his telling of
it illuminates elements in the synoptic narrative which might otherwise be obscure. The fact—for example—that the parable of
the Wicked Husbandman is immediately capped (in all three synoptics) by the words: "The stone which the builders rejected has
become the head of the corner" becomes luminous if we recall
the word of Jesus: "Destroy this temple, and in three days I will
raise it up" (2:19).

Jesus leaves the hill country of Galilee and comes down to
the lakeside town of Capernaum where—according to the tradition—much of his ministry was to be centered. He stays with
his mother and brothers and disciples "for a few days," but very
soon leaves the family and goes (presumably in view of v. 17
accompanied by the disciples) up to Jerusalem for the Passover.

The miracle at Cana had been a hidden sign for his disciples
only. Now he will proceed to a public action at the time and
place which are so central to the life of Israel that what is done
there must reverberate through the whole nation.

What is done is described—and this is characteristic of the
Fourth Gospel—with much more precise detail than in the synoptics. The merchants and the animals are driven out with a whip.
The money-changers' tables are overthrown and their coins scattered. Orders are given to carry out of the Temple the cages of
pigeons.

What reason is given? This was legitimate business. If the

provisions of the law were to be carried out, animals had to be available to the pilgrims coming from near and far. If the Temple tax was to be paid in the Tyrian coinage as required, pilgrims must be able to change their money. It is not suggested that the merchants were dishonest—as the synoptics indicate by their quotation from Jeremiah about a den of thieves. In place of this John reports Jesus as saying only, "You shall not make my Father's house a house of trade." Is there an echo here of the closing words of the prophet Zechariah which promise that "there shall no longer be a trader in the house of the Lord on that day" (Zech. 14:21)? Is this, then, a kind of messianic manifesto in action? It is difficult to interpret it otherwise, for it seems to announce not just a judgment upon corrupt and dishonest religion, but a judgment upon the whole apparatus of organized religion—at least in this form.

The disciples do not understand it so. Their perception is nearer that suggested by the synoptic record which sees the action of Jesus as in line with the great tradition of prophetic protest against corrupt religion. They remember one of the passages of Old Testament scripture which was to play an important role in the formation of the Church's understanding of Jesus. Psalm 69 portrays the suffering of God's righteous servant and is quoted several times in the New Testament. The words "Zeal for thy house will consume me" place the action of Jesus in that succession of prophetic protest, and also point forward to the passion. The cleansing of the Temple will—as the synoptics make clear—lead on to the passion. This understanding of the disciples is valid as far as it goes. But it does not go far enough—as we shall see in the following verses.

Now—understandably—"the Jews," the representatives of organized religion, ask for a sign. The meaning is substantially the same as that embodied in the corresponding synoptic passage: "By what authority are you doing these things?" (Mark 1:20). In the preceding story of the miracle at Cana we have seen the word "sign" used in a completely positive sense. Here we have our first example of its use in a much more ambiguous sense. "Jews demand signs," says St. Paul (I Cor. 1:22), and in that short phrase he is describing Jewish unbelief. The demand to see signs is portrayed in all the four Gospels as unbelief. To demand signs is unbelief because it is an attempt to validate the claim of Jesus by means of something else, something in the field of observation and experience which satisfies our self-set standards of what can be trusted. Faith, on the other hand, is always a gift of God. It is a work of the Holy Spirit, who himself—being "the Lord, the giver of life"—opens the heart to receive Jesus as lord over all our faculties. The fact that in exercising this lordship he is coming into his own, and therefore liberating these faculties for their true use, is something which we can only know afterward. Our freedom to know him for who he is, is itself his gift.

In the "Q" passage of the synoptics where Jesus is asked for a sign (Matt. 12:39; Luke 11:29) the answer given is that the only sign will be the sign of Jonah, interpreted as a prefiguring of the resurrection. Here the answer given also points to the resurrection, but in a still more indirect and hidden way: "Destroy this temple, and in three days I will raise it up." In Mark and Matthew (echoed in Acts 6:14) Jesus at his trial is accused of having said: "I will destroy the temple that is made with hands, and in three days I will build another, not made with hands" (Mark 14:58), but this is described as false witness. For John this phrase, truly understood, gives the clue to Jesus' action. It is not Jesus who will destroy Herod's temple; it will be destroyed by the unbelief and intransigence of the Jews. But there will be a renewed temple, a place where God dwells, where sin is taken away through the offering of a sacrifice not of sheep and oxen but of Jesus himself— the one who is both priest and victim (see 17:19 and cf. Heb. 8–10). John's readers already know this temple. They know that they—the believers gathered in the name of Jesus—are that temple (see, e.g., I Cor. 3:16 and Eph. 2:19-22). So the ironic imperative ("Go ahead and destroy this temple") has a double meaning: it refers both to Herod's great buildings which would in fact be destroyed, and to the body of Jesus which would be nailed to a cross. And this double reference rests upon a real interlocking of historical events—the rejection and crucifixion of Jesus and the end of the Jewish state. This interlocking can be understood at two levels. Jesus saw in the rejection of his message of the kingdom the final judgment of God upon Jerusalem. The Son himself has come and the tenants have rejected him. The Lord of the vineyard can only reject them and give the stewardship of the vineyard to others. So Jesus in the synoptics weeps over Jerusalem because she does not know the time of her visitation.

But the two references are also interlocked at a deeper level.

The Temple is the place of sacrifice, where God has provided the "mercy seat" at which sin is put away and men and women can come into the presence of God. But with the death of Jesus the one true sacrifice is offered and there is no more need for the blood of sheep and oxen. The Temple is the place of God's tabernacling where his glory dwells. But in Jesus the word of God has come to tabernacle among us and we have seen his glory (1:14). The flesh and blood of Jesus, this man, is the temple where God dwells in the fullness of grace and truth. The Jews will destroy the Temple, but Jesus will raise it up (not build another one as in the "false witness" quoted by the synoptics). This man's body will be the true temple, built of living stones and always growing up into fullness (Eph. 2:19-21).

So the action of Jesus is more than an example of prophetic protest against corrupt religion. It is a sign of the end of religion. The Father's house is no place for this apparatus. But neither the Jews nor the disciples could understand the sign then. Jesus points (as he does also in the synoptics when a sign is demanded) to that which is still future—to that manifestation of power and glory which will be given "on the third day" after the Jews have "destroyed this temple." And John comments that it was only after the resurrection that the disciples understood and believed.

This comment of the evangelist directs attention to something which affects all our study of the Gospels. What does it mean to "understand" the words and acts of Jesus? There is a kind of "critical-historical" study of the Gospels which seems to regard as the ideal to be aimed at such an "understanding" as we would have if a videotape record of all that was said and done were available to us. Implicitly the whole New Testament contradicts this approach to "understanding." There is hardly a single saying or action of Jesus about which we can be quite certain of the details. Is this something to be regretted? Is it a defect to be overcome? On the contrary, it belongs to the proper nature of the gospel itself. The gospel is good news of the events which have made it possible for men and women to live in the relation of trust, love, and obedience with the Father, through participation in the life of his Son, to which we are introduced by the work of the Spirit. Jesus in his ministry took no steps to provide a written body of teaching. He created a community which would be enabled by the Spirit, after his death and resurrection, to grow into an ever fuller understanding of him and of his message, and so to live as children in the Father's house. All the four Gospels are written, and could only have been written, as interpretations of the tradition about Jesus' words and deeds in the light of the resurrection and within the Spirit-filled fellowship. But it is the Fourth Gospel which makes this most explicit. At this point, at the opening of Jesus' public ministry, John emphasizes the fact that the disciples could only understand the works and words of Jesus in the light of the resurrection. In the passion discourses he reports that Jesus told his disciples that they had much more to learn about him, but that it would be the work of the Holy Spirit to teach them (16:12ff.). And at the end of his work he says that what he has told is only a small selection of the available material, but that it is told so that the readers may receive the gift of faith in Jesus as the Christ, the Son of God, and believing may have life—the life that God is and gives—in his name.

It is clear that the Church only slowly began to "understand" the meaning of what Jesus was and did and said. It was, for example, a long time before it was realized that the apparatus of Jewish religion—Temple, Sabbath, circumcision, the law—had been done away in Christ. It was not without struggle and conflict that the understanding was reached. And the struggle goes on while the Church pursues its mission through all generations to all peoples—for we do not fully "understand" Jesus until that day when his work shall be complete, all nations shall worship him, and every tongue confess him Lord. Until that day the Church can never absolve itself of the task of reexamining old patterns of understanding in the light of new experience of the work of the Spirit in bringing new peoples and new generations to confess in their own tongues that Jesus is Lord to the glory of God the Father.

4

NICODEMUS
(2:23–3:21)

IN NARRATING THE TWO PREVIOUS INCIDENTS JOHN HAS
shown us Jesus beginning to unveil his glory to the disciples and
beginning to reveal himself as the one in whom judgment is
exercised and new creation is promised. He has shown us the
beginnings of faith in the disciples, a faith which, however, has
not yet reached full understanding. Now we are introduced to a
kind of response to Jesus which can be described as belief, but
which cannot be accepted as an adequate response to the coming
of the light. It represents rather a twilight area between the light
and the darkness and therefore must be on the way either to day
or to night.

We come also to the first of the long discourses which char-
acterize the Fourth Gospel and which are in sharp contrast to the
short, crisp parables and aphorisms of the synoptics. It is obvious
from the reading of the Johannine epistles that the language of
these discourses owes much to the evangelist himself. On the
other hand, all attempts to mark off in detail the contribution of
the evangelist from the *ipsissima verba* of Jesus break down. In the
present passage, for example, various proposals have been made
in this regard, and the translators of the Revised Standard Version
have placed quotation marks at the end of verse 15, thus indicating their opinion that what follows is to be understood as the
comment of the evangelist and not the words of Jesus. The truth
surely is that what we are hearing from the beginning to the end
of the discourses is "Jesus speaking through the evangelist"
(Brown). Close study of the discourses reveals both that there are
many points of contact with the synoptics which point to a source
in the common tradition, and also (perhaps even more important)

35

that the Johannine interpretation of the words of Jesus illuminates those given in the other three Gospels.

2:23-25

Now when he was in Jerusalem at the Passover feast, many believed in his name when they saw the signs which he did; but Jesus did not trust himself to them, because he knew all men and needed no one to bear witness of man; for he himself knew what was in man.

The fact that Jesus performed many miracles of healing is assumed in all versions of the tradition. The synoptics devote much space to those which were performed in Galilee; John— without giving details—implies that Jerusalem was also the scene of such activity and states that as a result "many believed in his name." In the light of what is said in 1:12, where the same phrase is used, this might seem to be an extremely promising development in the mission of Jesus—an early and impressive example of successful evangelism. But it is not so. This belief is based upon "things that are seen"; it is not that faith which is a work of the Spirit who is not seen, and who comes—like the wind— as he will, and comes not from the solid ground below but from above. Jesus—who knows the heart and does not look on the outward appearance (I Sam. 16:7)—does not "believe in" them, even though they "believe in" him.

3:1-3

Now there was a man of the Pharisees, named Nicodemus, a ruler of the Jews. This man came to Jesus by night and said to him, "Rabbi, we know that you are a teacher come from God; for no one can do these signs that you do, unless God is with him." Jesus answered him, "Truly, truly, I say to you, unless one is born anew, he cannot see the kingdom of God."

There is one of these "believers" who sincerely desires to learn more. He is a man of standing and authority. He has a big stake in the established order—the order which Jesus had so openly and drastically attacked by his actions and his words in the Temple. Yet he believes enough to want to inquire further. He comes to Jesus "by night." It is a very understandable precaution, given his position as a public figure of the establishment. In the perspective of the evangelist he is a man who is drawn to the light but not yet able to leave the darkness.

His opening words express the belief of those who have just been described, those who believe because they have seen the "signs" that Jesus has wrought. These form the foundation on which one can build the conclusion that Jesus is "a teacher sent from God." The word "God" is, of course, already a well-understood word because there have been many teachers in the history of the human race who have taught about God. Jesus is one of this class. His miracles authenticate the designation. He is "one of the prophets" (in the language of the synoptics); in the language of our contemporary culture he is one of the world's religious leaders. In making this statement we are on solid ground—the sort of ground which makes it possible for a theologian to be a respected member of the department of religious studies of a secular university.

Nicodemus is in fact a theologian, a "teacher of Israel" (v. 10), and he addresses Jesus as a fellow theologian: "Rabbi." He has come for serious theological discourse. Jesus therefore begins at once with the central theme of Jewish theology—the kingship of God. This phrase, so central in the synoptic Gospels, occurs only here in the Fourth Gospel—although Jesus will speak later to Pilate about "my kingship." The central question for all sincere seekers is the question about the manner of God's kingship, of how it is manifested, so that it may be "seen" and "entered into"—that is, experienced as a reality from within.

Jesus immediately, solemnly, and without preamble affirms that the question will not be answered on the basis of the formulation which Nicodemus has indicated. There is no "building up" of a secure structure of affirmation from this starting point. There is, on the contrary, only the possibility of something coming down from above, a gift—in fact the gift of a new creation, a new begetting "not of blood nor of the will of the flesh nor of the will of man, but of God" (1:13), "not of perishable seed but of imperishable" (I Pet. 1:23). There are two distinct points involved here. First, that to experience the kingship of God as a present reality (not merely a future hope) can only be the result of an act of God himself. It is always a miracle, a mystery, an action "from above." It is not and can never be the direct result either of the reasoning of the theologian or of the technique of the "successful" evangelist. Secondly, to experience the kingship of God as a present reality is not simply a matter of illumination; it is a matter of regeneration. It is not just new seeing but new being. A theology which would seperate seeing from being has debarred itself from reality at the outset.

3:4

Nicodemus said to him, "How can a man be born when he is old? Can he enter a second time into his mother's womb and be born?"

The response of Nicodemus is one of bewilderment. There has been no "point of contact" with his opening statement; how then can rational discussion continue? He seizes on the word which in Greek can mean both "again" and "from above." (There is, apparently, no Semitic word which has the double meaning. Evidently the evangelist is interpreting the teaching of Jesus on the Semitic theme of the kingship of God through the use of thoroughly Greek language and thought forms.) Nicodemus takes up the first of these two senses and points out the absurdity of supposing a repetition of the process of human birth. Like his colleagues who thought that Jesus was proposing an impossible architectural feat on the temple hill (2:20) Nicodemus suggests a sort of obstetric *reductio ad absurdum*. Birth cannot be repeated. I am the person who was born on a certain day and has grown up in a certain way. All this cannot be simply cancelled. It is as this person that I am, that I want to "see" the kingship of God. The message must be addressed to this person that I am. This is a serious discussion between theologians, not a revivalistic campaign!

3:5-8

Jesus answered, "Truly, truly, I say to you, unless one is born of water and the Spirit, he cannot enter the kingdom of God. That which is born of the flesh is flesh, and that which is born of the Spirit is spirit. Do not marvel that I said to you, 'You must be born anew.' The wind blows where it wills, and you hear the sound of it, but you do not know whence it comes or whither it goes; so it is with every one who is born of the Spirit."

In reply Jesus (in typically Johannine manner) simply repeats the original affirmation in a strengthened form. Nicodemus has shown that his mind is moving in a flatland world. The meaning of "from above" is beyond his present perception. He can only think of "again"—a new start on the same flat earth. What is needed is to awake him to the reality and therefore the possibility of that wholly other dimension which is expressed in the phrase "from above." In the synoptics we find Jesus dealing with exactly the same problem in his discussion with the theologians of his time. When challenged by them to show his authority he replies by asking, "Was the baptism of John from heaven or from men?" (Mark 11:30). They were unable to answer, and therefore Jesus told them that he was not in a position to show them his authority. The baptism of John was one of the "earthly things" of which Jesus speaks (v. 12). It was a matter of ordinary water. The theologians were, however, unable to recognize that it was also "from above," and because they were blind to the reality and therefore the possibility of an action of the Spirit "from above," Jesus could say nothing to them of his authority.

John's baptism is the starting point of the ministry of Jesus according to all the traditions, and it forms the inescapable background for these opening chapters of the story. This action of John in turn rested (as we have seen) on the ancient promises of a future day when Yahweh would cleanse his people with water and pour out upon them his Spirit. John's baptism was explicitly baptism in water—a sign, and no more than a sign, pointing to that "day of the Lord" when the Spirit would descend as fire from heaven. The established theologians of Israel had rejected the sign. Jesus had humbly accepted it, and in that moment the sign and the thing signified had come together. Jesus had been baptized in water and the Spirit, the heavens had been opened, and there had come a voice "from above" affirming that he was the Son of God. What Jesus offered to all who came to him, and what he offers now to Nicodemus, is the possibility of being received into a like sonship by a "birth" from above, a begetting by the power of the Spirit who is (like the wind) invisible, but a begetting which is nevertheless no mere mental evolution from previous processes of thought or experience, but is linked through the baptism of Jesus by John in the river Jordan to the humble, concrete "earthly" action of baptism in water.

"No mere mental evolution," for our mental processes— even the most refined—are "flesh," and flesh does not evolve into Spirit. The words "flesh" and "Spirit" do not refer to parallel and analogous realities in our experience, such as "visible" and "in-

visible" or "lower nature" and "higher nature." "Flesh" denotes
the whole of our creaturely being insofar as it seeks to organize
itself and to exist in its own power and apart from the continually
renewed presence and power of God, "from above." In this sense
a vast amount of theology is "flesh." On the other hand an authentic "entering into" the kingship of God can only be the result
of an action of God himself "from above." And that action of
God is Spirit, not apart from but rather employing such "earthly"
realities as the water of baptism.

Flesh does not beget Spirit. There is no way to capture that
action of God which is Spirit by extrapolation from human reason. The enterprise of "building a tower with its top in heaven"
(Gen. 11:4) ends in the confusion of tongues—and this is emi-
nently true when the tower is an exercise in systematic theology.
But there is an analogy with our "earthly" experience that can
help to open our eyes to the possibility of another dimension.
The wind is invisible. But it is powerful and when it blows we
cannot question its reality even though we cannot locate its source
or control its movement. It is indeed mysterious, yet we cannot
doubt its reality. Why, then, think it impossible that the wind of
God, the mighty breath by which life itself is given to the lifeless
flesh, should be equally real and equally mysterious? Why refuse
the testimony of those who can speak of the kingship of God
from within the experience of a new birth?

3:9

Nicodemus said to him, "How can this be?"

For the third time Nicodemus speaks as one who is groping
for the truth. "How can this be?" might be a mere expression of
bewilderment, or it might be (and the ensuing discourse suggests
this) the serious question of a man who wants to know what has
to happen in order to make this new birth possible. Jesus responds
with a very full exposition of the central themes of the gospel.
It is true that from this point onward Nicodemus "fades into the
darkness whence he came" (Brown), yet he reappears twice later
in the story as one who is willing to distance himself from the
ecclesiastical establishment out of loyalty to Jesus (7:50; 19:39).
Nicodemus came to Jesus by night, but he is represented as one

who seeks the light and to whom Jesus speaks freely of those things which belong to the light.

3:10-15

Jesus answered him, "Are you a teacher of Israel, and yet you do not understand this? Truly, truly, I say to you, we speak of what we know, and bear witness to what we have seen; but you do not receive our testimony. If I have told you earthly things and you do not believe, how can you believe if I tell you heavenly things? No one has ascended into heaven but he who descended from heaven, the Son of man. And as Moses lifted up the serpent in the wilderness, so must the Son of man be lifted up, that whoever believes in him may have eternal life."

Yet Jesus' first response to Nicodemus' last question is to lay upon him, an authorized theologian, the charge that he is ignorant of the realities which he wants to discuss. This is because these realities cannot be known except by listening to the testimony of those who have actually received the new birth from above. In fact, as we shall hear later, this testimony is in truth the work of the Spirit himself (15:26; 16:7-15; Mark 13:11). In spite of the impression created by the confidence with which some theologians make their assertions about heavenly things, no one, and no theologian, has actually ascended into heaven and come back to tell us what he has seen. There is in fact only one way to know the realities of which we speak, and that is by attending to "earthly things" and specifically to the completely human figure of "the Son of man," who speaks in parables of earthly things and whom we meet not "with the clouds of heaven" (Dan. 7:13) but on earth, not by trying to ascend into heaven but by following him who humbled himself and went down among a crowd of sinners to be baptized in the water of the Jordan. The essential precondition for real theology is to listen to the testimony of those who have followed Jesus in the way of descent and thereby received in him the gift of the new birth from above. Theology can be done only in action—this action, because God is action—this action. When we try to fit this action into a preconceived idea of God, we become simply ignorant.

There *is*, however, an ascent, a lifting up to heaven—but it is not of the kind that the theologians expect. It is not an ascent into the heavens to receive "dominion and glory and kingship" (Dan. 7:13), but a very different kind of lifting up, for which the

Old Testament prefiguring is to be found in the bronze serpent which Moses lifted up on a pole in the midst of the people of Israel. The serpent expressed in symbol the very character of that which was destroying them. Jesus the Son of man must be "made sin on our behalf" (II Cor. 5:21). He must share to the limit the place of sinful, God-forsaken man. Only so can the "righteousness of God" become ours. Apart from this we could not grasp it because our very understanding is distorted. This "lifting up" is in fact the completion of Jesus' baptism in the Jordan, and it makes possible the pouring out of the Spirit and the gift of eternal life to those who believe (20:19-23; cf. 7:37-39).

So the "going up into heaven" by which the secret of the kingship of God might be grasped by the theologian is in fact accomplished only by a going down to the very depths. The descent of Jesus into the depths of our sin and death is—paradoxically but truly—the "lifting up," the glorifying which leads to the victory of life over death. But we can only know this by listening to the testimony of those who have followed this way. To "enter into the kingship of God" can only be by the gift of a new life, the life of God himself, and that gift can only be made available by the descent of God himself to pour out his life in death for the life of the world.

3:16-21

For God so loved the world that he gave his only Son, that whoever believes in him should not perish but have eternal life. For God sent the Son into the world, not to condemn the world, but that the world might be saved through him. He who believes in him is not condemned; he who does not believe is condemned already, because he has not believed in the name of the only Son of God. And this is the judgment, that the light has come into the world, and men loved darkness rather than light, because their deeds were evil. For every one who does evil hates the light, and does not come to the light, lest his deeds should be exposed. But he who does what is true comes to the light, that it may be clearly seen that his deeds have been wrought in God.

And that is what God has in fact done. God is known in this action because God is action—the action of love reaching out to the unlovely and the unlovable. We know this because of what he has done; it is not an extrapolation from our own ethical insights.

God's love is known to us because he has given his only Son so that whoever believes might have life. The uniqueness and the universality are counterparts of each other. To reject both in the alleged interest of mutual tolerance among the world's religions is to deny the message at its center. If there are many different revelations, then the human family has no center for its unity. If the Krishna of the Puranas and the Jesus of the Gospels are both revelations of God, then we must say (and this is what Hinduism in the end does say) that God is unknown and unknowable. Each of us is—in the end—shut up in his own world of ideas. He must find God in the depths of his own being because there is no action of God by which he gives himself to be known by us.

The uniqueness ("his only Son") corresponds to the universality ("whoever") because God is love in action—the love of the Father and the Son in the unity of the Spirit. But this love does not coerce. It is addressed to men and women who must receive it by a willing belief, and who can also withhold that belief and therefore choose death rather than life. The coming of Jesus, who is the "only Son" of the Father, thus confronts those to whom he comes with the possibility of receiving the gift of life—of "entering into the kingship of God," and also with the terrible possibility of refusing the gift and choosing death. The purpose of his coming is to bring life, not death. Yet the gift of life must be accepted and can be refused.

The coming of Jesus is thus like the coming of light into a dark place. The very presence of light also creates shadows. But these exist only where something has been interposed to shut out the light. Light of itself shines on to infinity. The light shines in the darkness, and the darkness does not overcome it. But it is possible to shut out the light and to create an area of darkness where evil deeds can be done without being recognized as evil.

In the synoptics (e.g., Mark 3:1-6) we read again and again of how the presence of Jesus created a double movement—a movement of those who came to him to receive blessing, and of those who withdrew from him into corners to plot his destruction. John sums this up in his first epistle by saying that the substance of the Gospel is that in the coming of Jesus light has come into the world (I John 1:5). There is thus provided in the midst of human affairs a concrete criterion by which all human action is to be judged. All human beings are continually engaged in making judgments. We have standards of behavior by which

43

we mark off the styles of living which we accept from those which we do not accept. We thus justify ourselves and condemn others. Jesus, as the synoptic Gospels so clearly show, upset these standards. Those who justified themselves were condemned. This was why they sought to destroy Jesus. By his coming the right of judgment has been taken out of our hands and we are required to acknowledge that he alone is the judge because he is the light. Therefore it is those who put their trust in him who are justified, and those who refuse this trust are condemned (v. 18).

But this "justification by faith" does not mean a severance of faith from works, for (a) those who refuse this trust in fact do so because they prefer to live in a world where they can justify themselves rather than to be exposed to that terrible light in which even the best of our good works are shown to be infected with evil (vv. 19f.); and (b) those who do put their trust in Jesus do so in order "that it may be clearly seen that their deeds have been wrought in God" (v. 21). Such deeds claim no justification of their own. They are incomplete in themselves. They are only tokens of our allegiance, "acted prayers for the kingdom of God" (Schweitzer). They thus belong to the light. They seek no shadow world where some kind of self-justification is possible in the company of those who inhabit the same shadow worlds. They look to the day when all things will be manifest in the clear light of God. Those who "come to the light" will be those who—in this sense—"do the truth."

Nicodemus is one of those who—even under the cover of darkness—is coming to the light. He had perhaps come—as one theologian to another—for a quiet discussion about "heavenly things." He is left—and the reader is left—face to face with the final judgment, with the alternatives of life and death, of light and darkness, and with the final reminder that it is only he who "does the truth" who comes to the light.

Theology is, after all, serious business.

5

JESUS AND JOHN
(3:22-36)

THEOLOGY, HOWEVER, IS ONLY ONE FORM OF HUMAN
activity. There is also the whole business of practical religion—
including rites of purification which were (as we know especially
from the literature of the Qumran communities) a matter of burning interest at the time.

And there is plenty of room for discussion. Three kinds of
practice are going on concurrently. There are the regular rites of
purification prescribed in the law and carefully carried out by
devout Israelites. There is the movement of people to the baptism
of John—with its disturbing eschatological overtones. And there
is the new movement gathering around Jesus from Nazareth. We
are introduced to a growing religious pluralism. Here is a typical
example of the situation in which theological principle becomes
inextricably entwined with the tensions—not to say jealousies
and ambitions—of churchmen, of evangelists, and of religious
people of all kinds.

3:22-30

*After this Jesus and his disciples went into the land of Judea; there he
remained with them and baptized. John also was baptizing at Aenon
near Salim, because there was much water there; and people came and
were baptized. For John had not yet been put in prison.*

*Now a discussion arose between John's disciples and a Jew over pu-
rifying. And they came to John, and said to him, "Rabbi, he who was
with you beyond the Jordan, to whom you bore witness, here he is,
baptizing, and all are going to him." John answered, "No one can receive
anything except what is given him from heaven. You yourselves bear me
witness, that I said, I am not the Christ, but I have been sent before him.*

He who has the bride is the bridegroom; the friend of the bridegroom, who stands and hears him, rejoices greatly at the bridegroom's voice; therefore this joy of mine is now full. He must increase, but I must decrease."

The synoptics begin their account of Jesus' ministry only after John's has been terminated by imprisonment (Mark 1:14). This leaves no room for parallel or competing missions—although there are indications of tension between the two movements (Matt. 11:2-19; Luke 7:18-35). John, however, asserts that a ministry of baptism was carried on by Jesus, or at least by his disciples (4:21), concurrently with that of John, though in a different part of the country.

This appearance of rivalry between religious movements prompts the report to John by his disciples. The original question—which was about purification—now is submerged by the question about the relative strength of the two movements. John's answer to the report of his disciples is twofold. First, if people are going to Jesus it is because the Father draws them (v. 27; cf. 6:44, etc.). "Church growth," if it is genuine, is not a human achievement; it is a gift of God. There is therefore no place for rivalry, for jealousy, or for boasting. Secondly, if the disciples had understood their master they would have known that there could be no question of rivalry between the two movements. John's mission was simply to serve, to point to, to prepare the way for the coming of Jesus. The bridegroom may have many friends (it appears that contemporary custom provided two "friends of the groom" at a wedding). But there can only be one lawful bridegroom who becomes the husband of the bride. The "friend" is simply one who assists—even if, like St. Paul, he has a big part in the betrothal (cf. II Cor. 11:2). There can be no question of rivalry between the bridegroom and his "best man"— unless the latter is guilty of infamous treachery. The situation is misunderstood if Jesus is understood as one of a class which includes other leaders of religious movements. He, and he alone, is the true husband, and John, who is a true friend of the bridegroom, rejoices to see the bride pass into the care of her lawful husband.

3:31-36

He who comes from above is above all; he who is of the earth belongs to the earth, and of the earth he speaks; he who comes from heaven is above all. He bears witness to what he has seen and heard, yet no one receives his testimony; he who receives his testimony sets his seal to this, that God is true. For he whom God has sent utters the words of God, for it is not by measure that he gives the Spirit; the Father loves the Son, and has given all things into his hand. He who believes in the Son has eternal life; he who does not obey the Son shall not see life, but the wrath of God rests upon him.

In fact we are here in the presence of the same radical distinction between "from above" and "from below" with which Jesus deals in his discourse with Nicodemus. This section is in effect a recapitulation and development of the latter part of that discourse in the light of the controversy in which John's disciples were involved.

This radical dichotomy, this separation of "from above" and "from below," was familiar to the religious world of the first century. It expressed the familiar dichotomy between the spiritual or mental world and the material world, between the world of the mind and the world of the senses. But to apply that dichotomy to parallel religious movements on the same plane of history was as offensive in that century as it is in this. The Jews were hated in that world because they refused to blur the distinction between Yahweh and the gods of the nations, and the disciples of Jesus would later incur the same hatred. When the world is so full of a number of religions, the easiest thing is to assume that the truth must lie somewhere among them or beyond them. This is convenient, for it permits each of us to formulate his mental picture of that truth in the privacy of his own mind. There is in fact, however, no necessity of thought which requires us to reject the possibility that God might have revealed himself in certain specific events which are on the plane of public history and which cannot be molded to suit private convenience. But such a revelation would require a decision which is also public—one way or the other—and would remove religion from the private sector.

The "natural" human decision is to reject this possibility—for such a revelation sets a boundary to my mental excursions. So it is said of the one who is "from above" that "no one receives his testimony." To receive this is not a possible accomplishment of that distorted human nature which tries to find its good within itself, which looks for a "beyond" only "within." But there are, nevertheless, those who do receive this testimony (cf. 1:11-13). Such persons have "set their seal to this, that God is true." How

47

is it possible that this should happen? If human nature as it is cannot receive the testimony, how can there be those who receive it? Only by a work of the Spirit by whose operation the words that Jesus speaks are authenticated as true. God himself has set his seal upon Jesus (6:27) in anointing him with the Spirit. It is because the Spirit dwells in Jesus fully and without limit (cf. 1:32) that Jesus speaks the words of God. The Spirit is the witness because the Spirit is the truth (I John 5:7). So through the presence of the Spirit, who is God's "seal" upon Jesus, believers are enabled to respond with a like attestation "that God is true." For God's utterly trustworthy "Yes" has been spoken to man in Jesus and "that is why we utter the Amen through him to the glory of God"—God who has "put his seal upon us and given us his Spirit in our hearts as a guarantee" (II Cor. 1:20-22). The limitless fullness of the Spirit is given to Jesus (1:32), and therefore Jesus himself is able to communicate that fullness to others (1:33). For the Spirit who is truth is also love, the love of the Father for the Son, a love which is also without limit because the Father has given all things to the Son (cf. 17:2). But this universality of God's love brings with it the necessary implication of judgment, for if we turn our backs upon universal love where shall we go but into death? If we turn our backs upon light where shall we go but into darkness?

6

SAMARIA AND GALILEE
(4:1-54)

4:1-6

Now when the Lord knew that the Pharisees had heard that Jesus was making and baptizing more disciples than John (although Jesus himself did not baptize, but only his disciples), he left Judea and departed again to Galilee. He had to pass through Samaria. So he came to a city of Samaria, called Sychar, near the field that Jacob gave to his son Joseph. Jacob's well was there, and so Jesus, wearied as he was with his journey, sat down beside the well. It was about the sixth hour.

The Spirit who is "from above," and who "blows where he will," inspires also a movement outward—from Jerusalem to "all Judea and Samaria and to the uttermost parts of the earth" (Acts 1:8). The story of Jesus must move from the Jerusalem rabbi to the semi-pagan peasant woman of Sychar, and finally to the vision of a harvest which is gathered by Jesus as the Savior of the world (vv. 35 and 42). There is, then, a theological as well as a geographical necessity implied in the statement that Jesus "had to pass through Samaria." He comes, however, not as the leader of a crusade for world evangelization but as a refugee from the wrath of the religious leaders of his people.

4:7-15

There came a woman of Samaria to draw water. Jesus said to her, "Give me a drink." For his disciples had gone away into the city to buy food. The Samaritan woman said to him, "How is that you, a Jew, ask a drink of me, a woman of Samaria?" For Jews have no dealings with Samaritans. Jesus answered her, "If you knew the gift of God, and who it is that is saying to you, 'Give me a drink,' you would have asked him,

*and he would have given you living water." The woman said to him,
"Sir, you have nothing to draw with, and the well is deep; where do
you get that living water? Are you greater than our father Jacob, who
gave us the well, and drank from it himself, and his sons, and his cattle?"
Jesus said to her, "Every one who drinks of this water will thirst again,
but whoever drinks of the water that I shall give him will never thirst;
the water that I shall give him will become in him a spring of water
welling up to eternal life." The woman said to him, "Sir, give me this
water, that I may not thirst, nor come here to draw."*

Tired, thirsty, utterly vulnerable, he is found by a village
woman sitting by the well in the intense heat of midday. He is
a helpless stranger in a land which does not acknowledge the faith
of Judah and whose people are so deeply compromised with paganism that their vessels are unclean to a devout Jew. However
terrible his thirst, a Brahmin will not drink from the well in the
Harijan quarter or from the cup that the Harijan offers. So it is
with astonishment that this village woman receives the stranger's
request for a drink.

Her question is perhaps half-mocking, half-teasing. His reply
is full of mysterious suggestion. "Living water" is water that
bubbles up fresh from the spring as contrasted with the stagnant
water of a cistern (Jer. 2:13). It is the life-giving stream that will
one day flow down into the desert to bring life where there was
death (Ezek. 47:1-12). It is the Torah—the life-giving instruction
of God for his beloved people. It is the Spirit of God himself.
"Living water" might suggest all of these—but not here surely.
Is this exhausted traveler really pretending that he can do better
than the great patriarch whose presence hallowed this countryside
and whose well is here—the well from which he was content to
drink and which was generous enough for all his cattle? Does this
man think he can immediately find a spring on the spot where
Jacob had to dig so deep to find water?

The reader of the Gospel understands that this woman is
standing—all unsuspecting—on the brink of a much deeper gulf
than that which divides Jew from Samaritan; it is the gulf between
him who is the author of life and the world which is thirsty for
that life. The woman does not—cannot yet—understand the offer
which Jesus has made. It is the offer of that which quenches not
just the natural and ever recurring thirst of the body, but the
eternal thirst which can only be quenched by the living God
himself (Ps. 42), who has made us for himself so that nothing

else can satisfy us. The living water which the traveler offers is indeed the true Torah and the living Spirit, forever renewed in the heart of the believer. But—like the Jews who were fed in the desert (6:25-34)—the woman can only think of a permanent satisfaction for the recurring thirst of the body. That, indeed, would be a wonderful gift of God, and she boldly asks for it. Despite the crudeness of her perception she is willing—unlike Nicodemus—to trust the stranger and to make her petition with confidence. This is faith—not yet a mature faith, but nevertheless the faith which can become the beginning of understanding. The act of turning in trust to Jesus—however far short it may fall of full understanding—is the indispensable starting point for understanding. Even "rice Christians" can be on the way to becoming mature Christians and authentic witnesses. And so this dialogue will lead to a conclusion far different from the conversation with Nicodemus. It will lead on to the confession of Jesus as Savior of the world (v. 42).

4:16-26

Jesus said to her, "Go, call your husband, and come here." The woman answered him, "I have no husband." Jesus said to her, "You are right in saying, 'I have no husband'; for you have had five husbands, and he whom you now have is not your husband; this you said truly." The woman said to him, "Sir, I perceive that you are a prophet. Our fathers worshipped on this mountain; and you say that in Jerusalem is the place where men ought to worship." Jesus said to her, "Woman, believe me, the hour is coming when neither on this mountain nor in Jerusalem will you worship the Father. You worship what you do not know; we worship what we know, for salvation is from the Jews. But the hour is coming, and now is, when the true worshippers will worship the Father in spirit and truth, for such the Father seeks to worship him. God is spirit, and those who worship him must worship in spirit and truth." The woman said to him, "I know that Messiah is coming (he who is called Christ); when he comes, he will show us all things." Jesus said to her, "I who speak to you am he."

Turning to Jesus means turning to the light. In him there is no darkness at all. When he comes, that which is hidden becomes manifest. The woman's need for water is not just for herself but—presumably—for her household. So there can be no surprise when his first response to her petition is "Call your husband." And now things hidden are brought to light. The disordered human relationships of the Samaritan woman are an accurate reflection of the disorder of Samaritan religion. From the time when the king of Assyria overran Samaria and planted there the worship of the gods of the nations, Samaria's religion had been a thoroughly promiscuous affair. And even the worship of the God of the patriarchs is no true worship when it accepts coexistence with this promiscuity. The reader of the Gospel knows that Samaria is the home of all kinds of gnostic cults, and is not surprised to find this disorder mirrored in the life of a Samaritan woman.

The woman realizes that she is in the presence of a more than natural perception of realities—that she is in the presence of one who sees things as they are and "knows what is in man." She has her own resources for dealing with the situation. This stranger is a prophet. He has done what true prophets have always done— exposed the sin which sin itself seeks to hide. The woman does not seek to defend herself or to hide the sin. She has placed her trust in the stranger and she does not draw back. On the contrary she rightly presses forward. Where sin has been exposed one must ask about the possibility of atonement, of forgiveness. A prophet can bring no healing if the ministry of the priest is not available, if there is no "mercy seat" where sacrifice can be accepted and sin put away. Where is that mercy seat, that true temple, where true worship may be offered by consciences cleansed from sin? Is it on Mount Zion as Jews believe, or on Mount Gerizim where the Samaritans worship? This is no irrelevance to deflect attention from the woman's sin; it is the proper pressing of the question which must be asked when sin has been brought to the light and exposed.

The serious, even if uninformed questioning of the woman opens the way for Jesus to unfold the central reality of God's new and decisive action in history. Jesus' words in verses 21-25 have been frequently used in the interests of a post-Enlightenment pri- vatized religion, as though he were saying that religion was an inward affair of the human spirit, to which disputes between Judea and Samaria are irrelevant. This is to abandon altogether the context of the words; their context is still the ultimate contrast between living water and the water which cannot give eternal life, between the Spirit and the flesh, between that which is from above and that which is from below. The dispute between Mount Zion and Mount Gerizim is not an irrelevance. The syncretistic worship of Samaria is worship in ignorance. It is worship of an unknown god (Acts 17:22-23). A god who can be equally represented by all the contradictory images of man's religious imagination is not God. To this whole world of religious imagination God remains unknown. But God—the living God—has made himself known in Judah. John, who is emphatically no anti-Semite, confesses the same faith as Paul that to the Jews belong "the sonship, the glory, the covenants, the giving of the law, the worship, and the promises" (Rom. 9:4). A discussion of "comparative religion" is not in order here. "Salvation is from the Jews."

But a new reality is now impending. A new hour approaches. It is now present although its full reality will only be manifest when the hour comes for the glorifying of the Son in the cross, the resurrection, and the outpouring of the Spirit. Then both Jews and Samaritans, and indeed all the world, will be summoned to the true worship. This will be an action of the Father. He himself will seek such worshippers and he himself will "draw" them to the Son in whom the truth is present (e.g., 6:44, etc.). This action of the Father is the Father himself in action, for God is Spirit, and Spirit is action—the mighty action which is "from above" and which, like the wind, is invisible and yet unmistakable in its presence and its powerful effects. God is not essence but action. His being is action, and the action is the seeking of true worshippers out of Jewry and out of Samaria and out of every nation.

And the Spirit is the one who brings the truth. It is he who "convicts the world" in respect of its fundamental religious beliefs (16:8ff.) and leads the Church into all the truth (16:13ff.). This new reality which displaces both Zion and Gerizim from the center of the religious map is at hand. It is in fact already present, for Jesus who is speaking to the woman is himself the truth; he speaks the truth because the Spirit is given to him in fullness. Indeed he is the truth as he is also the life (14:6). The hour of this new revelation is impending and it is now present: impending because Jesus is not yet glorified; present because it is Jesus himself who is speaking.

The woman rightly recognizes that her first answer to the question "Who is this stranger?" was inadequate. This goes beyond the language of the prophet. This is the language of eschatology, of the last things, of the Messiah. The Samaritans looked for the coming of a Messiah (the Taleb) who would be more a teacher after the manner of the promise of Deuteronomy (18:15f.) than a ruler of the Davidic line for whom Judah waited. She is willing to wait for his coming to hear the truth. And to this expression of faith and hope Jesus replies: "I who speak with you am he." Jesus had not—it seems—unambiguously accepted identification with the Davidic Messiah of the Jews; he is, however, content to identify himself in response to the sincere questioning of this semi-pagan, loose-living villager as the one who would speak truly the things of God.

To say that God is Spirit means: "God has run towards us with open arms, as the father ran to meet the prodigal son" (Bornkamm). And because the Spirit brings the truth, the truth about the woman and the truth about Jesus can be revealed and accepted. "If we walk in the light, as he is in the light, we have fellowship with one another, and the blood of Jesus cleanses us from all sin" (I John 1:7). And so true worship becomes possible.

4:27-38

Just then his disciples came. They marveled that he was talking with a woman, but none said, "What do you wish?" or, "Why are you talking with her?" So the woman left her water jar, and went away into the city, and said to the people, "Come, see a man who told me all that I ever did. Can this be the Christ?" They went out of the city and were coming to him.

Meanwhile the disciples besought him, saying, "Rabbi, eat." But he said to them, "I have food to eat of which you do not know." So the disciples said to one another, "Has any one brought him food?" Jesus said to them, "My food is to do the will of him who sent me, and to accomplish his work. Do you not say, 'There are yet four months, then comes the harvest'? I tell you, lift up your eyes, and see how the fields are already white for harvest. He who reaps receives wages, and gathers fruit for eternal life, so that sower and reaper may rejoice together. For here the saying holds true, 'One sows and another reaps.' I sent you to reap that for which you did not labor; others have labored, and you have entered into their labor."

Now there is a movement of the characters on the stage. The woman hurries away to the village, leaving behind her waterpot, taking with her not the water "from below" which might have served for a few hours, but the news of something which might be—perhaps—the living water, the gift promised at the last day to quench every thirst forever. And to the front of the stage come the disciples, bringing food which may stave off hunger for an hour or two, but which is not the food that Jesus desires. They are shocked to see their master talking to a Samaritan woman, but they dare not question him. Instead they press upon him the food they have brought—while the woman's empty pot stands as a silent witness against their misunderstanding of what it is that can finally satisfy. Jesus has only one overmastering hunger—a hunger only fully satisfied when he gave a great cry from the cross: "It is finished." He who is the "bread of life" is he who came "not to do my own will, but the will of him who sent me" (6:35-39). It is those who "eat this bread" that have "eternal life"—the life of God himself. For man shall not live by bread alone but by everything that proceeds out of the mouth of God—namely, by keeping his commandments and doing his work (cf. Deut. 8:3 with Deut. 8:2).

In fact this life of God is already being offered to the world. The harvest to which prophets had looked forward with longing is already ripe. The promise that "the ploughman shall overtake the reaper" is already being fulfilled (Amos 9:13). It is no longer a matter of long, patient waiting for the harvest to be ready. The seed is producing an instant harvest. The word spoken to the woman is already bringing a great crowd of Samaritans to the feet of Jesus. The word of God is a seed capable of producing an immense harvest. The one who sows the seed and the one who reaps may be quite different—may even be unknown to one another. The "others" of verse 38 cannot be certainly identified, and this is typical of the experience of the missionary who finds himself reaping a harvest where others unknown and forgotten have sown the seed. It is the reaper who receives the reward, but the joy of sower and reaper is the same—joy in doing the Father's will and finishing his work.

4:39-42

Many Samaritans from that city believed in him because of the woman's testimony, "He told me all that I ever did." So when the Samaritans came to him, they asked him to stay with them; and he stayed there two days. And many more believed because of his word. They said to the woman, "It is no longer because of your words that we believe, for we have heard for ourselves, and we know that this is indeed the Savior of the world."

Now the scene shifts once again. The disciples disappear and the front of the stage is filled with the crowd of Samaritan villagers. They have been brought to Jesus by the testimony of the woman, inadequate as it is. They, too, are willing to trust him and to ask him to "abide" with them (not yet knowing what this "abiding" will mean), and finally to "believe." This belief rests not on the woman's report but on the word of Jesus, the word which is truth. And so they are led themselves to a true confession, that this travel-weary and thirsty stranger is more than a prophet, more than the Messiah king of the Jews or the promised teacher of the Samaritans. He is the one whose dominion is to the ends of the earth. He is the Savior of the world. And so what was hidden from the wise and understanding Nicodemus is revealed to these spiritual babes, and while scribes and Pharisees stand aside, the pagan world flocks into the kingdom.

4:43-54

After the two days he departed to Galilee. For Jesus himself testified that a prophet has no honor in his own country. So when he came to Galilee, the Galileans welcomed him, having seen all that he had done in Jerusalem at the feast, for they too had gone to the feast.

So he came again to Cana in Galilee, where he had made the water wine. And at Caperna-um there was an official whose son was ill. When he heard that Jesus had come from Judea to Galilee, he went and begged him to come down and heal his son, for he was at the point of death. Jesus therefore said to him, "Unless you see signs and wonders you will not believe." The official said to him, "Sir, come down before my child dies." Jesus said to him, "Go; your son will live." The man believed the word that Jesus spoke to him and went his way. As he was going down, his servants met him and told him that his son was living. So he asked them the hour when he began to mend, and they said to him, "Yesterday at the seventh hour the fever left him." The father knew that was the hour when Jesus had said to him, "Your son will live"; and he himself believed, and all his household. This was now the second sign that Jesus did when he had come from Judea to Galilee.

Jesus, who is both Lord and Savior of the world, comes to his own and his own reject him. The proverbial saying that a prophet is not honored by his own people is used in the synoptics to refer to Galilee, which was (as John well knows) the human homeland of Jesus of Nazareth. However, the fourth evangelist here applies it (so it would seem) to Judah, for "salvation is from the Jews" and Judah is the proper home of the Savior. Though Jesus had done many signs in Jerusalem (cf. 2:23), however, Judea did not receive him, and so he pursues his journey northward from Samaria to Galilee where—as is well known—no prophet is to be expected (7:52). And the Galileans welcome him, having seen the signs wrought in Jerusalem.

But the character of this welcome has still to be tested to see whether it is genuine faith or only the kind of welcome which is always given to one who can work wonders. This necessary but delicate process of discrimination is immediately brought to the reader's attention by an incident with which he is perhaps already familiar. In the collection of the sayings of Jesus upon which both Matthew and Luke drew there is just one story of a miracle—the story of the military officer in Capernaum who sent to Jesus to ask for the healing of his servant (Matt. 8:5-13; Luke 7:1-10). John now describes in his own way what may well be the same incident as it has come to him through the common tradition, and tells it in such a way that the true and false understandings of "signs" are brought into clear contrast.

This royal official, perhaps a soldier, is in deep personal distress because his son is desperately ill. He therefore comes to Jesus with an appeal for help—an appeal which is not based on any theological concern about whether Jesus is really a worker of miracles but simply upon a deep human need and a faith—however uninformed—that Jesus can help.

The first response is an abrupt rebuff. As with his mother's approach at the marriage feast, and as with the petition of the Syrophoenician woman (Mark 7:27), so here Jesus rejects the first appeal. However, his words are rather a comment on the kind of belief he is encountering ("unless you [plural] see signs and wonders . . .") than on the appeal of the soldier. They are a comment on what he has found in Israel (cf. Matt. 8:10) and—as the sequel will show—they serve to discriminate between the misdirected belief of the majority and the rightly directed even if inadequately developed faith of the soldier.

A belief which requires signs and wonders is one which lays down in advance the conditions which are required to authenticate any alleged revelation of God. It is thus guilty of putting the constructions of the human imagination—often a very pious imagination—in the place of God. The belief is not a response to God as he actually reveals himself, for God's revelation may com-

57

pletely contravene our predetermined view of what God must be and do. It is a projection of our own imagination—perhaps of an image of power fashioned on the basis of our experience of weakness, or of omniscience fashioned on the basis of our experience of ignorance. Such projections are characteristic artifacts of religious persons and theologians.

But this man is not a theologian and probably not a religious person. He is simply a human being in desperate need, and he appeals to Jesus as he would appeal to anyone likely to help. He is not willing to be silenced by Jesus' rebuff. He persists—almost peremptorily: "Sir, come down before my child dies." He is a man of the practical world; he wants action.

Jesus responds with a word which is also an action: "Go; your son will live." The official, like the centurion of whom the synoptics speak, instantly recognizes the voice of authority. He knows what it is both to give and to receive orders. Without a word he turns on his heel and goes.

This is an action of belief. It is not yet the full belief to be described in verse 53, but it is true belief because it is based on the *word* of Jesus, not on visible signs, and because it is at the same time obedience to that word. Persistent intercession in the face of disappointment has led the man to the point where he becomes a hearer and doer of the word of Jesus, one to whom the word which is action and the action which is word is spoken straight from the heart of Jesus to his own heart. And that word, because it is the word of God, has power and bears the fruit of faith and obedience.

Why should there be a distinction between "seeing" and "hearing"? Why does John so often stress this contrast right up to the decisive word of Jesus to Thomas: "Blessed are those who have not seen and yet have believed" (20:29)? And why does the Old Testament combine such an emphasis upon the *word* of God with such a horror of visible representations of God? What is at stake in this contrast between seeing signs and believing the word? Perhaps—without going too far beyond the present text—one may attempt to answer as follows. The demand for a visible sign means that the one who makes the demand keeps ultimate sovereignty in his own hands. He has himself prescribed the tests by which divinity must prove itself. So the demand for signs and wonders is refused. To this man, however, in his simple human need and distress, the word of Jesus carries in itself a sovereign authority which commands obedience. One does not obey an image or a picture; one obeys (or disobeys) a word. For this practical man, accustomed to the voice of authority, the word of Jesus is enough. He accepts and obeys, leaving to Jesus the sovereign freedom to fulfil his word as he will. His own insistent and urgent cry for help is stilled by a word which shifts the center and takes the control out of his anxious hands into those of Jesus. And so he turns and goes home.

And then there follows what the evangelist does not hesitate to call the "sign." When the officer meets his servants (who are also—it is to be assumed—accustomed to obeying orders) he learns that the word of Jesus was indeed a word with authority. And this authentication of his trust in Jesus' word leads him and his whole household to become believers in the full sense of the word as the readers of the Gospel understand it.

The evangelist links this to the earlier miracle at Cana and calls it the "second sign"—in spite of all that has been said since then about signs wrought in Jerusalem. At that wedding in Cana there had been a similar sequence: a simple request arising from an ordinary human need, a rebuff, an order given and obeyed, and a "sign" which those who had obeyed the order recognized and which "manifested his glory." So the signs which are demanded as a proof of authenticity are no part of the path to faith. That faith begins with obedience to the words of Jesus. But to those who take that path there are indeed "signs" which lead believers on to a fuller and more understanding faith. And to those who struggle along the path of obedience it may be necessary to say: "Believe me that I am in the Father and the Father in me; or else believe me for the very works' sake" (14:11). Within a context of obedient discipleship Jesus does graciously grant signs which enable the disciple to go forward on the path of faith. Even when Thomas—that doubting but loyal disciple—says, "Unless I see I will not believe," Jesus grants his request, acknowledges the faith that has depended on sight, but immediately adds the decisive words "Blessed are those who have not seen and yet have believed" (20:29).

In the first miracle at Cana Jesus had shown himself as the giver of joy. In the cleansing of the Temple he had declared himself the new temple, the true place of meeting between God and his people. To Nicodemus he had revealed himself as the giver of a new birth from above. To the people of Samaria he had become known as the Savior of the world. And now to the officer in Capernaum he had become a giver of life from the dead. Three times the phrase is repeated: "Your son lives." That threefold repetition prepares us for the following sections in which Jesus is revealed as the giver of eternal life.

7

THE SON
AND THE FATHER
(5:1-62)

THE READER OF THE GOSPEL HAS ALREADY BEEN MADE aware of the vast and mysterious issues raised by the attempt to answer the question "Who is this man?" He has been hailed as the Lamb of God, as the Messiah, as the Savior of the world. He has acted and spoken in such a way as to suggest immense claims. Now the evangelist leads us on to a series of actions, followed in each case by long interpretative statements in which Jesus repeatedly uses the mysterious formula "I am." In these statements Jesus defines his own person in increasingly sharper contrast to his hearers and provokes them to ever firmer formulations of the charge that he is a blasphemer, claiming equality with God. Some of his statements—"Before Abraham was, I am" (8:58), "I and the Father are one" (9:30)—in fact lead the Jews to attempt without delay to inflict the punishment prescribed for the blasphemer—death by stoning.

It is no more than right to acknowledge at once that these long monologues present real problems for the reader who is part of contemporary Western culture. Such a reader—like "the Jews" of 5:18—is tempted to say, "This man is making himself equal to God." The resolution of these problems can only arise from a careful study of the text, but it may be useful to make four points before this study begins.

1. The reader must remember the purpose with which the Gospel is written: it is that the reader may come to believe that Jesus is the Christ, the Son of God, and that believing he may have life.

2. Everything in the story must be read, and can only be understood if it is read, in the light of the cross, resurrection, and

Pentecost. The one of whom we are reading is the one who was finally rejected with unique unanimity by the representatives of all the forces that control human behavior (cf. I Cor. 2:8), was subjected to that death which implied the curse of God as well as of men, was raised to new life, and became the author of new life for all who believed. It is this man whose identity is being defined in these passages.

3. As in all serious attempts to interpret a document from the past we must refrain from imposing upon it our own prior beliefs about what "must have been." For those whose tradition commits them to believing that Jesus is the ideal man, and whose concept of the ideal man excludes this apparently harsh and egotistical language, there is a strong compulsion to find some other explanation than the simple one that these words represent the actual claim of Jesus. The most often preferred explanation is that this language reflects the later conflicts between church and synagogue. Without denying the probability that this conflict has affected these presentations of the words of Jesus, one must still ask: Is the language wholly to be explained as a projection backward from these later conflicts, or are these conflicts to be explained as consequences of the claim embodied in this language? The facts of history, and especially the fact of the cross, lead this expositor at least to the latter view.

4. This leads to a final point which is the most important one. By interpreting these words as a projection backward from later conflicts one successfully evades the thrust of this part of the Gospel. We have already drawn attention to the dangers of failing to recognize that "the Jews," as they are portrayed in the Gospel, are not uniquely blind or stubborn people. They represent established religion. They represent us. If the cross is the bearing of the sin of all men, and not just of the Jews; if the question "Were you there when they crucified my Lord?" must be answered with an awestruck and whispered "Yes" by every human soul, then—equally—these words of Jesus are addressed not to Jews only, but to all. The strategies by which "the Jews" seek to exclude the possibility that the living God himself might be confronting them in this man are but local and temporary examples of the strategies by which all human beings seek to protect themselves within their worlds of thought and belief. Because these chapters portray Jesus as being in fact such an actual confrontation of men and women with the presence of God; because such a confrontation

calls in question all our established positions, including both our concepts of what it is to be human and our concepts of the world and history; and because—notwithstanding these texts—the name of Jesus is too precious to be removed from our affections, we are tempted to exempt Jesus from responsibility for the words and to place the responsibility upon the evangelist and—through him—on the later conflicts of church and synagogue. By this stratagem we both evade the impact of the living God in Jesus upon all our intellectual and spiritual securities, and project the guilt of our evasion upon the Jews, or upon the early Church.

5:1-9a

After this there was a feast of the Jews, and Jesus went up to Jerusalem.
Now there is in Jerusalem by the Sheep Gate a pool, in Hebrew called Beth-zatha, which has five porticoes. In these lay a multitude of invalids, blind, lame, paralyzed. One man was there, who had been ill for thirty-eight years. When Jesus saw him and knew that he had been lying there a long time, he said to him, "Do you want to be healed?" The sick man answered him, "Sir, I have no man to put me into the pool when the water is troubled, and while I am going another steps down before me." Jesus said to him, "Rise, take up your pallet, and walk." And at once the man was healed, and he took up his pallet and walked.

The fact that Jesus habitually healed sick people is one of the most prominent elements in the tradition. One-fifth of all the material in the four Gospels is concerned with the healing of physical disease. (The virtual ignoring of this work of healing during most of Christian history is one of the astonishing facts which the theologian and the historian must try to explain.) John has already spoken of "the signs" which Jesus did, and we have heard about (but not seen) the healing of the nobleman's son. Now the work of healing is brought to the front of the stage.

"There is in Jerusalem . . . a pool." Apparently the remains, with the five porches, have now been identified by archaeologists. John is telling a story which has similarities to that of the paralytic in Mark 2:1-12, but also many differences. Here Jesus takes the initiative, not the friends of the sick man. The man (as subsequent events will prove) has nothing to recommend him except his need. Jesus knows this need in advance, puts a question to evoke at least the beginnings of personal trust and hope, and then, with a simple word of command, heals. The man's obedience to the

63

word of Jesus is his healing. On Jesus' side it is an act of loving concern; on the man's side, of obedience. This double strand of love and obedience is, as we shall learn again and again, what binds Jesus to the Father and the disciples to Jesus.

5:9b-18

Now that day was the sabbath. So the Jews said to the man who was cured, "It is the sabbath, it is not lawful for you to carry your pallet." But he answered them, "The man who healed me said to me, 'Take up your pallet, and walk.' " They asked him, "Who is the man who said to you, 'Take up your pallet, and walk'?" Now the man who had been healed did not know who it was, for Jesus had withdrawn, as there was a crowd in the place. Afterward, Jesus found him in the temple, and said to him, "See, you are well! Sin no more, that nothing worse befall you." The man went away and told the Jews that it was Jesus who had healed him. And this was why the Jews persecuted Jesus, because he did this on the sabbath. But Jesus answered them, "My Father is working still, and I am working." This was why the Jews sought all the more to kill him, because he not only broke the sabbath but also called God his Father, making himself equal with God.

After the healing is complete we learn that it was the Sabbath. That Jesus healed on the Sabbath was well known to John's readers. The full significance of these actions of Jesus is now to be expounded.

The law of the sabbatical rest was perhaps the most important of all the bulwarks by which Judaism was protected from erosion by the encompassing paganism. The blood of the martyrs had been freely shed to hallow it. The man, in obeying Jesus's word, was violating the Sabbath law. When charged (unlike the blind man of ch. 9) he immediately incriminates his unknown benefactor. This does not lead Jesus to remain incognito but—on the contrary—leads him to make himself known to the man he has healed. Healing and forgiveness belong together—as in Mark 2:1-12—for the work of Jesus is an attack upon the whole power of evil which manifests itself both in sickness and in sin. In obeying Jesus the man has been turned toward that which delivers from evil. But it is possible to turn back. The gift of salvation brings with it also the reality of judgment. The coming of light may lead people to seek the protection of darkness.

Therefore the man must be warned. But the warning does

not prevent him from immediately proceeding to report Jesus to the authorities. Predictably they are incensed because (not on this occasion only) Jesus made a practice of healing on the Sabbath and thus systematically violating the law. Why? That is now the question.

In the synoptic Gospels the replies of Jesus to those who ask the question are varied. They do suggest, however, the greatness of the claim: "Something greater than the temple" is present (Matt. 12:6). Here, however, the claim is much sharper and more vast in its implications. "My Father is working still, and I am working." It seems to have been accepted by the rabbis that God's Sabbath rest did not mean that he had ceased to give life—for babies are born on the Sabbath and rain falls. Nor did it mean that he ceased his work as the moral governor of the universe. God is always—even on the Sabbath—the giver of life and the judge of all. This never-ceasing work of giving life and of judging is the work of God; therefore it is the work of Jesus. What has happened to the crippled man is this work of God who is—on the Sabbath also—always the giver of life.

This, therefore, is something much more serious even than the violation of the Sabbath. It is—or it appears to be—a direct assault upon the central affirmation of the Old Testament: "The Lord our God is one Lord," and upon the command which necessarily follows: "You shall have no other gods before me." For a man to "make himself equal with God" is the ultimate blasphemy, with which there can be no compromise.

Jewish monotheism was always threatened by the open or subtle assaults of various kinds of syncretism and polytheism—assaults which equally threaten monotheism today. Any claim—however genial and broad-minded—which blurs the distinction between God and that which is no god necessarily threatens to put man back in the central place where he can make his own gods and so destroy the seriousness of the encounter of the one and only living God with man who is creature and not creator. The words of Jesus—if they mean what they appear to mean—can only be a declaration of war to the death.

In fact they do *not* mean what the Jews take them to mean, and Jesus at once embarks upon a long exposition which has been described as "a defence of Christian monotheism" (Lightfoot).

5:19-24

Jesus said to them, "Truly, truly, I say to you, the Son can do nothing of his own accord, but only what he sees the Father doing; for whatever he does, that the Son does likewise. For the Father loves the Son, and shows him all that he himself is doing; and greater works than these will he show him, that you may marvel. For as the Father raises the dead and gives them life, so also the Son gives life to whom he will. The Father judges no one, but has given all judgment to the Son, that all may honor the Son, even as they honor the Father. He who does not honor the Son does not honor the Father who sent him. Truly, truly, I say to you, he who hears my word and believes him who sent me, has eternal life; he does not come into judgment, but has passed from death to life."

The Jews have used the word "equal." Jesus bypasses this word altogether. The unity of Father and Son is not one of "equality" but of love and obedience. Jesus is utterly dependent upon the Father, and precisely because this is so Jesus is entrusted with the fullness of the Father's power both to give life and to judge—a power which the Father is exercising "till now" and which the Son will therefore also exercise in absolute obedience to the Father, and which he is able to exercise because the Father's love is given to him in fullness.

The Jews have understood the words of Jesus to be a claim to equality with God. In his reply Jesus shows that what is being revealed is not equality but unity. The unique intimacy which is conveyed in Jesus' constantly repeated phrase "my Father" implies a perfect unity which is not equality. These are two quite different and even opposed patterns of relation. The ideal of equality (which our culture has espoused from the rationalist elements in our pagan heritage) leads on to independence. Those who are in all respects equal do not need to depend on each other but can stand on their own feet. In spite of the fact that paternity appears to be a fact of life, paternalism is condemned as a violation of human dignity because it rests on inequality and involves dependence. Our ideal of human dignity is in fact the very ancient one advocated by the Serpent (Gen. 3:5), needing nothing and independent of any judgment of good and evil other than our own. In total contrast to this vision of equality, Jesus speaks of a relation between himself and his Father in which filial obedience is as complete and total as is paternal love. Unlike other men (cf. 1:18) Jesus "sees" what the Father does because the Father "shows" him, and so Jesus can offer total obedience to the Father—like a faithful son who is apprenticed to his father in the same craft. Just because this is so, the works of Jesus in healing and in judgment are the works of the Father. In accepting or rejecting Jesus men are accepting or rejecting God. In saying and doing what he has said and done Jesus is not usurping the place of God. He is manifesting the glory of God in actions which because they are completely obedient are completely effective instruments of the Father's love. On the other hand all ideas about what the word "God" means, whether on the lips of first-century rabbis or on those of twentieth-century theologians, must be tested by what is to be seen in the words and deeds of this totally humble and obedient man. That we have here the germ of the doctrine of the Trinity will be obvious. What should also become clear is that it is only in the trinitarian form that monotheism is ultimately defensible in the face of the power of evil in the world. Is it possible that the term *homoousios* (of one substance with the Father), introduced at Nicea, has in our contemporary Western culture given room for a misunderstanding? According to a Jewish proverb (quoted by Lightfoot, *ad loc.*), "a rebellious son is one who makes himself equal to his father." The total unity between Jesus and his Father is not to be understood as equality but only as love and obedience.

John's readers are among those who have had experience of the "greater works" (v. 20) of which Jesus speaks. They have known what it is to pass from death to life through faith in Jesus. And they know that this new life is constituted by a relation of love and obedience which binds them to Jesus as Jesus is bound in love and obedience to the Father (15:9-10).

5:25-29

"Truly, truly, I say to you, the hour is coming, and now is, when the dead will hear the voice of the Son of God, and those who hear will live. For as the Father has life in himself, so he has granted the Son also to have life in himself, and has given him authority to execute judgment, because he is the Son of man. Do not marvel at this; for the hour is coming when all who are in the tombs will hear his voice and come forth, those who have done good, to the resurrection of life, and those who have done evil, to the resurrection of judgment."

John's readers know what it is to have received life from the dead through the gift of forgiveness (e.g., I John 5:9-11; Eph. 2:1; Col. 3:1-4), but they know also that there is still something to look forward to. The Jews to whom Jesus speaks believe in a future resurrection and judgment, and Jesus does not set that belief aside. The new reality which now confronts them is that the one who is author both of resurrection and of judgment is present. He is present as "a son of man." The use of this phrase without the definite article is unique here in the Gospel, but it is found in the original vision (Dan. 7:13) from which this mysterious title is probably taken. It is to "one who has been in all points tempted as we are, yet without sin," to one who "learned obedience," that the Father has entrusted the authority both to give life and to be the judge. There is still a judgment to come— for believer and unbeliever alike. "We must all stand before the judgment seat of God" (II Cor. 5:10), and we look for a resurrection which is still to come (II Cor. 5:1ff.). This future hope is not eliminated by the element of "realized eschatology" in the Fourth Gospel. Because the one who is both life-giver and judge is present in person, there is already given to believers here and now ("the hour is coming *and now is,*" v. 25) an actual experience of life from the dead and deliverance from judgment in the present time. But there is also a real future ("the hour is coming," v. 28) when the life-giver and judge will have his final word in respect of all that has been, is, and will be. And this is none other than Jesus who is speaking to these hearers (v. 24).

5:30-40

"I can do nothing on my own authority; as I hear, I judge; and my judgment is just, because I seek not my own will but the will of him who sent me. If I bear witness to myself, my testimony is not true; there is another who bears witness to me, and I know that the testimony which he bears to me is true. You sent to John, and he has borne witness to the truth. Not that the testimony which I receive is from man; but I say this that you may be saved. He was a burning and shining lamp, and you were willing to rejoice for a while in his light. But the testimony which I have is greater than that of John; for the works which the Father has granted me to accomplish, these very works which I am doing, bear me witness that the Father has sent me. And the Father who sent me has himself borne witness to me. His voice you have never heard, his form you have never seen; and you do not have his word abiding in you, for you do not believe him whom he has sent. You search the scriptures, because you think that in them you have eternal life; and it is they that bear witness to me; yet you refuse to come to me that you may have life."

These stupendous claims are being made by "a son of man." Jesus is—after all—just the carpenter from Nazareth. How can such claims be tested? There have been others who have made such claims. Indeed history is full of the bizarre stories of men and women claiming divine authority. Most reasonable people dismiss such claims as absurd. Devoutly religious people are likely to reject them as blasphemous. In the synoptic Gospels the question of Jesus' authority is raised. It is noted that "he spoke with authority" and that this authority manifested itself in the healings and exorcisms. But there were also those who said that the authority was demonic. Here Jesus faces the question directly.

Jesus has no authority of his own (v. 30). He is the bearer of his Father's authority simply because he claims no independent judgment but is the totally obedient agent of the Father's will. The only authentication of this which is possible is one given by the Father himself. It cannot be authenticated by reference to something else, to some element in the already existing experience of the hearer. This is the problem of divine revelation. How can God reveal himself to man in such a way that the revelation is accepted as true in mind and conscience? If I approach the alleged revelation with the apparatus of my own critical intelligence which is itself a product of the particular culture in which I happen to live and apply the tests which this apparatus suggests, am I not guilty of trying to sit in judgment on God who is the one who must judge me, my reason, and my conscience? A true revelation of God must necessarily call in question all the criteria by which—in normal affairs—I judge what is possible, what is reasonable, what is admirable. But if on the other hand my reason and conscience are set aside, how can the revelation become true for me in any meaningful sense? The ultimate answer to the problem can only be given in terms of a trinitarian doctrine of God—of the Father who is the source of all being and of all truth, of the Son by whose perfect obedience the being and truth are present in a human life as part of public history, and of the Spirit of the Father and the Son by whose sovereign and gracious action my reason and conscience are enabled to acknowledge the Son and through him to join in glorifying the Father.

This trinitarian model was slow to develop but the seeds of it are in the Gospel, and it is proper to seek to understand what is here with the help of that into which it later grew.

A claim to authority by Jesus himself in his own name would be rightly rejected as inadmissible (v. 31). But in fact the authentication comes from the Father himself (v. 32). In the last analysis the authentication is part of the gift of life just referred to (v. 25). Those who have been called out of death into life cannot fail to acknowledge the voice of him who called them. "This is the testimony, that God gave us eternal life, and this life is in his Son" (I John 3:11). However, God does not leave himself without witnesses. These cannot "prove" the authenticity of Jesus' claim, but they do provide witnesses to it. There is, first, the witness of John the Baptist (vv. 33-35). He was not "the light coming into the world" (1:9), but he was a witness to that light (1:8). The Jews did give a welcome to John, but in the end they turned away from him and left him to his fate. By their turning away from that auxiliary witness the Jews had excluded themselves from the possibility of recognizing the true light. (Exactly the same point is made in the debate about authority in Mark 11:27-33.)

Secondly, there is the witness of the "works" of Jesus (v. 36). For those with eyes to see, these works are signs that the reign of God is present (cf. Luke 7:18-23). But for some they are not signs of the kingdom but causes of offense (Luke 7:23). Such people are offended because "they do not have [God's] word abiding" in them and so they do not recognize them as witnesses of the Father's approval (vv. 37f.). None of these "signs" can demonstrate the truth of Jesus' words. Only the presence of God's word in the heart can do this (cf. 3:32-36), but they do bear witness that Jesus is indeed one sent by God, as even Nicodemus had recognized (3:2).

And, thirdly, there is the witness of the scriptures (vv. 39f.). These also—rightly understood—point to Jesus as the one who gives life. If they are understood as themselves the source of life, they are misunderstood. In fact, so understood, they can lead only to condemnation and death. As Paul testifies: "The very commandment which promised life proved death to me" (Rom. 7:10). The true function of the Torah is not to be itself the source of life, but to lead the one who accepts it to Jesus who gives life (Gal. 3:23ff.). But the guardians of the religious establishment refuse this leading. The fundamental reason for this refusal will now be set forth.

5:41-47

"I do not receive glory from men. But I know that you have not the love of God within you. I have come in my Father's name, and you do not

receive me; if another comes in his own name, him you will receive. How can you believe, who receive glory from one another and do not seek the glory that comes from the only God? Do not think that I shall accuse you to the Father; it is Moses who accuses you, on whom you set your hope. If you believed Moses, you would believe me, for he wrote of me. But if you do not believe his writings, how will you believe my words?"

Here we come to the heart of the matter. It is a matter of true and false glory. The glory of God is his actual presence in such a manner that it needs no other witness. This glory is present in Jesus precisely because he neither seeks nor receives glory from men, makes no claim for himself, but is the totally humble, obedient, self-effacing, and therefore transparent bearer of the glory of the Father in whose name alone he has come. As long as men and women seek to be something in the eyes of one another they are stopped from recognizing that the only true glory is to be found in total self-emptying (v. 44). It is because Jesus seeks nothing for himself that he is the complete manifestation of the glory of the Father. It is because he is the Lord of all that he is also the slave (13:2-5; 12:1-5). But this is such a total subversion of all human ideas of greatness, of divinity, that it is rejected, and so the gift of life is refused (v. 40). The scriptures are misunderstood if they are taken to be a guide enabling people to have in themselves the truth and the righteousness of God, and therefore to be able to judge one another's achievements and so to receive glory from one another (cf. I Cor. 4:1-5; Rom. 10:1-4; Matt. 7:1f.). Those who follow this way may indeed be full of zeal (Rom. 10:2), but in fact scripture itself condemns them, for they are violating its most fundamental law: "Thou shalt love the Lord thy God." They do not, in fact, have the love of God within them. At heart it is self-love which leads them to claim a righteousness of their own and receive glory from one another. Therefore it is not necessary for Jesus to accuse them. They stand condemned by the scriptures on which they rely.

The glory of Jesus is "the glory of the only Son from the Father" (1:14). The glory is manifest in him just because he does not "make himself equal with God" (cf. Phil. 2:1-11). Those who seek and receive another kind of glory will refuse to come to this place of total self-effacement where alone life is to be found. Whether they be ecclesiastics defending their establishment, or theologians defending their systems, or "men of the world" defending their interests, they will fail to recognize this, the only true glory. But those who "hear and believe" (v. 24) will know that they have been delivered from death and will need no further authentication.

8

BREAD FROM HEAVEN
(6:1-71)

IN PURSUIT OF HIS PURPOSE TO LEAD THE READER INTO the faith that Jesus is the Son of God, and the giver of life, the evangelist proceeds to recount events which were already a part of the common tradition and to bring out their full meaning.

The synoptic Gospels—whether or not John is dependent on them—are evidence that Jesus had an extensive ministry in the area around the Sea of Galilee; that somewhere in its vicinity a great multitude was miraculously fed; that in the course of various crossings of the lake the disciples were caught in a storm and miraculously rescued by Jesus; that the feeding of the multitude led on to a demand by the Jews for a sign, to argument among the disciples about food and about the teaching which is symbolized by food, to Peter's confession of Jesus, and to the identification of a presence of Satan among the twelve (Matt. 12:13-33; 5:32–16:23; Mark 6:30-51; 8:1-33; Luke 9:10-22).

These memories of Jesus' ministry evoked still older memories enshrined in the tradition of Israel: that God had miraculously led his people through the waters; that he had fed them miraculously in the desert; that both their hunger and its satisfaction by "bread from heaven" (Ps. 78:21-25) were occasions of murmuring, of disputation, and of testing. The people had murmured against God and against Moses, and Moses had doubted God's power to feed such a multitude (Num. 11). In fact, God himself had tested his people. "He humbled you and let you hunger and fed you with manna, which you did not know, nor did your fathers know; that he might make you know that man does not live by bread alone, but that man lives by everything that proceeds out of the mouth of the LORD" (Deut. 8:3). The miraculous gift of food in the desert had been the occasion of testing the reality of faith and of exposing the existence of unbelief.

Even more immediate than these memories, however, was the fact that during his last meal with the disciples on the night of his betrayal, Jesus had spoken mysterious words which identified the bread and wine of their supper with the flesh and blood given for them and for the world, and that these actions and words were at the heart of the life of the fellowship of believers in which the evangelist is bearing his witness. At the Supper Jesus had both expounded his "new commandment" (John 13:34) and identified his blood to be shed on the cross as the blood of a "new covenant"—just as the giving of the law through Moses had been sealed by the shedding of blood (Num. 24:1-11).

And finally the evangelist tells us that the deeds and words of Jesus which he is about to recall were done and spoken on the eve of the Passover, the festival when lambs would be slain and blood sprinkled and the families of Israel would be gathering in their households to eat flesh and drink wine in celebration of their deliverance from bondage. The evangelist writes as one who knows that "Christ, our paschal lamb, has been sacrificed" (I Cor. 5:7), and he will recount these well-remembered events in Jesus' ministry in the light of these memories and this knowledge, and in such a way as to make still clearer the nature of faith and unbelief.

6:1-15

After this Jesus went to the other side of the Sea of Galilee, which is the Sea of Tiberias. And a multitude followed him, because they saw the signs which he did on those who were diseased. Jesus went up into the hills, and there sat down with his disciples. Now the Passover, the feast of the Jews, was at hand. Lifting up his eyes, then, and seeing that a multitude was coming to him, Jesus said to Philip, "How are we to buy bread, so that these people may eat?" This he said to test him, for he himself knew what he would do. Philip answered him, "Two hundred denarii would not buy enough bread for each of them to get a little." One of his disciples, Andrew, Simon Peter's brother, said to him, "There is a lad here who has five barley loaves and two fish; but what are they among so many?" Jesus said, "Make the people sit down." Now there was much grass in the place; so the men sat down, in number about five thousand. Jesus then took the loaves, and when he had given thanks, he distributed them to those who were seated; so also the fish, as much as they wanted. And when they had eaten their fill, he told his disciples,

"Gather up the fragments left over, that nothing may be lost." So they gathered them up and filled twelve baskets with fragments from the five barley loaves, left by those who had eaten. When the people saw the sign which he had done, they said, "This is indeed the prophet who is come into the world!"

Perceiving then that they were about to come and take him by force to make him king, Jesus withdrew again to the hills by himself.

The reader knows that the healing miracle recounted in the previous chapter is only one example of the healing which Jesus practiced wherever he went. It is natural that a crowd will flock to one who has powers of healing; but this "following" is not faith. It has not penetrated behind the healing to the mysterious person of the healer in whom God is offering his own eternal life.

So Jesus, like Moses before him, is surrounded by a vast crowd. And like Moses he asks where food enough for them is to be found (cf. Num. 11:21f.). But unlike Moses, he puts the question not in scepticism, not "to put the LORD God to the test," but because he knows what he will do. The question is put to the disciples to test their faith in God. The response of Andrew is a small but genuine response of faith struggling against a background of scepticism. He offers what in effect is material for one man's picnic. Jesus accepts the offer, takes the bread into his hands, offers the prayer of thanksgiving to the Father (and the word used is "eucharist"), and distributes the bread and the fish to the multitude. Like the disciples at the Last Supper (but unlike the crowds in the synoptic narratives) they receive the food direct from his hands and not through intermediaries. The bread is barley bread—the food of the poor, used in the eucharistic practice of the early Church. The entire multitude is satisfied. The resources of God are enough and far more than enough for human need; there is a vast surplus which the disciples are instructed to gather carefully—for nothing that the Father gives is to be lost.

The crowd had followed Jesus because they saw him as a healer, as one who could satisfy their needs. The feeding confirms their opinion. Moses, who had led Israel out of slavery and had called down manna from heaven, had also promised that the Lord would send another prophet like himself who would speak God's word (Deut. 18:15ff.), and it seems to have been a common belief that he also would bring down manna from heaven. Jesus must be this promised prophet. The long-awaited day of a new deliverance is at hand. The enthusiasm of the crowd rises; they will seize him forthwith and make him their leader.

This is not faith but unbelief. They have not understood who Jesus is. Jesus will not be the instrument of any human enthusiasm or the symbol for any human program. To say "Jesus is king" is true if the word "king" is wholly defined by the person of Jesus; it is false and blasphemous if Jesus is made instrumental to a definition of kingship derived from elsewhere. Jesus has come "to proclaim liberty to the captives," but he will not become the mascot for a people's movement of liberation. At the very moment when the cry "Make Jesus king" is rending the air Jesus abruptly disappears, leaving both the crowds and the disciples with no visible goal for their enthusiasm. And on that scene of disappointed hope night falls. Jesus is alone with his Father. The crowds are left on the hillside, and the disciples are left without an answer to the question "Where has he gone?" They are—in every sense—in the dark.

6:16-24

When evening came, his disciples went down to the sea, got into a boat, and started across the sea to Caperna-um. It was now dark, and Jesus had not yet come to them. The sea rose because a strong wind was blowing. When they had rowed about three or four miles, they saw Jesus walking on the sea and drawing near to the boat. They were frightened, but he said to them, "It is I; do not be afraid." Then they were glad to take him into the boat, and immediately the boat was at the land to which they were going.

On the next day the people who remained on the other side of the sea saw that there had been only one boat there, and that Jesus had not entered the boat with his disciples, but that his disciples had gone away alone. However, boats from Tiberias came near the place where they ate the bread after the Lord had given thanks. So when the people saw that Jesus was not there, nor his disciples, they themselves got into the boats and went to Caperna-um, seeking Jesus.

The evangelist recounts this story, in spite of the fact that it interrupts the transition from the feeding to its interpretation, because it is securely fixed in the tradition which has been received (Mark 6:30-52). But if we keep steadily in mind the evangelist's purpose we shall see how important is the retelling of this incident at this point.

Who is Jesus? That is the central question. There is a multitude ready to answer with the acclamation "He is our king." Jesus has—by his abrupt departure—disowned that ascription. The disciples, perplexed and at a loss, bereft of their master, decide to escape from the clamor of the crowd and to find their way home across the lake under cover of darkness. Deeper than the darkness is the fact that they are bereft. "It was now dark, and Jesus had not yet come to them." More violent than the storm that threatens to drown them are their doubts and perplexities. And then—at the moment of greatest distress—they behold Jesus and they hear the words "It is I; do not be afraid." Who, then, is this? To make a path through the sea is the prerogative of the one whose name is "I am." It is he who "made the depths of the sea a way for the redeemed to pass over" and who says "I, I am he that comforts you" (Isa. 51:10, 12). It is he of whom it is said that he stills the storm and brings the travelers to the haven where they would be glad because they have quiet (Ps. 107:29f.). This "gladness" the evangelist records; there is nothing corresponding to Mark's statement at this point that "they did not understand about the loaves because their hearts were hardened" (Mark 6:52). John reserves a long discussion about the proper "understanding about the loaves" for the next section of his narrative.

For this purpose he returns to the crowd left throughout the night on the hillside. When dawn breaks they find that the disciples have left by the only available boat and that Jesus has left by means unknown; they cross the lake in search of him and find him in Capernaum. The scene is now set for a long discussion "about the loaves."

6:25-34

When they found him on the other side of the sea, they said to him, "Rabbi, when did you come here?" Jesus answered them, "Truly, truly, I say to you, you seek me, not because you saw signs, but because you ate your fill of the loaves. Do not labor for the food which perishes, but for the food which endures to eternal life, which the Son of man will give to you; for on him has God the Father set his seal." Then they said to him, "What must we do, to be doing the works of God?" Jesus answered them, "This is the work of God, that you believe in him whom he has sent." So they said to him, "Then what sign do you do, that we may see, and believe you? What work do you perform? Our fathers ate the manna in the wilderness; as it is written, 'He gave them bread from

*heaven to eat.' " Jesus then said to them, "Truly, truly, I say to you,
it was not Moses who gave you the bread from heaven; my Father gives
you the true bread from heaven. For the bread of God is that which comes
down from heaven, and gives life to the world." They said to him,
"Lord, give us this bread always."*

The crowds who had been fed on the hills above the lake
were presumably Galileans. In the ensuing discussion, however,
the participants are referred to as "the Jews." Moreover, the opening address to Jesus—"Rabbi"—in verse 25 does not seem to
accord with the proposal of the Galileans to make him king. It
has been suggested that the core of what follows is an exposition
of the verse in Psalm 78 ("He gave them bread from heaven to
eat") in a style commonly employed by the rabbis. We know
from the synoptics that Jesus was accustomed to teach in the
synagogue. It may well be that the evangelist has in fact placed
such an exposition given by Jesus "in the synagogue" (v. 59) at
this point in his work. The title "Rabbi" shows that the discussion
is concerned with the teaching of Jesus as well as with the miraculous feeding, and in fact these two themes—teaching and
feeding, hearing and eating, word and sacrament—are woven
together throughout the ensuing dialogue.

The opening question (v. 25) implies that there is a mystery
about the way Jesus has crossed the lake, but Jesus ignores this
and goes straight to the question which his interlocutors must
face: What are they really seeking?

The deeds of Jesus, such as the one they have just witnessed
(vv. 26f.), are both "mighty works" and "signs." They are effective actions which liberate people from disease, hunger, and
death, and they are signs which point beyond these immediate
effects to the kingly rule of God present in Jesus. The crowd has
enjoyed the effect, but has failed to see the sign. And the effect—
like all such effects—is transient. The hungry man is fed, but he
hungers again. The sick man is healed, but he will die. The victim
of oppression is delivered, but he becomes the slave of other
"principalities and powers." These visible acts of liberation are
not to be made the prime object of desire and labor; they are signs
pointing to a gift that is never exhausted, a satisfaction that never
passes. This is the gift of the "Son of man," the one who comes
as a man—Jesus the son of Joseph (v. 42)—but who is at the
same time the bearer of the seal of the Spirit, of that gift "from
above" which comes from the Father and abides in the Son (1:32f.).

If you see only the visible effect and fail to see the sign, your life will be an endless "rat race" in pursuit of satisfactions which never endure. Why, then, "do you spend your money for that which is not bread, and your labor for that which does not satisfy" (Isa. 55:2)? The true bread which gives eternal satisfaction will be the gift of the Son of man when he has been lifted up and pours out upon believers the life-giving Spirit.

Like the Samaritan woman, the crowd are sufficiently interested to ask the obvious question: What has to be done to achieve this satisfaction? What is the program? What is the path that will take us out of the meaningless maze of satisfactions pursued and achieved only to be forgotten in an ever-new dissatisfaction? What is the work God wants of us? (v. 28).

The answer (v. 29) is that it is not a "work" at all. No works can achieve what we know we desire above all else. It can only be a gift received in trust. This is the "work of God"—not only in the sense that it is the work God desires but in the sense (which will be made clear as we proceed) that it is the work which God does. For to receive in trust God's gift of himself in the man Jesus is not something which I can of myself accomplish. It is strictly "a work of God" that I believe in him whom he has sent, for "no one can come to [Jesus] unless the Father draws him" (v. 44). This is so because it is impossible that my perceptions, distorted as they are by the fact that I make myself the center of my world, could of themselves recognize and receive the presence of God in this man. Consequently "the flesh is of no avail" (v. 63). Only that which is from above, the Spirit, can give life. Here is the terrible paradox of human nature. We know that love alone is the supreme good. Yet to seek that good directly as an achievement of the self-centered ego is to shut oneself in the prison of self-love. That which is our supreme need can only be a gift. But the "heart turned in upon itself" will demand proof of the reality of the gift when it is offered.

It follows therefore that a sign is demanded (vv. 30f.). A sign is something which validates the claim of an alleged revelation by showing that it accords with the requirements of reason, conscience, and experience as I recognize them. It is—in other words—something which subordinates the alleged revelation to the prior requirements of my human mind and conscience. It is what enables "flesh and blood" to grasp and accept something new. The "prophet who is to come into the world" like Moses will call down bread from heaven as a sign that the new age has really dawned. Can the man from Nazareth do likewise? If so, we can believe.

In reply to this demand (vv. 32f.) Jesus directs their attention to the text which they themselves have quoted from the 78th Psalm: "He gave them bread from heaven to eat." What is the real meaning of these words? Who is the subject? Not Moses but God, for only God who is in heaven can give the bread of heaven. And what is this bread? What is it, in fact, that gives life? Was it not made clear to the men of old that the manna itself was a sign designed to test those who received it, to teach them that it is not by bread but by the word of God that life is given (Deut. 8:3)? In fact, it was a common thought that the real manna which gives life is the living word of instruction in the Torah. "Thou gavest thy good Spirit to instruct them, and didst not withhold thy manna from their mouth" (Neh. 9:20). But in truth the Torah has not given life. Only God himself can give life. Only if he who is in heaven comes down from heaven can the true life be made available to the world. But that inconceivable happening is in fact the present reality which is now confronting them. "My Father is now giving you the true bread from heaven"—the reality which is "from above" and which is (life-giving) Spirit and truth. Only now is the real meaning of the text from Psalm 78 being revealed.

Like the Samaritan woman ("Give me this water, so that I may not thirst, nor come here to draw") the people eagerly but without understanding reach out for what they think is being offered—satisfaction on their own terms (v. 34). They are ready to believe that Jesus can give what they seek; they have yet to learn that he *is* what they *need*.

6:35-40

Jesus said to them, "I am the bread of life; he who comes to me shall not hunger, and he who believes in me shall never thirst. But I said to you that you have seen me and yet do not believe. All that the Father gives me will come to me; and him who comes to me I will not cast out. For I have come down from heaven, not to do my own will, but the will of him who sent me; and this is the will of him who sent me, that I should lose nothing of all that he has given me, but raise it up at the last day. For this is the will of my Father, that every one who sees the Son and believes in him should have eternal life; and I will raise him up at the last day."

Jesus is now ready to unveil the central mystery. He is in his own person, this man of flesh and blood, the presence of the one who alone gives life. His invitation is without limit. For all who come, without exception, he is the secret of eternal satisfaction. Here the promise is fulfilled which the law could not fulfil. Here the invitation is valid "Ho, every one who thirsts, come to the waters; and he who has no money, come, buy and eat!" (Isa. 55:1).

The invitation is without limit in its generosity. But it is not coercive. Jesus can speak these amazing words not because he exercises any powers of his own, far less because he claims to be "equal with God" (5:18). The exact opposite is the case. Jesus can speak these words because he claims nothing for himself but is simply the humble, meek, obedient child of his Father. It is in his nothingness that his fullness consists, because only so is he the bearer of the true life which does not seek to climb up to heaven but comes down from heaven.

Jesus therefore has no attractive power in himself. "He had no beauty that we should desire him" (Isa. 53:2). On the contrary he testified to his questioners: "You have seen me and yet do not believe." Jesus exercises no power of his own over others. He is not a god walking on earth in the style of a Hindu *avatar*. The "heart turned in upon itself" which finds the center of the universe in itself, seeks a god in its own image. How, then, can the true and living God reveal himself otherwise than in the form of a contradiction of every human image of godhead? But if the revelation is only by a contradiction, how can it ever be grasped as revelation? If those who see Jesus do not believe, how shall anyone come to him?

Only if the Father himself "draws them" (v. 44) and "gives them" (v. 37) to Jesus. Only a secret work of God in the heart of a person can bring that person to see in this humble, obedient man the presence of the sovereign Lord of all. No one can call Jesus Lord except by the Spirit of God (I Cor. 12:3). The claim that the sovereign wisdom of God is revealed in a crucified man is scandalous or meaningless except to those who have been called and commissioned by God to be the hearers of the claim (I Cor. 1:23f.). But they will themselves contradict their own calling if they imagine that by their own power or wisdom they can draw men to Christ. For them also the promise of being filled with the fullness of God will be realized only in their nothingness (I Cor. 1:26-31).

To those whom the Father so gives to Jesus that they become believers, there is a triple promise. First, that he will receive them and will not cast them out. The penitent thief on the cross is received instantly and unconditionally into the fellowship of Jesus. The love of Jesus is total and without limit. Secondly, they will receive now the gift of eternal life. They will share already in the life of heaven because they share the life of Jesus in whom the life of heaven is present in the form of loving obedience to the Father. Thirdly, they can look forward with assured certainty to sharing in the victory of Christ "at the last day." Thus the past, the present, and the future are secure. The sin of the past has been blotted out and the believer is accepted forthwith into the fellowship of Jesus. The present is lived in that fellowship with Jesus which is a sharing in the life of heaven. The future is secure because Jesus whose resurrection is the dawning of a new age will raise up those who belong to him at the end.

6:41-51

The Jews then murmured at him, because he said, "I am the bread which came down from heaven." They said, "Is not this Jesus, the son of Joseph, whose father and mother we know? How does he now say, "I have come down from heaven'?" Jesus answered them, "Do not murmur among yourselves. No one can come to me unless the Father who sent me draws him; and I will raise him up at the last day. It is written in the prophets, 'And they shall all be taught by God.' Every one who has heard and learned from the Father comes to me. Not that any one has seen the Father except him who is from God; he has seen the Father. Truly, truly, I say to you, he who believes has eternal life. I am the bread of life. Your fathers ate the manna in the wilderness, and they died. This is the bread which comes down from heaven, that a man may eat of it and not die. I am the living bread which came down from heaven; if any one eats of this bread, he will live for ever; and the bread which I shall give for the life of the world is my flesh."

All the Gospels bear witness to the fact that Jesus' contemporaries were scandalized by the apparent incongruity between the vast claims implied by his words and deeds and the fact that he was just a working man from a well-known village. This incongruity is found equally scandalous by many theologians. How can contingent happenings in a particular time and place be

determinative for all times and places? How can a man whose
origins are known say "I came down from heaven"? How can a
man with a known name and address be God?

Everything depends upon whether the meaning of the word
"God" has already been fixed with reference to the general religious experience of the human race. As far as we know, there is
no human language which does not have some equivalent for the
English word "God." There is therefore a vast body of data available from which it is possible to draw conclusions about the
reality of human experience which is embodied in this word.
From these conclusions it is then possible to proceed to an as-
sessment of the records about Jesus, and of the claim "I have
come down from heaven." The results will vary greatly according
to the religious and cultural presuppositions of the investigator.
One thing, however, is certain: they will not lead to the conclusion that Jesus is what these verses imply (vv. 41f.).

The writer of the Gospel is not writing on the basis of these
presuppositions. He is one of those whom the Father has drawn
and given to Jesus and who has believed. From this point of view
he is bearing witness to what he has seen. And from this point
of view it is clear that the general religious experience of the
human race is not a basis from which it is safe to start because it
is in fact sinful experience and was shown to be such in the rejection and condemnation of Jesus by its representatives. From
this point of view, therefore, one has to begin to learn the meaning of the word "God" by "coming to Jesus" and learning from
him of the one he calls "my Father." From this point of view it
is clear that a knowledge of God could not come by induction
from the religious experience of the race, but could only come
by the presence, in flesh and blood in the world of ordinary
human secular experience, of one who confronts us in the concrete particularity of a man with a known name and address.

And if, then, these two points of view are placed side by
side and compared, and if one asks "How do I choose between
them?", the only possible answer is that you do not choose; you
are chosen. "No one can come to me unless the Father who sent
me draws him" (v. 44). There is no method of demonstration,
persuasion, or psychological manipulation by which this choice
may be programmed. It is strictly a work of God, and the only
demonstration will be "at the last day."

But this does not mean that the Father is niggardly or sparing in his action of drawing men to Jesus. As the prophet Isaiah said, he has promised that all shall be taught of God (Isa. 54:13). Yet this does not take away the responsibility that rests upon each to hear and learn from the Father (v. 45).

But this "hearing and learning" does not mean that the believer "sees the Father." Only of the Son can it be said without reserve that he "sees" the Father. The direct immediate vision of the Father could only shatter the perception of sinful men and women. But because Jesus has come "in the likeness of sinful flesh" (Rom. 8:3) it is possible for sinful men and women to believe and so to share in the life of God, the life which has come down from heaven and is present in Jesus (v. 46).

In the exposition of the text "He gave them bread from heaven to eat," we have learned that the giver is the Father, that the bread is Jesus, and that for "gave" we must read "is giving." We have now to consider the last two words of the text. In what way does one "eat" this bread? Up to this point the language has mainly suggested that it is by "learning," "hearing," and "believing" that one receives Jesus (v. 47). This is fully in line with the strand of Old Testament teaching which identified the manna with the Torah. But now we turn to look at the words "to eat."

Jesus is himself "the bread of life" (v. 48). This means not merely that he lives but that he is the giver of life. Consequently, while those who ate the manna had their hunger temporarily assuaged but eventually died, those who "eat" Jesus will not die because Jesus is the life-giving power of God "come down" into the life of the world. And if it is asked: "What is the bread that has to be 'eaten'?", Jesus answers: "My flesh." The deliberately crude and shocking word forces the reader to look beyond the language of hearing and believing, beyond the language of the Torah, of teaching and instruction, and to ask "What more is implied?"

For the Christian reader of the Gospel the indications are clear. He is accustomed every week to share an action of reading and expounding the law and the prophets, hearing and believing. But he is also accustomed to an action which goes beyond this, to an eating and drinking of bread and wine identified in the words of Jesus with "my flesh" and "my blood." There have in fact already been in the earlier part of the discussion hints which pointed in this direction. And in moving from Torah, teaching, to sacramental action the Christian believer is not departing from the pattern found in the Old Testament when the reading of the law is followed and sealed by the sprinkling of the blood (Ex. 24:7f.).

Nevertheless these words necessarily provoke a still sharper debate in which not only "the Jews" but also "the disciples" are involved. The word "flesh" emphasizes in the sharpest possible way the "materialism" of Jesus' words. While Greek has two distinct words for "body" and "flesh," Aramaic has one. If, as we must assume, the words spoken at the Last Supper were spoken in Aramaic, then—in contrast to the translation "body" used elsewhere in the New Testament—we have here the deliberate use of the translation "flesh" which shifts the content of what it means to receive Jesus as the bread of life away from a purely mental and spiritual hearing and believing, in the direction of a physical chewing and swallowing.

We have already learned that "the bread" is Jesus. We now learn, more precisely, that the bread is his flesh and that it is given for the life of the world—that is, in order that the world may have life. This life-giving work is accomplished by the death of Jesus; only so can he give life. But this life is received only by "eating" this bread which is the flesh of Jesus. We have here the Johannine version of the words spoken at the supper when Jesus gave the bread to the disciples and said, "Take and eat: this is my body [my flesh] given for you." By eating this bread they become participants in his dying and so in his risen life. It is thus that Jesus "gives life to the world."

But these words, spoken in this context, are unintelligible and cause still sharper controversy.

6:52-59

The Jews then disputed among themselves, saying, "How can this man give us his flesh to eat?" So Jesus said to them, "Truly, truly, I say to you, unless you eat the flesh of the Son of man and drink his blood, you have no life in you; he who eats my flesh and drinks my blood has eternal life, and I will raise him up at the last day. For my flesh is food indeed, and my blood is drink indeed. He who eats my flesh and drinks my blood abides in me, and I in him. As the living Father sent me, and I live because of the Father, so he who eats me will live because of me. This is the bread which came down from heaven, not such as the fathers ate and died; he who eats this bread will live for ever." This he said in the synagogue, as he taught at Caperna-um.

To eat human flesh ("this man," v. 52) is something unthinkable. To drink human blood (v. 53) is even worse. Yet Jesus insists that it is only by eating the flesh and drinking the blood of "the Son of man" that the life he promises is to be had. To say that Jesus is the life-giving bread is not only to say that to hear and believe his teaching is to have life. It is to say that Jesus in his concrete humanity (flesh and blood) is the actual presence of the life of God in the midst of the contingent happenings of human history. But the life of God is present not in any form of self-sufficiency but only in the form of unlimited self-surrender. It is made available to the world only by being given away—the flesh and blood of this man given up to death. It follows that there can be no participation in the life of God except by an equally concrete factual participation in the self-surrender of Jesus—in his broken body and his shed blood. The hearing and believing of the words of Jesus properly lead on to an act of communion, of eating and drinking in accordance with his own words which constitute this act as an effective sign and means of participation in his death and therefore in his life. And—for the first readers of the Gospel— this act of communion carried with it the constant possibility of actual suffering and death, and the total commitment to be faithful in following the way of the cross to the end. Those who thus "bear about in the body the dying of Jesus" have also the life of Jesus . . . manifested in their bodies" (II Cor. 4:10). In this way they live "because of Jesus" just as Jesus "lives because of the Father" (v. 57). And the resurrection of Jesus from the dead is their pledge that this "living through dying" will be consummated in the end by a victorious life from the dead (v. 54).

This, and nothing less than this, is the real meaning of the text "He gave them bread to eat." The giver is the Father. The bread is Jesus. It is eaten by actual participation in the midst of history in his own total self-giving which is the manifestation of the life of God in the life of the world. And the end result is the resurrection of the dead to a new and eternal life. Such was the. way in which Jesus "in the synagogue" expounded these words of scripture (v. 59).

6:60-65

Many of his disciples, when they heard it, said, "This is a hard saying; who can listen to it?" But Jesus, knowing in himself that his disciples murmured at it, said to them, "Do you take offense at this? Then what if you were to see the Son of man ascending where he was before? It is the spirit that gives life, the flesh is of no avail; the words that I have spoken to you are spirit and life. But there are some of you that do not believe." For Jesus knew from the first who those were that did not believe, and who it was that should betray him. And he said, "This is why I told you that no one can come to me unless it is granted him by the Father."

The "murmuring" which has been the background of the whole discussion—as it was the background of the giving of the manna to Israel—now begins to infect the disciples. In what respect is the word of Jesus a "hard" saying? From the parallel passages in the synoptics we know that Jesus' teaching about his death created a crisis of faith among his closest disciples. We know also from the Johannine epistles that the emphasis upon the "flesh" of Jesus was the cause of division (e.g., I John 4:1-3; II John 7). Both of the causes of offense (and they are of course interrelated) are present in the discourse. The response of Jesus to this incipient unbelief is to direct attention to the future. When Jesus washed the disciples' feet and Peter protested, Jesus told him, "What I am doing you do not know now, but afterward you will understand" (13:7). Indeed, "flesh and blood"—which are "from below"—cannot understand the mystery of Jesus. Only the Spirit from above can bring illumination (cf. 3:5-8) Jesus has yet to "ascend where he was before" (v. 62), and only then will the Spirit be poured out upon the disciples (cf. 7:39 and 20:19-23). Only the Spirit can give life; apart from the Spirit words are mere words and flesh is dead flesh.

"Unless you eat the flesh of the Son of man and drink his blood, you have no life in you" (v. 53). "It is the Spirit that gives life, the flesh is of no avail" (v. 63). In the juxtaposition of these two statements lies not evidence of textual dislocation or incompetent editing, but the heart of the whole matter—the heart, in fact, of the gospel.

That which is born of flesh is flesh. The heart of man, turned in upon itself so that its center is mistaken for the center of the universe (*atma* = *brahma*), is quite capable of entertaining an infinite variety of images of God. However lofty and "spiritual" they may be, they are—in biblical language—flesh. How can this ego, imprisoned in itself, be met, called, and liberated by the living God? Only if that meeting and calling takes place in the sphere where man is: only if the word is made flesh; only in the presence of one who is a son of man, a man of flesh and blood. But if it is to be a real meeting with the living and true God, who is not a product of human "spirituality," there will necessarily be a contradiction, a scandal. The sovereignty of the ego will be questioned by something which contradicts its claims and which resists the demand to be co-opted for its own purposes ("they were about to come and take him by force to make him king"). How, then, is the contradiction to be overcome? How can there be a revelation of the living God which is other than a contradiction? And if it is a contradiction, how can it be received as a revelation? Only if there is an action of the living God himself, God as living and active Spirit, which makes of human words and a human life (flesh, blood) the place where the true life "from above" is present. Only if the Spirit quickens the flesh.

Materialism and spiritualism are both evasions of this meeting. They are alternative strategies by which man seeking sovereignty in his own will evades the calling of him who is Creator and Lord of all things visible and invisible. The first supposes that the visible and measurable world is the ultimate reality and that man is free to impose his own meaning and therefore his mastery upon it. The second supposes that the ultimate reality is mental or spiritual and that it is by formulating true ideas that man can reach his proper goal as a spiritual being. In fact—however—both of these strategies leave man at the center of his own universe and therefore a prisoner. His liberation can come only when he is met by a real human life sharing his own world ("flesh and blood") which yet totally contradicts his own dream of mastery, and when by the acts of the living Spirit of God himself this "flesh and blood" becomes the place of a new life "from above." This can only be an act of God himself ("No one can come to me unless it is granted him by the Father"). But this act has happened. There are believers who bear witness as the evangelist is doing. There is no way by which the action "from above" can be dispensed with. Neither word nor sacrament is a means by which people can secure the life of heaven for themselves or for others. Words are words, flesh is flesh. But the words of Jesus are "spirit and life." When Jesus took bread and wine and said: "This is my body, given for you," his words were not empty. They were—and are—actions of the living Spirit of God. The words of the living God are themselves creative: they effect what they say. Those whom the Father draws will "draw near and receive" the flesh of Jesus, knowing that there is being given to them something which is far more than they can grasp, the life of God given for the life of the world. But this "knowing" will be a matter of believing. It depends from first to last upon a faith which trusts where it does not see. The flesh remains flesh. It does not become something which can be used or manipulated to secure the gift of God. But neither is it simply a symbol of a "spiritual" (i.e., mental) reality, of my own religion. It is received by faith as the concrete gift of the flesh of the Son of God given for the life of the world. It is a reality, given "from above" ("he gave them bread from heaven to eat"), which is always more than my understanding can grasp but which I receive in faith—a faith which leads on to obedient following.

"In faith." There are believers. But there are also unbelievers—and unbelievers within the circle of disciples. Revelation in flesh and blood must be contradiction of flesh and blood. It must involve "scandal." The rock which is the cornerstone is also the rock of offense. The words of Jesus therefore cause division in which those who had been "disciples" are shown to be in fact unbelievers. They stumble at the "scandal" of the flesh of Jesus. If the language here reflects the experience of the Johannine communities (e.g., I John 4:2f.; II John 7), unbelief springs from the desire for a more "spiritual" religion. The "flesh" of Jesus—the concrete humanity of the Son of man—is the stumbling block because it forbids the kind of "spirituality" which leaves each man free in the privacy of his own thoughts to give his allegiance to the "truth" as he has himself discovered it. That kind of "spiritual religion" is exactly "the flesh" in biblical language. It is unbelief, and it is present in the midst of the disciples.

6:66-71

After this many of his disciples drew back and no longer went about with him. Jesus said to the twelve, "Will you also go away?" Simon Peter answered him, "Lord, to whom shall we go? You have the words of eternal life; and we have believed, and have come to know, that you are the Holy One of God." Jesus answered them, "Did I not choose you, the twelve, and one of you is a devil?" He spoke of Judas the son of Simon Iscariot, for he, one of the twelve, was to betray him.

Unbelief cannot remain permanently hidden. It issues eventually in open apostasy. The faithful exposition of the meaning of scripture has led not to "church growth" but to its opposite. The testing goes on relentlessly until it touches the central core of Jesus' company—"the twelve." In the synoptic account it is the explicit teaching about the cross which causes the crisis of faith, and it is Peter who is identified as the "Satan" (Matt. 16:21-23). Here the necessity of Jesus' death is contained within the language about the flesh and blood of Jesus. But here Peter speaks on behalf of the twelve, making a full confession of faith in Jesus as the holy one of God and the giver of life, and it is Judas who is identified as "a devil." But how close Peter and Judas are! Well might the disciples ask at the end, "Is it I?" (Mark 14:19). All of them have been chosen by Jesus, and they are with him by his choice, not by theirs. Yet belief and unbelief both remain as realities within the company of his choice. So it is, and so it has been from the beginning. Jesus has chosen and called them, but they are free—free to be with him or to leave him. Jesus will never cast out any who come to him. But neither will he cajole, persuade, or bribe anyone to remain. His company will therefore always include those who do not believe and who will in the end betray. To believe is to have been brought to the place where one knows that one has to rely completely on Jesus, and on Jesus alone.

9

LIGHT AND DARKNESS
(7:1–8:59)

WE HAVE SEEN HOW THE WORD OF JESUS HAS THE POWER to test men's desires and to sift their thoughts so that true believers are distinguished from those who follow Jesus because they are attracted by his miracles. We have seen the sifting and testing pressed right into the center of Jesus' company, to the twelve themselves. We now come to a long passage in which the crisis created by the presence of the light in the midst of the darkness of the world creates an almost unbearable tension. We see the light shining in the darkness, and the darkness seeking to destroy it. Like the parallel passages in the synoptic Gospels, this confrontation between Jesus and "the Jews" is located in the Temple. But whereas the synoptics place it in the week of the passion, just before the Passover, the Fourth Gospel places it during the Feast of Tabernacles. This was the most popular of the annual festivals and drew vast crowds to Jerusalem. It was originally the celebration of the completion of the harvest, but it had become filled with a strong element of eschatological expectation. It was a foretaste of the age to come, of the final harvest. Its central ceremonies made use of the symbolism of water and light. Each day water was drawn from the pool of Siloam and carried up to the Temple in procession, while the words of Isaiah 12:3 were sung ("With joy you will draw water from the wells of salvation"). The prophecy of Zechariah 14:8 that "on that day" living waters would flow out from Jerusalem was recalled. And at night the Temple courts were brilliantly lit up—recalling the preceding verse (Zech. 14:7) with its promise of unending daylight. The form of Jesus' teaching on this occasion is clearly governed by these festival themes of "living water" and light.

91

Its content is based upon the healing of the paralytic on the Sabbath, recorded in chapter 5. While the synoptics speak of many miracles of healing, it is characteristic of the Fourth Gospel that the evangelist takes one such miracle and probes its meaning to the deepest level. He wants the reader not only to see the effect but to understand the sign and to believe. But the parallel with the synoptics is close. Mark (3:1-6) records an occasion when Jesus was confronted in the synagogue on the Sabbath by a man with a paralyzed arm. The authorities see it as an opportunity to test Jesus' obedience to the law. With a simple and direct word Jesus exposes the murderous intent that lies behind their religious zeal. So far from being upholders of the law they are in fact murderers—and forthwith they set about plans to kill Jesus. Such is the crisis created by the fact that "light has come into the world." What Mark compresses into a brief recital is—in the Fourth Gospel—developed with ruthless logic in these long arguments with and among Jesus' contemporaries. Whether in Mark or in John they are to be understood only in the light of the cross and resurrection.

Another, less prominent, theme also runs through both the Marcan and the Johannine accounts—the theme of secrecy. In Mark, when Jesus is on his way to Jerusalem, the disciples are repeatedly warned both of the necessity of his death and of the need for complete secrecy. They are to tell no one who he is. Why is this so? Because the revealing of the living God can only be also a veiling. The word must become flesh. There can be no direct vision of the glory of God. The Johannine account takes up these hints from the older tradition about secrecy and develops their full theological meaning. It is to be noted that this whole section contains no reference to the disciples. It is an account of the interaction between "the light" and "the world."

7:1-9

After this Jesus went about in Galilee; he would not go about in Judea, because the Jews sought to kill him. Now the Jews' feast of Tabernacles was at hand. So his brothers said to him, "Leave here and go to Judea, that your disciples may see the works you are doing. For no man works in secret if he seeks to be known openly. If you do these things, show yourself to the world." For even his brothers did not believe in him. Jesus said to them, "My time has not yet come, but your time is always here. The world cannot hate you, but it hates me because I testify of it that its

*works are evil. Go to the feast yourselves; I am not going up to this feast,
for my time has not yet fully come." So saying, he remained in Galilee.*

The reader has already been told that "the Jews" are seeking
to kill Jesus on account of his Sabbath healing and of the claim
which it seemed to imply (5:18). However, the death of Jesus—
when it comes—will not be their act but his. ("No one takes [my
life] from me; I lay it down of my own accord," 10:18). But this
will take place only at the hour appointed by the Father. This
hour has not yet come, and therefore Jesus has withdrawn to
Galilee.

But now the time for the great festival has come. Jesus'
brothers evidently know—and, therefore, in a sense believe in—
Jesus' power to perform "works." It seems obvious to them that
the festival is the proper occasion for achieving the maximum
publicity for Jesus and his message. If Jesus has a message for the
world, why not use the available means for "getting it across"?
Is it not foolish and counterproductive to ignore the "media"? A
revelation is no revelation if it is not revealed!

The reply of Jesus contains three themes which—in their
interlocking reference—take us to the heart of the problem of
revelation: the hatred of the world, the time of Jesus, and the
meaning of his "going up." To state the first theme at its sharpest,
the mark of a true revelation of God is that it will be rejected by
the world. The findings of communication theory cannot be applied to God's self-revelation to the world. That revelation must
create a crisis for the world because it destroys the world's estimate of itself. Revelation must involve contradiction. Jesus has
already been tempted to secure men's allegiance by meeting their
demand for food and for leadership (6:34 and 15). Now he is
being tempted to secure it by a great public manifestation in the
Temple. But these are all rejected (cf. Luke 4:1-12). Jesus cannot
and will not seek glory from men.

But the hatred of the world does not have the last word. It
is true that in the "time" of the world there is no escape from it.
The world which seeks its own glory is condemned to live in a
time to which there is no end and therefore no meaning. It is
endless time and therefore meaningless time. It is controlled by
the pursuit of an illusion—namely, of a wisdom and righteousness which man could have as his own possession. But a new
time—God's time—now confronts this time of the world. It is

the new time of the reign of God (Mark 1:14f.). This new time will be established when Jesus "goes up" or "is lifted up" (e.g., 3:14; 12:32) on the cross and goes to the Father. This will be the point at which the hatred of the world is finally turned upon Jesus. And here, precisely at the point where the righteousness and wisdom of God are veiled in the figure of a condemned and excommunicated man, is the event of its decisive unveiling, the event which makes it possible to live in the new time, the time of the reign of God. This new time is not meaningless because it looks to a real end—the glory of God.

The brothers can go to the festival as and when they will. No moment can be really decisive in their time, the time of the world. But Jesus must await the time which his Father will set for his "going up." It is not his business to seek the approval of the world. "Public opinion" is not the criterion by which his moves are to be determined. He looks only to his Father, and awaits his command to "go up."

7:10-13

But after his brothers had gone up to the feast, then he also went up, not publicly but in private. The Jews were looking for him at the feast, and saying, "Where is he?" And there was much muttering about him among the people. While some said, "He is a good man," others said, "No, he is leading the people astray." Yet for fear of the Jews no one spoke openly of him.

As on other occasions (e.g., 2:1-11; 4:46-54) Jesus declines to act on the instigation of others, but acts in his own way at his own—or rather at his Father's—time. He goes to Jerusalem not for a public demonstration but simply as one of those participating. Immediately we are introduced to the two groups who will figure in the ensuing discussion—"the Jews" and "the people." All are—of course—Jews, but the former group comprises the authorized leaders and the latter the "people of the land," often regarded as illiterate and incompetent in matters of the law. Among the latter there is—as usual—a variety of opinions about Jesus. But there is no faith in the proper sense.

7:14-24

About the middle of the feast Jesus went up into the temple and taught. The Jews marveled at it, saying, "How is it that this man has learning,

94

*when he has never studied?" So Jesus answered them, "My teaching is
not mine, but his who sent me; if any man's will is to do his will, he
shall know whether the teaching is from God or whether I am speaking
on my own authority. He who speaks on his own authority seeks his
own glory; but he who seeks the glory of him who sent him is true, and
in him there is no falsehood. Did not Moses give you the law? Yet none
of you keeps the law. Why do you seek to kill me?" The people answered,
"You have a demon! Who is seeking to kill you?" Jesus answered them,
"I did one deed, and you all marvel at it. Moses gave you circumcision
(not that it is from Moses, but from the fathers), and you circumcise a
man upon the sabbath. If on the sabbath a man receives circumcision, so
that the law of Moses may not be broken, are you angry with me because
on the sabbath I made a man's whole body well? Do not judge by appearances, but judge with right judgment."*

The festival lasted for a week. In the middle of the week
Jesus goes up into the Temple itself to teach—as the synoptics
inform us that he did during the last week. Immediately the question of authority is raised. Matthew notes that his teaching created
astonishment among the people, "for he taught them as one who
had authority and not as their scribes" (Matt. 7:29). The scribes
were authorized teachers trained and accredited by the accepted
teachers before them. Jesus did not have this authorization. He
had not taken the proper training. The natural inference is that
he was simply propagating his own ideas.

Jesus disclaims any such arrogance. If the case were as stated,
Jesus would be seeking to establish his own reputation, to build
up a "school" of followers. But he is not doing so. He speaks
only as the representative of the one who sent him—the Father.
His only desire is that men should glorify God. But how is this
to be known? It cannot be proved from some other source of
authority: there is no bar of judgment before which God can be
summoned. Only he who does God's will can know whether the
teaching is from God. And what does it mean to "do God's will"?
We have already been told in 6:29; it is to "believe in him whom
he has sent." What is in question here is not the ethical condi-
tioning of spiritual insight. This is not a call to salvation by good
works. It is the call to total commitment in obedient and loving
faith. There is no other way by which God's revelation of himself
can be received. Any attempt to validate the claim by reference
to some generally accepted criteria is to foreclose the possibility
of revelation and to return to "the world."

Revelation thus creates a crisis in which all theology is involved. "The Jews" are not an exceptional case. They are—here as elsewhere—the representatives of us all. There is no way of receiving God's revelation of himself except one which involves the abandonment of every intellectual and spiritual security in order to "come to Jesus." At this point there is required a simplicity which must appear to the philosophers of religion at best naive and at worst arbitrary and even arrogant. The theologian who would be a Christian must become an evangelist and say "Come to Jesus," yet this "coming" is always in fact the work of God who "draws" men to him. Those who do accept and obey the calling of God—who do his will—know that they are in touch with the truth. They cannot prove it; they can only bear witness.

The authority upon which the teaching of "the Jews" rests is that of the Torah given through Moses. It is this which they are claiming to uphold against a claim which seems to challenge it. But in fact under cover of zeal for the law there is lurking a terrible violation of the law. Their zeal is a murderous zeal. They do not yet recognize this, but in fact—as the sequel will show— they are on a course which can only lead to murder (cf. Mark 3:1-6). This murderous zeal is a response to an act of healing which caused astonishment. It shows that they have not understood the real intention of the law which they seek to uphold against a supposed violation. (The words translated "at it" in v. 21 probably belong properly to the following sentence, which should read: "This is why Moses gave you circumcision. . . .") It was accepted by the rabbis that the rule of circumcision on the eighth day had precedence over the Sabbath law. Since God—the giver of life—continues to cause babies to be born on the Sabbath (see 5:17) it follows that they may and must be circumcised on the following Sabbath, and the work so required is lawful. And if it is lawful, then the greater work of restoring life is lawful. Thus the law points beyond itself to its fulfilment in Jesus, for its purpose is not death but life. It follows that in their judgment upon Jesus the Jews are—under cover of an appearance of legality—in fact violating the law. He gives life; they want to kill. This is what happens, and will always happen, when the attempt is made to capture the revelation of God and make it a possession of men.

7:25-31

Some of the people of Jerusalem therefore said, "Is not this the man whom they seek to kill? And here he is, speaking openly, and they say nothing to him! Can it be that the authorities really know that this is the Christ? Yet we know where this man comes from; and when the Christ appears, no one will know where he comes from." So Jesus proclaimed, as he taught in the temple, "You know me, and you know where I come from? But I have not come of my own accord; he who sent me is true, and him you do not know. I know him, for I come from him, and he sent me." So they sought to arrest him; but no one laid hands on him, because his hour had not yet come. Yet many of the people believed in him; they said, "When the Christ appears, will he do more signs than this man has done?"

The words of Jesus inevitably provoke the question about his person: Who is he? This is a question which sounds through all the four Gospels and is pressed to its conclusion in the trial scenes which lead to his death. Here also the impending death of Jesus is the background. The people know that the "authorities" are plotting his death. But they have not arrested him. Why? Is he really the Messiah? No—that is impossible. It is universally accepted that the coming of the Messiah will be a mystery. His origin will be unknown. "The Lord whom you seek will come suddenly to his temple" (Mal. 3:1). But there is no mystery about this man: he is Jesus the carpenter from Nazareth in Galilee.

We are to understand that these discussions are going on in undertones in the crowd and that Jesus—as always—is aware of what is in men's hearts. Therefore he loudly and solemnly proclaims the truth about himself. The truth is that they both know and do not know the secret of his origin and his person. Once again we are dealing with the paradox of revelation, that it must be both a veiling and an unveiling if it is to be true. If God is to be revealed in such a way that the revelation can be grasped, then it must be in an actual life lived at a particular place and time in the continuum of world events. The revelation must be flesh— Jesus, the man from Nazareth. But if Jesus is simply perceived "according to the flesh"; if he is perceived simply as "this man" who can be "placed" in the appropriate category provided by the experience of the world, then there has been no revelation. For this man of flesh and blood, the carpenter from Nazareth, is at the same time the one who has been sent by, comes from, and

97

knows the Father in a sense which is not true of any other. "No one knows the Father except the Son and any one to whom the Son chooses to reveal him"; therefore, "Come to me, all who labor and are heavy laden" (Matt. 11:27f.; Luke 10:22). The world does not know God and cannot know God because it seeks its own glory. Jesus knows God because he seeks only the glory of his Father (17:25). This knowledge is unique, for Jesus is the "only Son who is in the bosom of the Father" and he has revealed him (1:18). Apart from this there cannot be revelation; the revelation can only be by means of the "veiling" in flesh. But the presence of revelation in the flesh—in a particular human being—necessarily creates a crisis and a confrontation, for the flesh—the ordinary wisdom of the world—does not and cannot admit such a claim. It immediately leads to a renewed attack. The authorities seek to arrest Jesus. An "idea of God" creates no crisis. It is part of my mental furniture and therefore part of "the world" in which the self is sovereign. But a man of flesh and blood, a man whose name and address and occupation are a matter of ordinary knowledge, and who at the same time makes these claims, necessarily creates a crisis. The "rulers of the age," as Paul calls them (I Cor. 2:8), are incapable of accommodating such a claim because it challenges all the structures of wisdom and power by which they are sustained. And so they "crucify the Lord of glory" in the name of the wisdom and righteousness of the world—the accumulated religious and moral and political experience of the human race.

The attempted arrest fails, for Jesus' hour has not yet come. Till it comes, human plans directed against Jesus are powerless (cf. Luke 22:53). Among the crowd there are some who "believed in him," but their belief rests on the great number of his miracles and not upon a true understanding of his person and his origin. A true understanding of one of the "signs" would have been enough to lead them to the secret of his person and his origin and so to a true and life-giving faith.

7:32-36

The Pharisees heard the crowd thus muttering about him, and the chief priests and Pharisees sent officers to arrest him. Jesus then said, "I shall be with you a little longer, and then I go to him who sent me; you will seek me and you will not find me; where I am you cannot come." The

Jews said to one another, "Where does this man intend to go that we shall not find him? Does he intend to go to the Dispersion among the Greeks and teach the Greeks? What does he mean by saying, 'You will seek me and you will not find me,' and, 'Where I am you cannot come'?"

The priests and the Pharisees—normally in opposed camps—combine in the presence of the challenge to "the powers"; Jesus must be removed! Yes indeed, he will be removed, for he will go to the Father at the hour appointed. And that "going" will also be an act of judgment. "Seek the Lord while he may be found; call upon him while he is near," said the prophet (Isa. 55:6). But the "powers" have not known the acceptable time—the "acceptable year of the Lord" (Luke 4:10). There is a time—"a little while"—when the opportunity is given. If it is rejected the opportunity is lost. Because it is God's revelation and not our investigation, the timetable is not in our hands. "The threat is always present, too late! For human research and enquiry cannot find the revelation; it is inaccessible" (Bultmann).

There is thus irony in Jesus' confirmation of the intention of the authorities to put a limit to his public ministry. There is a further irony in their misunderstanding of his words as a threat to emigrate, for the reader knows that in fact the message of Jesus—following his act of "going to him who sent me"—is being spread throughout the Greek-speaking world and that in very truth Jesus has gone to "teach the Greeks." But the Jews have excluded themselves from this ministry so that—in a sense they could not have understood—where he has gone they cannot come.

But the precondition of this Gentile mission is not only the "going" of Jesus to the Father by way of the cross, but also the pouring out of the Spirit upon the disciples which follows this. Jesus now utters a solemn promise of this gift.

7:37-39

On the last day of the feast, the great day, Jesus stood up and proclaimed, "If any one thirst, let him come to me and drink. He who believes in me, as the scripture has said, 'Out of his heart shall flow rivers of living water.' " Now this he said about the Spirit, which those who believed in him were to receive; for as yet the Spirit had not been given, because Jesus was not yet glorified.

The crowds participating in the festival will have watched day after day the procession of worshippers carrying water up to the Temple where it was poured out as a sign of the eschatological promises of Zechariah and Ezekiel. The symbolism of abundant water pouring forth from the Temple to bring life to the dead lands of the desert and the Dead Sea beyond (Ezek. 47) vividly expressed the longing for the outpouring of the life-giving Spirit of God which would mark the age to come. On the last of the seven days when the water ceremony was performed, Jesus solemnly announced the coming of that which had been portrayed in symbols.

At his baptism in the Jordan Jesus had been anointed by the Spirit and it was testified of him that the Spirit "descended and remained" on him (1:33). It was then promised that he was the one who would "baptize with the Holy Spirit." The fulfilment of that promise had to await the completion of Jesus' own baptism. What was accepted proleptically when Jesus went down into the water of the Jordan and accepted a baptism for sinful men had to be completed on Calvary when he took upon himself fully and finally the sin of the world. Only when that action was complete could Jesus return to his disciples and communicate to them the gift of the Holy Spirit (20:19-23). With that the new age foreshadowed by the ritual of the festival is to begin. Until then, as the evangelist explains in a very startling phrase, "The Spirit had not been given, because Jesus was not yet glorified." This is, clearly, not intended to contradict what has been said about the "descending and remaining" of the Spirit upon Jesus, nor what is said in the Old Testament about the men and women who were inspired by the Spirit to do and to teach the things of God. What this striking phrase does is to emphasize—as the later discourses will do (Chs. 14–16)—that a radically new presence of the Spirit is inaugurated by the completed work of Jesus on the cross. Once again, therefore, it is made clear that a new age to which the symbolism of Tabernacles points will be inaugurated when Jesus is "lifted up" to glorify God in his death.

The promise is—in the first place—a promise that the life-giving waters of the Spirit will flow from Jesus himself. He is, as Paul says, the rock which, being smitten, gives a stream of life-giving water (I Cor. 10:4; Ex. 17:1-7; Ps. 78:15f.). But—depending upon the punctuation—it may also be a promise that the same life-giving Spirit will flow from believers. Probably both

100

meanings are included. In any case, this claim made in these circumstances immediately sets in motion a fresh debate about the
person and origin of the speaker.

7:40-52

*When they heard these words, some of the people said, "This is really
the prophet." Others said, "This is the Christ." But some said, "Is the
Christ to come from Galilee? Has not the scripture said that the Christ
descended from David, and comes from Bethlehem, the village where
David was?" So there was a division among the people over him. Some
of them wanted to arrest him, but no one laid hands on him.*

*The officers then went back to the chief priests and Pharisees, who said
to them, "Why did you not bring him?" The officers answered, "No
man ever spoke like this man!" The Pharisees answered them, "Are you
led astray, you also? Have any of the authorities or of the Pharisees
believed in him? But this crowd, who do not know the law, are accursed."
Nicodemus, who had gone to him before, and who was one of them, said
to them, "Does our law judge a man without first giving him a hearing
and learning what he does?" They replied, "Are you from Galilee too?
Search and you will see that no prophet is to rise from Galilee."*

As in the earlier part of the chapter, we have two different
discussions going on at the same time. There is the discussion
among "the people" and there is the discussion among the authorities. Among the former (vv. 40:44) there is a variety of
opinions. Jesus is tentatively identified by reference to "the
prophet" promised in Deuteronomy, or—alternatively—by reference to the promised Messiah. The latter is ruled out by the
fact that Jesus is a Galilean. The crowd supposes that the question
"Who is he?" can be answered by reference to his place of birth.

The authorities, on the other hand, have already made up
their minds. They have retreated into the security of their religion,
and this gives them the confidence to reject the testimony of their
own agents that there is something in the words of Jesus for
which human analogies are inadequate, as well as to dismiss the
discussion of the people as worthless because outside the hedge
of the law. This security of theirs precludes all possibility of receiving the revelation. Even when one of their own members
protests that they are violating the law by their refusal to give the
accused a hearing, he is silenced. The report that Jesus is from
Galilee is enough to condemn his claims as false.

Thus while the people who "do not know the law" are at

101

least open to conviction, the guardians of the law, having made
of the law a bastion for their own security, are incapable of receiving the new and strange word of revelation. They illustrate
again the fact that "religion is unbelief" and that genuine revelation must involve contradiction.

8:12-20

*Again Jesus spoke to them, saying, "I am the light of the world; he who
follows me will not walk in darkness, but will have the light of life."
The Pharisees then said to him, "You are bearing witness to yourself;
your testimony is not true." Jesus answered, "Even if I do bear witness
to myself, my testimony is true, for I know whence I have come and
whither I am going, but you do not know whence I come or whither I
am going. You judge according to the flesh, I judge no one. Yet even if
I do judge, my judgment is true, for it is not I alone that judge, but I and
he who sent me. In your law it is written that the testimony of two men
is true; I bear witness to myself, and the Father who sent me bears witness
to me." They said to him therefore, "Where is your Father?" Jesus
answered, "You know neither me nor my Father; if you knew me, you
would know my Father also." These words he spoke in the treasury, as
he taught in the temple, but no one arrested him, because his hour had
not yet come.*

The scene is still the Temple. Specifically it is said to be "in
the treasury," and the reference is probably to the Court of Women
where the chest for the reception of offerings was kept and where
we know from the synoptics that Jesus taught (Mark 12:41ff.).
This was also the place where, during the festival, lamps were lit
which illuminated the whole Temple area and even the houses
beyond. Jesus then picks up the record of the two themes of the
festival, as adumbrated by Zechariah (ch. 14). He has said that it
is through him that the eschatological promise of life-giving water
will be fulfilled. Now, apparently in direct reference to the judgment which the authorities have passed (7:45-52), Jesus affirms
that it is in him that the eschatological promise of light, the promise that darkness will be banished (Zech. 14:8), is being fulfilled.

This is a staggering claim. The theme of light is so central
and pervasive, both in the Old Testament and in contemporary
religion (influenced by Persian, Greek, and Egyptian sources),
that these words could only be understood as conveying a claim
to cosmic significance. From any point of view they are such as
to demand some validation. If this man is simply making an

unsupported assertion, it must be rejected. The law—both the law of Moses and natural common sense—requires that some corroborative witness should be given. From this point of view the objection is unanswerable. "If I bear witness to myself, my witness is not true" (5:31). Within the ordered world of human moral and political experience there is no doubt that the assertion of a man about himself needs to be tested by the evidence of others. But—and this is the whole point at issue—what if this ordered world of human experience is, in fact, a world turned in upon itself and therefore a world in darkness, a world whose judgments are necessarily "according to the flesh"? In that case, the validation which is desired is—necessarily and in principle— not to be had. When the light shines in the darkness it cannot prove itself to be light except by shining. And how can I know that it is the light? I have only the testimony of Jesus: "I know whence I have come and whither I am going." This testimony necessarily places me at a point of decision, of crisis, which I cannot evade. I must either accept this testimony or else reject it because it is not corroborated by any witness from the world of human experience.

The rule that at least two witnesses are needed is in fact a sign of the real character of the world—that it is a world which is not ruled by the truth. If everyone spoke only the truth no second witness would be needed. And if he who is himself the truth speaks to this world, the possibility that he should need, or would accept, corroborative witness does not arise. Standing as I do within this world in which falsehood operates, I am confronted by the word of truth which requires me to make a decision to accept or reject it. If I seek to evade total responsibility for that decision by looking for validation from the accumulated experience of the world, I am in fact rejecting the truth.

Thus I am confronted by the reality of judgment. This part of the conversation between Jesus and the authorities begins with the judgment which the authorities have already passed on Jesus on the basis of their understanding of God's revelation (7:45-52). This is—in the context of Jesus' presence—a judgment "according to the flesh." Jesus makes no such judgment on others (v. 15). Nevertheless the presence of Jesus does bring judgment because it is God himself who is present where Jesus is present ("I and he who sent me"). Therefore the light itself is present, shining in the darkness, and those who do not wish the darkness of their world to be exposed and dispersed will retreat into their world. This is the judgment, and it is true judgment because God's own presence constitutes the ground of it. In a sense, therefore, the requirement of two witnesses is met because "I and he who sent me" are present. But in truth this exposes the fact that a law which is reasonable within "the world" cannot be applied when it is a question of God's revealing himself *to* the world. What witness can God call to validate his own revelation of himself?

The present paragraph stands in a close and subtle relation to the discussion in chapter 5. There the theme of judgment leads on to the theme of Jesus' witness to himself; here the witness of Jesus to himself leads to the theme of judgment. There Jesus says, "If I bear witness to myself, my testimony is not true" (5:31); here, "Even if I do bear witness to myself, my testimony is true" (8:14). There he says, "The Father judges no one, but has given all judgment to the Son" (5:22); here, "I judge no one. Yet even if I do judge, my judgment is true, for it is not I alone that judge, but I and he who sent me" (8:16). If Jesus is simply a man making assertions about himself and therefore seeking his own glory, his witness must be rejected in the absence of corroboration. But if Jesus is in truth the one sent by his Father, the one in whom is life and light, and who seeks only the glory of his Father, then the world cannot apply the tests to which it is accustomed. It cannot ask for corroborative testimony. It must either come to the light or turn away into darkness. This is the judgment (3:19). Not that the purpose is to judge the world in the way in which the religious and political authorities judge "the people of the land" and Jesus with them, because they do not conform to the law. In that sense Jesus judges no one—not even a woman caught in the act of adultery. Yet the coming of Jesus is the coming of judgment—not because he condemns anyone (he has come not to condemn but to save) but because by being present in the flesh, within and as part of the world which seeks its own glory, as one who seeks only the glory of the Father, his presence is the presence in the world of the light itself. The very nature of Jesus' witness, that it cannot be validated by any of the world's accepted norms, is what makes it the occasion of judgment.

The authorities, secure in their well-ordered world, reject something which would break that world open. They ask Jesus to produce his witness. "Where is your Father?" No doubt it is a question which malicious gossip could fasten on. But the real irony is different from anything that the questioners can understand. The only answer to the man who sincerely asks "Where is God?" is to say "Look at Jesus." And Jesus is standing right there. God is to be known in his revelation of himself. To know the revelation is to know the one who is revealed, and there is no other way of knowing. If they had known him, they would not have needed to ask the question. But then their secure world would have been shattered and they would have understood that by passing judgment on Jesus they had passed judgment upon themselves. For "none of the rulers of this world" understood the power and the wisdom of God. "If they had, they would not have crucified the Lord of glory" (I Cor. 2:8).

8:21-30

Again he said to them, "I go away, and you will seek me and die in your sin; where I am going, you cannot come." Then said the Jews, "Will he kill himself, since he says, 'Where I am going, you cannot come'?" He said to them, "You are from below, I am from above; you are of this world, I am not of this world. I told you that you would die in your sins, for you will die in your sins unless you believe that I am he." They said to him, "Who are you?" Jesus said to them, "Even what I have told you from the beginning. I have much to say about you and much to judge; but he who sent me is true, and I declare to the world what I have heard from him." They did not understand that he spoke to them of the Father. So Jesus said, "When you have lifted up the Son of man, then you will know that I am he and that I do nothing on my own authority but speak thus as the Father taught me. And he who sent me is with me; he has not left me alone, for I always do what is pleasing to him." As he spoke thus, many believed in him.

The reader of this long account of the dialogue between Jesus and his contemporaries cannot fail to feel all the time the presence in the background of a dark and menacing reality. It is the fact that "the world" as a whole is "in the power of the evil one." Human life as a whole is organized around a false center. It seeks its own glory rather than the glory of its maker and lord. Therefore its wisdom and knowledge cannot find God. Consequently the revealing of God to the world must be the occasion of crisis for the world.

This dark and terrible fact will become more and more clear as the discussion moves on. At this point, however, the attention is directed to the person of the one who bears the revelation and is therefore the occasion of crisis. The theme of Jesus' witness to himself is developed further.

We have just been told that the authorities could not seize Jesus because "his hour had not yet come." So there is still time— time to hear, to turn around, to face the light, to believe. But the time is not endless. There will not always be another chance. Jesus will go away—and he knows where he is going (v. 14). Then it will be too late. The people of the world will seek, but as they have rejected the one who gives the water of life (7:37) and the light of life (8:12) they will lose the possibility of life and die in that sin which consists essentially in unbelief—in the rejection of Jesus (cf. Mark 3:21-30). They will remain imprisoned in the world which is ruled by darkness and death.

The Jews, unlike Jesus, do not know where he is going. At an earlier point they had supposed that he was going to emigrate and start a mission to the Gentiles. Now their suspicions are darker. If Jesus is going to take his own life, then he is going down to Gehenna—and certainly these devout ecclesiastics are not going to follow him there! But as in the earlier exchange so now the reader is aware of a profound irony. Jesus is indeed referring to his death. It will be his own act of loving surrender to his Father, but it will also be their act of murderous rejection. And he will indeed "descend to the dead," but it will not be to remain there but for the "harrowing of hell" so that neither the living nor the dead may be excluded from the possibility of life.

The answer of Jesus (vv. 23-24) to their misunderstanding is twofold. First it is a restatement of the absolute distinction between "the world" and the life which is not of the world but "from above." "The world" is human power and wisdom organized around itself as center, seeking its own glory. Its wisdom is based upon accumulated human experience and therefore incapable by itself of comprehending that which is not of the world but from above. Secondly, Jesus' answer is the offer of the one and only way by which it is possible to pass out of this realm of darkness and death into the realm of light and life, and that is to "believe that I am."

What can these words mean? In the Old Testament the living God reveals his name to Moses as "I am," and the phrase is used at many points when God himself speaks (e.g., Deut. 32:39; Isa. 43:10). What can the words "I am" mean on the lips of this man?

The verb "to be" requires a predicate. Therefore the words "I am" need to be completed: "You are—who?"

How can that question be answered? What predicate can define the being of God? What word or name could be put forward here except one which embodied some part of the (sin-burdened) knowledge and wisdom and experience of the human race? There can be no predicate. Jesus can only reply: "I am—from the beginning what I have told you." In this sentence "from the beginning" means both "from before the foundation of the world" and "from the beginning of the ministry of Jesus" (cf. Mark 1:1 with John 1:1).

Is Jesus, then, claiming to be God? If the word "God" is introduced here as a predicate the meaning of which is determined by human experience in "the world," then the answer is No. If, to be specific, the word "God" means a monad who (which?) exists to seek his own glory, then Jesus is not that monad, for he explicitly states that he speaks only what he has received from the one who sent him, the one who is the truth. This one is the one whom Jesus calls "Father." By contrast the God who is a monad seeking his own glory is a typical product of "the world" which seeks its own glory. This "God," as Feuerbach rightly saw, is a projection of man's ego on the clouds. But the one who here uses the words "I am" is one who renounces all glory for himself and seeks only the glory of the one who sent him. And this is true godhead, for God is not the monad of man's imagination but an eternal spring ("living water") of self-emptying love—Father and Son in the unity of the Spirit by whom Jesus is anointed and whose anointing will be given to believers. This is not the projection of man's self-glorification but the contradiction of it, including very specifically the contradiction of man's religion which is the central citadel of his desire for self-fulfilment and therefore of his resistance to the God whose being is self-emptying.

There is no escape from the presence of unbelief except by the humble acceptance of the gift of self-emptying love in the person of the one in whom it is present as "flesh" in the world. Every spiritual resource which I myself might bring to the enterprise of escaping is itself part of the imprisonment. He—God made flesh—must wash my feet and I must simply accept (13:8). I must simply believe.

But how is belief possible? Jesus' words are not understood by the hearers—and indeed even the closest disciples cannot know

107

now but will understand only afterward (13:7). Belief in its fullness can only come when Jesus, the "Son of man," who is both flesh of our flesh and the one who is from above, has been lifted up. The final and complete self-emptying of Jesus on the cross, his resurrection from the tomb, and his impartation of the Holy Spirit to his disciples will be the necessary condition without which it is not possible to know—with full assurance—that Jesus is indeed the one who can and must say "I am." Once again this will not mean the manifestation of Jesus as a divine being in his own right clothed with his own glory in the manner of pagan deities. What will be manifest will be the "glory of the only Son from the Father," the one who says and does only what the Father teaches, who is eternally united in love and obedience to the Father who sent him, just as believers will later be united in love and obedience with Jesus who sends them into the world (15:9f.; 17:18).

Therefore (v. 26) although Jesus might say many things in judgment upon his hearers he does not do so, for he has not come to judge but to save. His one concern is to declare to the world the truth which he knows from the Father, and that declaration—not just to Israel but to the whole world—will be made when he is lifted upon the cross (cf. 12:32).

The result of these words of Jesus is that "many believed in him." Yet—as we have already learned on many occasions and as the sequel shows once again—the belief falls short of that assured knowledge which will be possible only after Jesus has been "lifted up." Till then no one, not even the closest disciple, can fully understand.

8:31-38

Jesus then said to the Jews who had believed in him, "If you continue in my word, you are truly my disciples, and you will know the truth, and the truth will make you free." They answered him, "We are descendants of Abraham, and have never been in bondage to any one. How is it that you say, 'You will be made free'?"

Jesus answered them, "Truly, truly, I say to you, every one who commits sin is a slave to sin. The slave does not continue in the house for ever; the son continues for ever. So if the Son makes you free, you will be free indeed. I know that you are descendants of Abraham; yet you seek to kill me, because my word finds no place in you. I speak of what I have seen with my Father, and you do what you have heard from your father."

To these new believers Jesus opens up two new themes which are, however, familiar to the reader of the Gospel, the themes of perseverance and liberation. The first is the theme of perseverance. "He that endures to the end shall be saved," said Jesus according to the synoptics, and in the parable of the Sower he gave vivid illustrations of how a promising start can prove abortive. It is those who not only hear and receive the teaching of Jesus but who "abide in it" so that it has "free course" in them, who are the real disciples.

And to them there is promised liberation through knowledge of the truth. Each of these words has the content which the Gospel gives it. The knowledge in question is that personal knowledge of him who is the truth which grows out of the believing and which is itself a sharing in the eternal life of God (17:3 and 8). The truth is that which is above all characteristic of God who is true, who is faithful and trustworthy and whose Spirit is the Spirit of truth (15:26; 16:13). He who is truth and in whom is no lie is alone able to deliver those who are captive to the power of the lie.

What exactly is the captivity from which we are set free? In Paul's writings it is described variously as bondage to sin, to death, to the law, and to decay. Here it is bondage to sin (v. 34).

The believers indignantly deny that they are or have ever been slaves. To be sure, Joseph was sold into slavery, but in his soul he was never a slave but always a free servant of Yahweh. The same could be said of Israel as a whole, which had preserved its inner freedom through centuries of foreign oppression. As the seed of Abraham they can proudly boast that they are not slaves. They are the supreme example of a people who have found in their traditional faith and practice a citadel within which they could maintain unbroken an inner resistance against all the powers that oppress and dominate the world.

But—and here is the supreme tragedy—this very security is their undoing, for it leads them to reject with furious anger the offer of freedom as a gift. The freedom of which they are proud is their own possession. They will defend it even to the extent of bloodshed—not only their own, but the blood of the one who offers freedom as a gift from above. And in the fact that they are bent on destroying Jesus (as the sequel will show) lies the proof that they are not free: they are under the power of sin. The man who is not able to receive his freedom as a gift of pure grace is not yet free.

Here the two themes of perseverance and liberation interact. There are many places in the New Testament and in the Gospel where a contrast is made between the son and the slave. The former offers loving obedience which is a response to the free gift of the Father's love; the latter offers slavish obedience which looks to rewards and punishments and is therefore still within the prison of the self. It is characteristic of the son that he will never leave the house. It is characteristic of the slave that he has no permanent place there (cf. Gal. 4:21-23). So the true disciple will be marked by the fact that he "continues" in the teaching of Jesus. This is the true freedom in which a man is wholly delivered from the prison of self and has his freedom as a constantly renewed gift of the Son. On the other hand those who fall away prove that they do not belong to the family. In fact they do not know the Father whom the Son knows and loves. They have a different father— as is proved by their murderous hatred of the Son. That they are descendants of Abraham cannot be denied. But the fact that they use this descent as a ground for claiming freedom as their own possession and therefore as a ground for pride proves that they are not true children of Abraham. For Abraham is the supreme example of the man of faith who believed God and trusted in the promised gift even when every possible ground of assurance had been taken away (Rom. 4). Their reaction to the words of Jesus indicates another paternity (cf. Matt. 23:15).

8:39-47

They answered him, "Abraham is our father." Jesus said to them, "If you were Abraham's children, you would do what Abraham did, but now you seek to kill me, a man who has told you the truth which I heard from God; this is not what Abraham did. You do what your father did." They said to him, "We were not born of fornication; we have one Father, even God." Jesus said to them, "If God were your Father, you would love me, for I proceeded and came forth from God; I came not of my own accord, but he sent me. Why do you not understand what I say? It is because you cannot bear to hear my word. You are of your father the devil, and your will is to do your father's desires. He was a murderer from the beginning, and has nothing to do with the truth, because there is no truth in him. When he lies, he speaks according to his own nature, for he is a liar and the father of lies. But, because I tell the truth, you

110

do not believe me. Which of you convicts me of sin? If I tell the truth, why do you not believe me? He who is of God hears the words of God; the reason why you do not hear them is that you are not of God."

The dialogue continues relentlessly on its way. The reader is required to face still more inescapably the meaning of the statement that the light shines in the darkness and the darkness does not and cannot either comprehend it or overcome it. We evade the whole thrust of the passage if we fail to recognize that "the Jews" are simply the representatives of ourselves, or if we allow the (very probable) reference to apostasy in the early Church (see I John 3 and 4) to lead us into thinking that this exhausts the meaning of the words ascribed to Jesus. We are dealing here with the deepest issues of the human situation in the presence of God's revelation of himself. The reader has missed the whole point if he does not know that he himself is being addressed.

"Abraham is our father." In a sense this is incontrovertible, as are the similar statements of Christians who claim to stand in the succession of prophets, apostles, and martyrs. But, at a deeper level, the claim is disproved by the spirit in which it is made. For there sounds through it the familiar note of a fanaticism which cannot tolerate anything which questions the man who makes the claim. Abraham believed God, even when ordinary. common sense would have denied belief. He trusted in the truthfulness of God's promise even when it was a promise of life from the dead (Rom. 4:17). Jesus has come as the one who speaks the truth of God and offers the life of God. His hearers do not believe his word and are on the way to taking his life. They cannot therefore invoke the name of Abraham to define their identity. They bear another identity—an identity which derives from that power which destroys life and denies truth, the power of death and darkness. In the name of Abraham they speak and act as children of the devil.

With another sly reference to the rumors about Jesus' paternity the Jews indignantly deny the implied charge. They are not bastards but true children of God. Not so, replies Jesus, for if they were they would receive Jesus as a brother. He has not come of his own will or in his own name, but simply as the child sent by his father to his brothers—as Joseph was sent by Jacob to seek the welfare of his brothers. Why, then, do they not receive him gladly? Why do they seek—like Joseph's brothers—to kill

the one who comes from their father? Why do they not understand? "It is because you cannot hear my word."

Here is the crux of the matter. The word "cannot" must be
taken with full seriousness (as at 13:36 where it is addressed to
Peter). The insertion of the Revised Standard Version "bear to"
weakens the thrust of the crucial sentence. We are here dealing
with the terrible reality of the bondage of the human will, and
this has as much to do with twentieth-century Christians as with
first-century Jews or early Christian apostates.

The life of man centered in the development of his own self,
in the unfolding of his own capacities, is the microcosm which
is reflected on the grand scale (as the word implies) in the cosmos,
the organized world of human culture in all its forms—philosophy, science, technics, economics, politics, and aesthetics. "The
world" represents on the grand scale man's attempt to understand
and to organize his life in such a way that he is in control of it.
Language, which is fundamental to the whole effort, provides the
"words" by which the business of understanding and managing
is carried on. The words of Jesus—his audible speech in one of
the languages of the world—are part of the world. His hearers
hear them. But they can only hear them as part of this world. In
that context they are intolerable and must be silenced. The Jews
are unable—literally unable—to hear his *logos*, the word which
he himself is. And this is because the *logos* is in fact the true source
and center of all that exists and its presence requires the abandonment of the whole enterprise of understanding and managing
the world from a center in the human ego. From this center belief
is simply an impossibility. It is not that the man in the world has
the free option to believe or not to believe. "The being of these
unbelievers is constituted by the will to unbelief" (Bultmann).
The being and the willing are not two separate things.

How, then, is belief possible? Only—as the whole Gospel
affirms—by a death and a rebirth, only when the adult man,
secure in the mastery which his philosophy, his science, and his
technology give him, becomes a child who must simply receive
life and truth as a gift. And this new birth is not a human possibility: it is a gift which will be available only when Jesus has
died and risen from the dead and has given to his chosen disciples
the gift of the Spirit. This is why Peter is told "You cannot follow
me now." And this is why the Jews are told "You cannot hear
my word." For the central citadel of man's enterprise in seeking

to understand and to manage his world is not his science, his technology, or even his philosophy: it is his religion. The Jews are at the center of this controversy not because they belong to the ethnic group of Semites but because they represent the highest form of religion.

"The truth" which Jesus speaks is the truth which he is. We are not dealing with statements about the world which may or may not correspond with what is the case. We are in the presence of the ultimate conflict between light and darkness, between the reign of God which is life and light and the power of the devil which is darkness and death. Man does not stand at a midpoint between the two, free to choose one or the other. He is part of "the world" which seeks to possess in itself light and life—the capacity to understand and the power to cope. Within this world it is impossible for him to receive the word of light and life which is present in Jesus. The truth which he speaks is heard as nonsense. The life which he offers is perceived as death. Yet the resulting rejection is not and cannot be based upon a judgment that Jesus is a sinner. He is the one who speaks and does the truth. But to receive this truth is a possibility only for those who are "of God" as Jesus is "of God," for those—in other words—who are called and sent by God into the world, consecrated in the truth to be the bearers of his truth in the world (cf. I Cor. 1:22-24 and John 17:16-19). There are such because Jesus has come not to judge the world but to save it, and for this it is necessary that he should "cast out the prince of this world" (12:32) and "destroy the works of the devil" (I John 3:8)

8:48-59

The Jews answered him, "Are we not right in saying that you are a Samaritan and have a demon?" Jesus answered, "I have not a demon; but I honor my Father, and you dishonor me. Yet I do not seek my own glory; there is One who seeks it and he will be the judge. Truly, truly, I say to you, if any one keeps my word, he will never see death." The Jews said to him, "Now we know that you have a demon. Abraham died, as did the prophets; and you say, 'If any one keeps my word, he will never taste death.' Are you greater than our father Abraham, who died? And the prophets died! Who do you claim to be?" Jesus answered, "If I glorify myself, my glory is nothing; it is my Father who glorifies me, of whom you say that he is your God. But you have not known him; I know him. If I said, I do not know him, I should be a liar like you; but I do know him and I keep his word. Your father Abraham rejoiced that he was to see my day; he saw it and was glad." The Jews then said to him, "You are not yet fifty years old, and have you seen Abraham?" Jesus said to them, "Truly, truly, I say to you, before Abraham was, I am." So they took up stones to throw at him; but Jesus hid himself, and went out of the temple.

But "the prince of this world" fights back. As in the synoptic Gospels (e.g., Mark 3:20-30) so here it is recorded that Jesus was accused of being himself an agent of the devil—even in his works of healing. The charge that Jesus has made is thrown back at him. And—for good measure—he is accused of being a Samaritan— no true Israelite but a bastard product of illegitimate union between Israel and paganism.

The reply of Jesus is a calm repetition of his total commitment to the honor of his Father. He will not seek to answer the accusation by vindicating his own honor. "When he was reviled, he did not revile in return; . . . but he trusted to him who judges justly" (I Pet. 2:23). The world, with "its boundless need for recognition and standing" (Bultmann), will always answer such charges by an effort at self-vindication. But there is no tribunal before which these rival accusations can be adjudicated except that of the Father whose humble and obedient messenger Jesus is. Jesus seeks only the glory of the Father, and the Father will— in due time—glorify Jesus by enabling him to die for the sin of the world and rise again. Those who do not reject the word of Jesus but "keep" it by trusting and obeying Jesus as he trusts and obeys the Father (v. 55) are delivered from the power of death as they are delivered from the power of the lie. They become partakers of the life of God himself, a life which death cannot destroy (17:22f.).

This reply, taken literally as a denial of the death of the body, only confirms the opinion that he is mad. It is obvious that Abraham and the prophets died. "Who do you make yourself?"

Once again we have to learn that Jesus' words have nothing in common with the claims that men make for themselves. He claims nothing for himself. In fact, he will himself "taste death for every man" (v. 52; cf. Heb. 2:9). But in and through that act God himself will glorify him and make him the source of eternal life for all who believe.

Jesus can say this because he knows God and keeps his word. The world does not know God (17:25). This contrast between knowing and not knowing God has to be stated with absolute

114

clarity. Not to state it, to be silent about it, would be collusion with the power of the lie which rules the world. In a world which is organized around the self and seeks its own glory the statement "I know God" will be seen as an outrageous piece of self-glorification. Agnosticism will be seen as a proper modesty. But this modesty does not provide any way of escape from the world which is centered in the self. Its genial tolerance ends abruptly in face of a claim that God has actually revealed himself in the flesh and blood of the man Jesus. That claim will appear as a shocking assault upon the sovereignty of the autonomous reason and conscience. The inevitable conflict is focused and resolved in the crucifixion of Jesus.

The Jews, however, are not agnostics. They are confident that, as descendants of Abraham, they are within the covenant which God made with Abraham and his seed. But they have misunderstood the nature of the covenant. It was and is a covenant of promise. It required Abraham to abandon every security upon which men rely. He was called to abandon home and kindred and traditional religion. He was denied the possession of a place of his own. He was without heirs until extreme old age, and then even his beloved son was demanded in sacrifice. He was the supreme example of the man who looks not to the past but to the future, whose only security is the promise of God, who—as a wandering migrant—"looked forward to the city . . . whose builder and maker is God" (Heb. 11:10). It is the consistent teaching of the New Testament in all its parts that the coming of Jesus is the beginning of the fulfilment of that promise by which Abraham and Moses and the prophets lived. All these "died in faith, not having received what was promised but having seen it and greeted it from afar" (Heb. 11:13). The joy of Abraham should have been fulfilled in his descendants to whom the fulfilment of the promise has come. Instead they use their descent from Abraham as the ground for rejecting that which Abraham longed for and saw by faith from afar. Where he looked forward, they look back. His security was in the faithfulness of the one who promised; they seek another kind of security based upon the faith of Abraham and not on the one in whose promise Abraham believed. Thus again and again (and certainly not only among the Jews) does "the world" seek to encapsulate the promise of the living God and make of it an asset among its own possessions and a security against the fresh action of God.

Once again the words of Jesus are taken with a crude literalism. How absurd to talk as if Abraham, and this man Jesus, living two thousand years apart, could have "seen" each other. Absurd, and yet—as so often in these discourses—the literalist misunderstanding opens the way for the unfolding of a deeper truth—in fact to the awesome climax of this whole series of exchanges in which the light has been making itself manifest in the darkness. "Amen, amen, I tell you" (it is the most solemn possible affirmation) "before Abraham was, I am."

Abraham, Moses, the prophets, and John the Baptist all "came to be" (1:6). They had their time. But before all time "the Word was in the beginning with God." The one of whom this is said is present in this man of flesh and blood. He is the one in whom the promise to Abraham is fulfilled because that promise is not an afterthought in the mind of God but is the end for which "all things were made" (1:3). The covenant of promise is the central meaning and end of all creation and therefore it is before its beginning. And that promise has not remained forever a vision "seen and greeted from afar" (Heb. 11:13); it is now present with the power of life and truth in the man Jesus, who is "not yet fifty years old."

According to Mark the decisive utterance of the words "I am" which fixed the charge of blasphemy upon Jesus was spoken at the trial (Mark 14:62). Here they form the climax of the encounter in the Temple. Like the equally mysterious title "Son of man"—which might or might not imply supernatural claims—this phrase evoked but did not necessarily require association with the divine name—a name too sacred to be uttered. In the context the Jews have no doubt about its meaning. They attempt without further investigations to inflict the punishment laid down for blasphemy—death by stoning (Lev. 24:16).

But the hour for Jesus' death has not yet come. He had come up to the festival not publicly but in private (7:10). In the midst of the festival he had openly presented himself as the source of life and light. In the face of total rejection he withdraws into the hiddenness which had marked his coming. The light has been manifested, but men loved the darkness rather than the light. The hour of judgment approaches, but it is not yet.

10

SIGHT AND BLINDNESS
(9:1-41)

AFTER THE ALMOST UNBEARABLE TENSION OF THE CON-
frontation between Jesus and the authorities recorded in the two
previous chapters, we pass to the account of an event which is
told with the utmost vividness and dramatic irony and which sets
before the reader in concrete form the central issue of the Gospel.

It is not useful to ask whether or not the happenings now to
be recounted followed immediately after the controversy in the
Temple during the Feast of Tabernacles. At the end of chapter 10
we are in the season of Dedication, two months later. John is not
writing a biography but selecting from the great store of memories of the words and works of Jesus a very limited number
which can be told so as to lead the readers to faith in him and to
life in his name. The controlling principle is theological, not
chronological.

The "signs" so far recounted have had as their general theme
the gift of life—abundant life through Jesus. He has been shown
as the one who heals the sick and the lame, who gives the living
water and the living bread, who turns water into wine and who
gives his flesh for the life of the world. But "the life" is also "the
light of men" (1:4). John has given us the words with which
Jesus, during the Feast of Tabernacles, had offered himself as the
source of living water and of light for the world. He now proceeds to tell the story of the healing of a blind man in such a way
as to bring out with intense dramatic force the fact that in Jesus
light has come into the world and that this coming of the light
also, and necessarily, brings judgment because men love darkness
rather than the light (3:19).

117

9:1-41

As he passed by, he saw a man blind from his birth. And his disciples asked him, "Rabbi, who sinned, this man or his parents, that he was born blind?" Jesus answered, "It was not that this man sinned, or his parents, but that the works of God might be made manifest in him. We must work the works of him who sent me, while it is day; night comes, when no one can work. As long as I am in the world, I am the light of the world." As he said this, he spat on the ground and made clay of the spittle and anointed the man's eyes with the clay, saying to him, "Go, wash in the pool of Siloam" (which means Sent). So he went and washed and came back seeing. The neighbors and those who had seen him before as a beggar, said, "Is not this the man who used to sit and beg?" Some said, "It is he"; others said, "No, but he is like him." He said, "I am the man." They said to him, "Then how were your eyes opened?" He answered, "The man called Jesus made clay and anointed my eyes and said to me, 'Go to Siloam and wash'; so I went and washed and received my sight." They said to him, "Where is he?" He said, "I do not know."

They brought to the Pharisees the man who had formerly been blind. Now it was a sabbath day when Jesus made the clay and opened his eyes. The Pharisees again asked him how he had received his sight. And he said to them, "He put clay on my eyes, and I washed, and I see." Some of the Pharisees said, "This man is not from God, for he does not keep the sabbath." But others said, "How can a man who is a sinner do such signs?" There was a division among them. So they again said to the blind man, "What do you say about him, since he has opened your eyes?" He said, "He is a prophet."

The Jews did not believe that he had been blind and had received his sight, until they called the parents of the man who had received his sight, and asked them, "Is this your son, who you say was born blind? How then does he now see?" His parents answered, "We know that this is our son, and that he was born blind; but how he now sees we do not know, nor do we know who opened his eyes. Ask him; he is of age, he will speak for himself." His parents said this because they feared the Jews, for the Jews had already agreed that if any one should confess him to be Christ, he was to be put out of the synagogue. Therefore his parents said, "He is of age, ask him."

So for the second time they called the man who had been blind, and said to him, "Give God the praise; we know that this man is a sinner." He answered, "Whether he is a sinner, I do not know; one thing I know, that though I was blind, now I see." They said to him, "What did he do to you? How did he open your eyes?" He answered them, "I have told you already, and you would not listen. Why do you want to hear it again? Do you too want to become his disciples?" And they reviled him, saying, "You are his disciple, but we are disciples of Moses. We know that God has spoken to Moses, but as for this man, we do not know where he comes from." The man answered, "Why, this is a marvel!

118

You do not know where he comes from, and yet he opened my eyes. We know that God does not listen to sinners, but if any one is a worshiper of God and does his will, God listens to him. Never since the world began has it been heard that any one opened the eyes of a man born blind. If this man were not from God, he could do nothing." They answered him, "You were born in utter sin, and would you teach us?" And they cast him out.

Jesus heard that they had cast him out, and having found him he said, "Do you believe in the Son of man?" He answered, "And who is he, sir, that I may believe in him?" Jesus said to him, "You have seen him, and it is he who speaks to you." He said, "Lord, I believe"; and he worshiped him. Jesus said, "For judgment I came into this world, that those who do not see may see, and that those who see may become blind." Some of the Pharisees near him heard this, and they said to him, "Are we also blind?" Jesus said to them, "If you were blind, you would have no guilt; but now that you say, 'We see,' your guilt remains."

That the blind will receive their sight is, in the Old Testament, one of the promises that belong to the messianic age (e.g., Isa. 29:18; 35:5), and the synoptic Gospels both record that Jesus gave sight to the blind and point to this as one of the signs of the dawning of the new age (Luke 7:18-23). John will now tell the story of such a healing—probably depending upon a tradition distinct from those embodied in the synoptics although having many similarities. In none of the synoptic accounts do we hear of a man blind from his birth. In the story as told by John this is the first matter to which our attention is drawn. The congenital blindness of this man will be interpreted both by the disciples (v. 2) and by the authorities (v. 34) as evidence of sin. By the time the whole story has been told we shall understand that the man is simply representative of the entire human situation. Until the true light comes, all men are in darkness. The distinction is not between those who are blind and those who see; it is between those who know that they are blind and those who claim that they see. But this distinction cannot come to light except when the light comes (v. 39).

Why was this man born blind? Whose fault is it? The asking of such questions is an inescapable part of our struggle to "make sense" of experience. That suffering and death are consequences of sin is a belief shared by a great part of the human race. It is a belief which has at least more of the seed of hope in it than the belief that these things are the result of blind fate or of mechanical causation. The Indian tradition has taken the link between sin and

119

suffering to its most completely logical conclusion in the doctrine of *karma*—the teaching that the immortal soul must work out to all eternity the consequences of its actions, enjoying the fruit of the good deeds and suffering that of the evil. It is probable that this doctrine was known at least to the hellenized sections of the population of first-century Palestine. That both the sinner himself and his descendants would suffer the consequences of sin was a common thought among the Jews, and without this belief the passion of Job would be unintelligible.

Whatever the cultural and philosophical background—Indian *karma*, Judaic theism, or Western positivism—the question "Why has this happened?" is one which can hardly be restrained by any human being faced with calamity. But if a good reason could be found for evil, then either the evil is not evil or the reason is no good. The attempt to "make sense" of a world which is under the power of sin and death by probing back into its antecedents is doomed to frustration. The only thing which can "make sense" of a dark world is the coming of light, and the light does not come from below but from above, not from the past but from the future. We have seen in the closing verses of chapter 8 how the darkness seeks to destroy the light. Now we see, by contrast, the light destroying the darkness, for "the darkness has not overcome it." But this light is—strictly—something new, something from above. It shines out of the future into the present like the dawning of a new day. We can "make sense" of a dark world only by allowing the light to come in, by turning to the light and believing in the one who comes as the light of the world. This is "the work of God," as we learned in 6:29. And "we"—Jesus and his disciples and the whole Church—must be active in doing this work "while it is day." Again we are reminded that it is possible to hear the terrible words "too late." We are not dealing with timeless verities in the life of the soul, but with a real happening in history, with real opportunities which must be seized or they will be lost. The Church is not sent into the world to explain the world but to change it. The *logos*, the true light which makes sense of the world, is not to be found by a study of the experience of the world, for the world, though it was made by him, does not know him (1:10). He has come and is coming and will come into the world. Only by being part of his movement into the world do we "make sense" of the world.

This "movement" is a real coming in history and therefore

subject to the "not yet" and the "too late" of real historical events. The life of the light in the flesh is subject to the strict limitations of time. "While I am in the world, light for the world am I." The emphasis here is not upon the subject but upon the predicate. Jesus has come as the light and therefore nothing must hinder the shining of the light in the time that is given, which is not eternity but strictly given and limited time.

So Jesus proceeds immediately to action. No questions are asked about the faith of the blind man. His faith will be the result—slowly matured—of Jesus' action, not its precondition. As in Mark (but not in Matthew and Luke) Jesus makes use of material means—dust and spittle. The act of anointing the eyes does not itself bring sight, but the man is ordered to go and wash in the Pool of Siloam. His going is itself an act of faith in Jesus—albeit faith at an elementary level. Unlike Naaman the Syrian in similar circumstances (II Kings 5:10-12) he obeys without hesitation, and receives the gift of sight.

The pool to which he is directed is the one from which the water was drawn for the Feast of Tabernacles. In moving from the theme of life to that of light, the evangelist continues to make use of the symbolism of water. He interprets the name of the pool—Siloam—as "sent." This is his constantly repeated designation of Jesus; he is the one sent, the apostle of God. "The waters of Siloam disappear in the living water of Christ" (Hoskyns). The light which has banished the man's darkness is the light of Christ himself, and (this is certainly in the mind of the evangelist) becomes the possession of the believer through the water of baptism in which men and women are incorporated into the "sending" of Jesus himself.

The new man in Christ is so changed that the neighbors are not sure that it is the same man whom they had known. Only the man himself can affirm that, although he is a new man, he is still the same person. What, then, has happened? How is it to be explained?

In reply the man can only refer to "the man Jesus," about whom he knows absolutely nothing except what he has done for him. Here is something that defies all ordinary explanation and so the case is referred to the proper authorities—those learned in the law of God. But when the radically new has come, the "proper authorities" of the old world are precisely the improper ones who cannot grasp the new unless they are willing to recognize that the old is passing away. Darkness has no means of explaining light.

As in the case of the healing of the paralytic (ch. 5), we learn only after the event that it had occurred on the Sabbath. The actions which Jesus had performed were expressly forbidden for the Sabbath. Here was something clear and intelligible. Jesus had transgressed the law. "We know where we are with him." But do we? Can a transgressor of the law give sight to a man born blind? It is a cruel dilemma for the authorities and—as before—they are divided. What is to be said about Jesus? Agent of God or of the devil? How to decide? Perhaps the man can give a clue. "What do you say about him?"

"He is a prophet." The man has moved on from his first position. "The man called Jesus" is acknowledged as "a prophet." He has still a long way to go, but he is moving toward the light.

The authorities, however, are moving in the opposite direction. They rightly perceive that the whole foundation of their world is threatened and look for any possible support. Perhaps the man was lying. Perhaps he never was blind. The parents should be able to give information. But this move, so far from helping them, pushes them further into a corner. The parents stubbornly affirm the facts but refuse to propose any solution to the problem. They are in the same world as the authorities—a world ruled by fear. They fear the authorities, and the "authorities" fear for their authority. The only liberated character is the man who is the center of the story, and both parties seek to hang all responsibility on him.

So, once again, he is interrogated—this time on oath (v. 24). The first move is a sheer assertion of official authority: "We know." Judgment has already been passed on *a priori* grounds. It is the typical move of the guardians of the established order. In the perspective of the Gospel it is the claim "We see" which is the proof of blindness. By contrast the man disclaims all capacity to pass judgment: "I do not know." He can do only one thing: he can be a witness to what has been done and to the one who has done it. He is not an authority, but he is a witness and he gives his witness in face of the threat of excommunication.

This very simple act of testimony causes the whole facade of official bluff to collapse. The concealed anxiety of the threatened authorities is obvious in the renewed questioning. The man does not hesitate to draw attention to the pittiful weakness which is now exposed. Since they are obviously at their wit's end, perhaps they would like to become Jesus' disciples?

At this, all pretense of judicial objectivity is thrown to the winds. The judges start reviling the witness. The fact that he was born blind, which they had sought to deny, is now used as a ground for refusing to listen to his testimony (v. 34). Again they repeat the claim to know God's revelation and in the same breath deny knowledge of the one in whom light has come into the world (v. 29). And finally, with unconscious irony, they testify to the fact that those born in sin will become—through the light which Jesus brings—the teachers of those who are still in darkness.

Here is the most vivid explication in the whole Gospel of the statement that the light shines in the darkness and the darkness neither comprehends it nor overcomes it. It continues to shine in the simple testimony of those who know what Jesus himself has done for them—even if they cannot yet adequately say who Jesus is. Those, however, who insist on saying "We know," apart from the acknowledgment of Jesus, are driven by that testimony to seek refuge in deeper darkness. This is the terrible reality of judgment, because—even though the light is healing light—its inevitable effect is to compel those who love the darkness to seek refuge in still deeper darkness. "If then the light in you is darkness, how great is the darkness!" (Matt. 6:23). The man who has received his sight from Jesus is cast out of the company of those who claim to know the truth apart from Jesus. This man does not yet know truly who Jesus is. But he is not left to find his own way. Jesus seeks him out—for he is, as we shall learn, the good shepherd who cares for his sheep.

He seeks him out in order that he may be able to come fully into the light. For this it is necessary that he should "believe in the Son of man." He has all along disclaimed any previous knowledge of who Jesus is. He has simply acknowledged, confessed, and built upon what Jesus has done for him (vv. 12, 17, 30-33). Now he is invited to declare his relation to Jesus himself. As "Son of man" Jesus is both "the man called Jesus" (v. 11) and the one to whom is given everlasting dominion (Dan. 7:9-14). Confronted by this self-manifestation of Jesus, the man offers him the worship which all men owe to the source of life and light.

Unlike this man who knew that he was blind until Jesus gave him sight, the authorities have all along claimed to see. "We know" has been their repeated assertion (vv. 24, 29). This claim to see is itself the judgment upon them because it has caused them to refuse and reject the coming of the light. Therefore their sin remains (v. 41). It is the sin which cannot be forgiven because the bearer of forgiveness has been rejected as an emissary of the devil (cf. Mark 3:20-30).

"Light has come into the world, and men loved darkness rather than light because their deeds were evil." If it is "the Jews" whose actions illustrate this fact, it is only because they are the representatives of us all—as Paul insists in Romans 2–3. Every achievement in "making sense" of the world, insofar as it succeeds, creates a claim to "see" which is threatened by the coming of Jesus who overturns all the "wisdom of this world," all the systems which are extrapolations from the experience of a world turned in upon itself. The coming of the light must always threaten every such system, for it can only be received in the simplicity of a child, in the simple gratitude of a man who says "One thing I know, that though I was blind, now I see." This kind of "seeing," this "wisdom from above" (James 3:17), begins and ends in worship, for the true light can never be a possession but only and always a gift.

11

THE GOOD SHEPHERD
(10:1-42)

THE COMING OF JESUS IS THE COMING OF LIGHT INTO THE world, and this inevitably means judgment. The false shepherds of Israel who do not love the sheep but on the contrary throw one of them out of the fold (9:34), are exposed by the coming of the light as "blind guides." But the purpose of Jesus' coming is not to judge but to give life. The revelation of God as light in whom is no darkness at all would be unbearable if it were not true that "the blood of Jesus cleanses us from all sin" (I John 1:5-7). After this vivid and terrible picture of Jesus as light bringing judgment we move without a break to the picture of Jesus as the one who brings life by the surrender of his own life. There is still inevitable division—between the shepherd and the thieves and brigands; between the shepherd and the hirelings; between those who receive the word of Jesus and those who reject it. But the purpose is "that they may have life, and have it abundantly."

The imagery of shepherd and sheep plays a very large part in the Old Testament and in the synoptic Gospels. The Lord is the shepherd of his people (e.g., Pss. 23, 80, 100; Isa. 40:11). He has chosen David to be a true shepherd of the flock (e.g., Ps. 78:71f.). He will punish and remove the false shepherds who behave like thieves and robbers (Ezek. 34). In the synoptics Jesus has compassion on the crowds because they are like sheep without a shepherd (Mark 6:34), and in the two versions of the parable of the Shepherd (Matt. 18:10-4; Luke 15:3-7) he gives an unforgettable picture of God as the loving shepherd who goes to all lengths for the sake of even one of his flock. In contemporary pagan literature also such imagery was common.

In St. John, as we might expect, the imagery is complex and mobile. Jesus is both the shepherd and the door of the sheepfold. Both images express the same fact, namely, that it is through Jesus alone that there is available both total freedom and total security—in fact, life in abundance.

10:1-6

"Truly, truly, I say to you, he who does not enter the sheepfold by the door but climbs in by another way, that man is a thief and a robber; but he who enters by the door is the shepherd of the sheep. To him the gatekeeper opens; the sheep hear his voice, and he calls his own sheep by name and leads them out. When he has brought out all his own, he goes before them, and the sheep follow him, for they know his voice. A stranger they will not follow, but they will flee from him, for they do not know the voice of strangers." This figure Jesus used with them, but they did not understand what he was saying to them.

In these verses the contrast is between the true shepherd and the brigands. It seems possible that two distinct parabolic sayings have been conflated here, since the gatekeeper referred to in verse 3 does not play any further part. As the passage stands, however, its purpose is clear. There are those who seek to rule the flock but they are false shepherds because they do not follow the one true way to leadership, which is the way of Jesus—the way which Jesus *is* (v. 7; cf. 14:6). World history is full of the records of those who have aspired to and achieved rule. For the most part they have been brigands who destroyed the flock, not shepherds who tended and nourished it. These self-appointed messiahs, saviors, "benefactors" have one thing in common. They do not follow the way of Jesus, which is—as we shall learn—the way of total self-giving. They "climb up some other way." It is not surprising that "leadership" has become almost a term of abuse and that those who try to exercise leadership are almost universally presumed to be corrupt.

But there is a proper and necessary leadership. The one who would exercise it must enter by the one true door which Jesus is, and which he has opened. The one who enters that way will be recognized and trusted and followed. Those who belong to him know him, because he is no stranger but "the light that lightens every man."

126

10:7-10

*So Jesus again said to them, "Truly, truly, I say to you, I am the door
of the sheep. All who came before me are thieves and robbers; but the
sheep did not heed them. I am the door; if any one enters by me, he will
be saved, and will go in and out and find pasture. The thief comes only
to steal and kill and destroy; I came that they may have life, and have
it abundantly."*

As in the synoptic record (e.g., Mark 4:10) so here the parable leads not to understanding but to its opposite. So with a renewed and solemn affirmation ("Amen, amen") Jesus spells it out. The door is a universally evocative symbol. It is the way of access from one world to another and therefore also the way by which the reality of that world may be communicated to this (e.g., Rev. 4:1). It is the way—the narrow way—which leads to life, and which one may easily miss (e.g., Matt. 7:13f.). It is the way by which entry is gained to the inner life of the soul (e.g., Rev. 3:20). Jesus is himself all that to which this image points. He is—as Son of man—the ladder by which traffic between heaven and earth is carried (1:51).

When Moses had reached the end of his journey he prayed: "Let the Lord, the God of the spirits of all flesh, appoint a man over the congregation, who shall go out before them and come in before them, who shall lead them out and bring them in; that the congregation of the LORD may not be as sheep which have no shepherd" (Num. 27:16f.). The man so appointed was Joshua, and it is a greater Joshua in whom the prayer finds its final answer. All men long both for security and for freedom, and often it seems that the one can be had only at the cost of the other. The liberator quickly becomes the dictator who can offer security only at the cost of liberty. And this world is full of self-appointed saviors who offer freedom and security on other terms than those which are embodied in the ministry of Jesus. Those who know his voice will not be seduced by these offers. On the contrary, they learn, as they follow the way which he is in, that he gives them both security and freedom, and that their needs are met abundantly, "good measure, pressed down, shaken together, running over" (Luke 6:38). As we shall learn further (14:1-6), the way, or door, which Jesus is, is both the way by which he comes to us and the way by which we move out of established securities to find new freedom in serving him in the world. We have the freedom to move in and out, and we find all our needs supplied.

10:11-13

"I am the good shepherd. The good shepherd lays down his life for the sheep. He who is a hireling and not a shepherd, whose own the sheep are not, sees the wolf coming and leaves the sheep and flees; and the wolf snatches them and scatters them. He flees because he is a hireling and cares nothing for the sheep."

But this abundance is a gift purchased at great cost. The metaphor of the door has been stretched to the breaking point, and it has to give place to another which has been all along in the background. Jesus is himself the good shepherd, the one who does for the flock what only God can do and what he has so often promised to do (e.g., Isa. 40:11; Jer. 31:10; Ezek. 34:11-16). But the fulfilment of the promise involves a price beyond the vision of the prophets. The shepherd must give his own life for the sheep; only so can they receive the superabundant life of God himself.

Here is the unmistakable criterion by which true leadership is to be distinguished from false. We are familiar with the kind of leadership which is simply a vast overextension of the ego. The ultimate goal—whether openly acknowledged or not—is the glory of the leader. The rest are instrumental to this end. He does not love them but he makes use of them for his own ends. He is a hireling—in the business of leadership for what he can get out of it.

By contrast the mark of the true leader is that of the cross. This is the only proof that Paul offers when his apostolic calling is questioned: he bears the marks of the cross in his own life (e.g., I Cor. 4; II Cor. 11). The good shepherd lays down his life for the sheep. Such true leadership must not be denigrated in the fashionable contempt for "elitism." The elite are, in biblical language, the elect, and they are chosen to go the way of the cross, following him who is—*par excellence*—God's chosen one, God's elite. If they put their own safety before the safety of the flock they are no true shepherds but hirelings and the coming of the true shepherd exposes them for what they are—whether (as here) the leaders of the legal and ecclesiastical establishment or the pseudo-messiahs who achieve a brief glory as purveyors of instant salvation outside the establishment.

10:14-18

"I am the good shepherd; I know my own and my own know me, as the Father knows me and I know the Father; and I lay down my life for the sheep. And I have other sheep, that are not of this fold; I must bring them also, and they will heed my voice. So there shall be one flock, one shepherd. For this reason the Father loves me, because I lay down my life, that I may take it again. No one takes it from me, but I lay it down of my own accord. I have power to lay it down, and I have power to take it again; this charge I have received from my Father."

The good shepherd knows his sheep and his sheep know him. This deep mutual knowing rests upon and is a participation in the mutual knowing which binds Jesus to the Father. In fact the mutual knowing is the abundant life which he gives (17:3). It is not just the "objective" knowledge which leaves the knower uncommitted. It is a knowledge which is only present in a total self-giving, and—once again—this is rooted in the total mutual self-giving which is the life of God. The Father gives his Son for the life of the world; the Son gives back his life to the Father, and thus the glory of God is revealed in the world. This alone is true shepherding, true leadership. Here is the one focus for the unity of mankind. The good shepherd has come not only to tend the flock of Israel but "to gather into one the children of God who are scattered abroad" (11:52). There is no other good shepherd, no other who can lead the entire human family into fullness of life, except him who has laid down his life for all. It is upon him that the love of the Father rests, the Father who longs to gather all his children together. The unity of the Church and the unity of mankind cannot be rightly considered in separation from each other. The former is to be sought and cherished as the sign and foretaste of the latter, for there is only one good shepherd who has laid down his life "to draw all men to himself" (12:32).

The action of Jesus in giving his life is an act both of complete freedom and of filial obedience. He is not the passive victim of other men's purposes. They imagine that they are in command and can make their own decision about whether and how and when he is to be eliminated (11:47-53). But the truth is otherwise. Jesus goes forward on the path which his Father has prepared for him, and does so with an obedient freedom and a free obedience. This path is that of unswerving witness to the truth, which necessarily draws upon itself the hatred of those who live by the lie.

Jesus in going this way offers his life to the Father in whose will is his joy (15:11), confident that what he has so offered cannot be lost but will be received back. This path of freely willed and obedient surrender to the Father is the way which Jesus is, and along which he leads his people. At every moment they face the powers which threaten to diminish and destroy life, but always they are masters of the secret alchemy by which loss is transmuted into free gift, death into life. At each step as they face the power that negates life they turn the negation into a triumphant affirmation, "No one takes this from me; I lay it down of myself," until the time comes to surrender life itself in glad obedience to the Father who will in his own time and way give back the free gift of eternal life. This is the way for all humankind, and to follow this way is to learn the only true leadership.

10:19-21

There was again a division among the Jews because of these words. Many of them said, "He has a demon, and he is mad; why listen to him?" Others said, "These are not the sayings of one who has a demon. Can a demon open the eyes of the blind?"

Once again there is a deep division among Jesus' hearers. These are words which we cannot expect to hear from any man. Whence, then, do they come—from the realm of darkness, or from the light? What criteria are there for recognizing light and distinguishing it from darkness? The "judgment of this world" (12:31) looms ever nearer.

10:22-31

It was the feast of the Dedication at Jerusalem; it was winter, and Jesus was walking in the temple, in the portico of Solomon. So the Jews gathered round him and said to him, "How long will you keep us in suspense? If you are the Christ, tell us plainly." Jesus answered them, "I told you, and you do not believe. The works that I do in my Father's name, they bear witness to me; but you do not believe, because you do not belong to my sheep. My sheep hear my voice, and I know them, and they follow me; and I give them eternal life, and they shall never perish, and no one shall snatch them out of my hand. My Father, who has given them to me, is greater than all, and no one is able to snatch them out of the Father's hand. I and the Father are one." The Jews took up stones again to stone him.

The Feast of Dedication was celebrated in the month of December to commemorate the cleansing and reconsecration of the Temple after it had been profaned by Antiochus Epiphanes. It was a time when cold east winds blew upon the exposed height of the Temple rock; and Solomon's Portico, on the east side of the walled enclosure, would be the most sheltered open space in Jerusalem. It was here that the infant Christian community was later to meet (Acts 3:11). It was also, according to Mark's version of the tradition, while Jesus was "walking in the temple" near the end of his public ministry, that he was challenged by the authorities to declare his credentials (Mark 11:27ff.) and that he went on immediately to warn them, in the parable of the Vineyard, that their intention to take his life would end in the taking away of their place of God's economy (Mark 12:1-12). This Marcan account also leads to an unsuccessful attempt to arrest Jesus.

In John's account the Jewish authorities gather around Jesus and demand a plain answer to a question which—of course—they formulate in their own terms. Is he, or is he not, the Messiah? The words "How long will you keep us in suspense?" translate a Greek verb which does not normally have this meaning but means rather to lift up, to bear, or to take away. A literal translation would be: "How long do you take away our life?" The same verb is used at verse 18 where Jesus says, "No man takes my life from me," and at 11:48 where the high priest warns his colleagues that the result of Jesus' work will be that "the Romans will come and take away both our place and our nation" (11:48 AV). It would be characteristic of John's style if indeed the same word is deliberately used in these three places. The effect is to align the questions of the Jews with the issue which—according to Mark—was so dramatically stated at the same time and place in the parable of the Wicked Husbandmen: the "taking away" of the life of Jesus will indeed mean the "taking away" of the Lord's vineyard from its present tenants.

The question of the Jews and the answer of Jesus raise again the fundamental problem of revelation. Jesus has spoken in parables; they demand a plain answer to a straight question: "Are you the Messiah?" This is to require that Jesus either accept or decline a place already prepared for him in their theology. But Jesus cannot take any place in a true theology except the determinative one. A true theology—that is to say, a true word about God—begins with him who is himself God's word. Jesus has in fact both spoken and acted in such a way that those whom the Father has given him do hear and believe. For them his words are lifegiving and his works are signs which reveal who he is. But for the rest, his words are riddles and his works are occasions of stumbling (Matt. 11:4-6). This fact is stated with even greater sharpness in Mark when Jesus in answer to a question about his use of parables quotes the terrible word of the Lord to Isaiah: "Go, and say to this people: 'Hear and hear, but do not understand; see and see, but do not perceive' . . . lest they turn and be healed" (Isa. 6:9f. and Mark 4:10-12). This is to state with extreme sharpness what is the constant theme of St. John, namely, that to recognize in the man Jesus, in all his weakness, humility, and vulnerability, the very presence of the glory of God can only be the result of a total conversion which none but God himself can bring about. There is no way by which Jesus can be accommodated within any theology which has its starting point elsewhere. To acknowledge him as who he is, is to accept a shattering of all other structures of confidence and belief, which is one aspect of what Paul describes as "being crucified with Christ." Using Paul's language again, it is only for those who are called that Jesus is recognizable as the power of God and the wisdom of God (I Cor. 1:23).

It follows, and here we revert to Johannine language, that those who do believe do so because the Father has called them, brought them to Jesus, and given them to him. They recognize his voice; they see his works as signs of glory; they follow him and they receive the gift of life out of death (as the raising of Lazarus will vividly show). They have no security except in him, but that security is complete because it is the Father himself who called them and gave them to Jesus. They do not depend for security upon their own faith, insight, or goodness, but simply on the one who called them. Those who are not so called remain within the structures of belief and conduct which are built around man's own search for certainty and security; they belong to "the world." The "straight question" formulated within these structures cannot possibly receive a "plain answer." To imagine that it can is to remain in the prison of the world.

Before the reader dismisses this as the unacceptable face of Johannine predestinarianism he should ask himself what is involved in rejecting it. Faced with the fact that for multitudes of his friends and neighbors the gospel seems to be a meaningless or irrelevant piece of ancient mythology, the Christian believer is tempted to meet the problem in one or other of two ways. The first is to judge the unbeliever as culpably blind; he is the one who refuses to take the step of faith. The second is to conclude that the believer and the unbeliever are equally seeking something which is beyond them both. The first road leads the believer down a path which separates him from Christ, who did not come as judge but as Savior—even though his coming does precipitate judgment. It leads the believer to search for some kind of moral defect lurking behind the pretensions of the unbeliever. He becomes a judge and not a friend. The second road abandons the claim to truth and leaves each person finally imprisoned in his own subjectivity.

Faced with the fact that I am a believer in Jesus, while other better and more devout than I are not, I can only fall back upon the fact that I have been called by one stronger than I who has so ordered my goings that I can find life only in Jesus. If I ask "Why has he called me and not another?" I have no clue to the answer. But if I ask "For what purpose has he called me?" the answer is clear. It is in order that I may be a witness. In the strongest statement of God's election which the Gospel contains, Jesus says to his disciples: "You did not choose me, but I chose you and appointed you that you should go and bear fruit" (15:16). What is said in the present passage about those who do and those who do not belong to Jesus must be read in the context of the whole teaching of the Gospel about the coming of light into the world. There is light and there is darkness; but these are not two zones separated from each other by a fixed boundary. The light shines in the darkness. It is not placed under a bushel but on the lampstand so that darkness may be banished (Matt. 5:14f.). The lighting of the lamp inevitably casts shadows, but the purpose is to fill the whole room with light. To ask why some men see and some do not is to ask the wrong question (9:2). The light has come into the world not just to expose the darkness but to banish it. Once again, we only begin to understand the world as we are involved in changing it.

The Jews had asked for a plain statement. They receive something which is not framed in the terms of their question, but is so plain as to lead straight to an attempt to stone him for blasphemy. The words about the Father and about the shepherd and his sheep come to rest in the terse statement: "I and the Father are one." This verse has figured so much in theological debate from the beginning, and is still so popular with those who would understand Jesus in terms of the Vedanta, that it is necessary to make an effort to see what it means in its context. Jesus is speaking of the security which believers have in him. He has said that it is in accordance with his Father's will that he lays down his life for them (vv. 17-18), that his works are done in the Father's name (v. 25), and that believers are given to him by the Father and cannot be snatched out of the Father's hand. His loving care of his flock is, in fact, the Father's love and care. No separation can be made between them. The security which the followers of Jesus have is the absolute security of dependence upon the Father, for the love of Jesus is in fact the love of God in action.

These words, which go far beyond the claim to Messiahship, lead immediately to the attempt to stone Jesus for blasphemy. But his hour has not yet come. There is still time for him "to work the works of him that sent me," and so Jesus gives them a calm reply.

10:32-39

Jesus answered them, "I have shown you many good works from the Father; for which of these do you stone me?" The Jews answered him, "We stone you for no good work but for blasphemy; because you, being a man, make yourself God." Jesus answered them, "Is it not written in your law, 'I said, you are gods'? If he called them gods to whom the word of God came (and scripture cannot be broken), do you say of him whom the Father consecrated and sent into the world, 'You are blaspheming,' because I said, 'I am the Son of God'? If I am not doing the works of my Father, then do not believe me; but if I do them, even though you do not believe me, believe the works, that you may know and understand that the Father is in me and I am in the Father." Again they tried to arrest him, but he escaped from their hands.

The works of Jesus have been works of blessing, bringing life, light, and health to those denied them. These are the gifts that God alone gives. The works of Jesus are, and should be seen to be, the works of the Father. Why should they be rewarded with the death penalty?

"Because you, being a man, make yourself God": with terrible irony the one who does the works of God is accused of usurping the place of God. Here is an accusation infinitely more

serious than that of claiming to be Messiah. These two charges
are those which, according to the synoptics, were investigated in
the trials before Annas and Caiaphas (see Mark 14:61; Matt. 26:63
and Luke 22:66-71). In Luke's account the two charges—Christ
and Son of God—are separated (vv. 67 and 70). John, on the
other hand, places this investigation in the context of the argument in the Temple. Consequently he gives only a very brief
account of the trial before "the high priest" and gives a very full
account of the trial before Pilate when the nature of Jesus' claim
is set in a universal and secular rather than a purely Jewish and
religious context.

In reply to the accusation of blasphemy Jesus quotes Psalm 82
in which God addresses those who are responsible for adminis-
tering the law with the words "You are gods, sons of the Most
High, all of you." If one reads the Old Testament as one element
in the comparative study of the world's religions it will be difficult
to see how this text provides any answer to the charge. But this
way of reading the Old Testament (a product of the movement
of European thought usually described—by Europeans—as "the
Enlightenment") was certainly unknown to the early Church, to
the evangelist, and to Jesus himself. From the earliest time of
which we have knowledge Christians believed that the work of
Jesus was to establish a "new covenant" which fulfilled the covenant made by God with Israel. The heart of that covenant was
the giving of the law. Those who interpreted and administered
the law, from Moses onward, did so in the name of the Lord
whose covenant it was. Hence to come before the judge was to
"come before God" (e.g., Ex. 21:6; 22:9; Deut. 19:17). The use
of such language rests upon the fact that God in his covenant has
shown himself as one who does not separate himself from his
people but binds them to himself, giving them an authority to
act in his name and so even to bear his name.

But—and this is of course the perspective of all the writings
which we call the "New Testament"—the covenant given on
Sinai points beyond itself to its fulfilment. When the time is fulfilled, the God who binds man to himself takes manhood upon
himself. Those to whom the word of the Torah came were, in
virtue of that fact, addressed as "God." How much more the one
in whom the word has become flesh! For the promise of scripture
cannot fail of its due fulfilment (v. 35). Jesus can therefore explicitly accept the title "Son of God" but must totally reject the

135

charge that he has usurped this title—"making himself God."
The exact opposite is the truth. It is God who has consecrated
him and sent him into the world. Perhaps the word has a special
force since this was the Feast of Dedication when the consecration
of the place of God's dwelling was celebrated. Jesus is himself the
one consecrated and sent into the world to be the place of God's
"tabernacling" among men (1:14). To affirm this is not to blas-
pheme the name of the covenant Lord, but to acknowledge that
the covenant is fulfilled in the very presence of God's own beloved son and in the works of blessing which he is doing in the
Father's name.

These works are, in fact, the evidence, if they will but see,
that Jesus is one with the Father. The language is not the meta-
physical language of later theology; the unity of which Jesus speaks
is one of perfect mutual loving and indwelling. For the works of
Jesus are "good" works (v. 32), works which ought to be clearly
recognizable as worthy of God's infinite goodness. Above all the
supreme work with which his ministry will be crowned, the
laying down of his life for the sheep, will be a "good" work
which is worthy of the "good" shepherd. Even if they cannot
believe him in the basis of his word, surely works of love should
be recognizable as the work of the Father.

Once more the appeal is rejected. Since his time has not yet
come, Jesus withdraws for a season. The proper time for his
crowning good work will not be the festivals of Tabernacles or
Dedication but that of the Passover. For that he waits. He will
not simply be trapped by his enemies in Jerusalem. He will come
of his own free will and at the proper time so that he may give
his life for his sheep and for the world (vv. 17-18).

10:40-42

*He went away again across the Jordan to the place where John at first
baptized, and there he remained. And many came to him; and they said,
"John did no sign, but everything that John said about this man was
true." And many believed in him there.*

The place of his retreat is the place where John the Baptist
had exercised that ministry which was the signal and the context
for the beginning of Jesus' own. John's baptism had been a symbol pointing to the greater reality which was impending, but not

a "sign" in the full sense in which the word is used in the Gospel—a deed in which the power of the kingdom of God is present to the faith of believers. But John's witness had been a true witness. The reality of wich he had spoken was present in Jesus. And though the authorities in Jerusalem had not believed in Jesus, there were among the people of the countryside many who did. Jesus stayed with them until the hour appointed for him by the Father.

12

LAZARUS
(11:1-57)

WE COME NOW TO THE LAST OF THE SEVEN "SIGNS" WHICH John records, signs which are selected and recorded in order that the reader may believe in Jesus and have life in his name (20:30f.). Of all the seven, this is the one which is most closely related to this purpose and therefore most fitted to be the climax of the series. "All Jesus' miracles are signs of what he is and what he has come to give man, but in none of them does the sign more closely approach the reality than in the gift of life. The physical life that Jesus gives to Lazarus is still not in the realm of the life from above, but it is so close to that realm that it may be said to conclude the ministry of signs and inaugurate the ministry of glory" (Brown).

There are, moreover, further reasons why this miracle most fitly concludes the series of signs and forms the transition to the story of the passion. First, it brings together the two themes of life and light. It is primarily concerned with the gift of life, but it is closely linked to the gift of sight to the man born blind (cf. 11:4, 9-10 with 9:3-5), and it strongly emphasizes the link between life and faith; the gift of life is linked to the perception of who Jesus is (11:25-27, 40). Secondly, it shows that Jesus gives life only by giving his life. The raising of Lazarus leads directly to the death of Jesus. It is at the cost of life that he gives life. The "abundant life" that he gives is life through death. He is the life only because he is the resurrection from the dead (v. 25). It is in this sense that the illness of Lazarus is for the glory of God (v. 4).

The synoptic Gospels report two instances of the raising of the dead by Jesus—that of the widow's son of Nain (Luke 7:11ff.)

and that of the daughter of Jairus (Mark 4:21-43). In the reply which Jesus sends to John, Jesus lists the messianic signs which are being wrought through his ministry as follows: "The blind receive their sight and the lame walk, lepers are cleansed and the deaf hear, and the dead are raised up, and the poor have good news preached to them" (Matt. 11:4; Luke 7:22). It is reasonable to think that the traditions regarding the ministry of Jesus included other cases of the raising of the dead besides the two recorded in the synoptics, that one of these concerned a man named Lazarus, and that John has placed this incident at such a point in his account of the ministry and told it in such a way as to bring to a climax his treatment of Jesus' "sings." This would be especially appropriate in that the synoptic passages just quoted have as their "punch line" the words "Blessed is he who takes no offense at me" (Matt. 11:6; Luke 7:23). John portrays the raising of Lazarus as the decisive cause of offense which precipitated the decision to destroy Jesus.

This seems more probable than the suggestion that John has developed the parable of the Rich Man and Lazarus into the story of a real resurrection in view of the closing words of the parable: ". . . neither will they be convinced if one rise from the dead" (Luke 16:31). Since there is no other parable of Jesus in which one of the characters is given a personal name, it is much more likely that the name has been affixed to the parable than that the parable has given birth to the story.

11:1-4

Now a certain man was ill, Lazarus of Bethany, the village of Mary and her sister Martha. It was Mary who anointed the Lord with ointment and wiped his feet with her hair, whose brother Lazarus was ill. So the sisters sent to him, saying, "Lord, he whom you love is ill." But when Jesus heard it he said, "This illness is not unto death; it is for the glory of God, so that the Son of God may be glorified by means of it."

The names of Mary and Martha, and the fact of their relation to Jesus, are presumed to be already known to the reader. The name of Lazarus is introduced as though the knowledge of it could not be presumed. The message from the sisters is an implied appeal for help on the basis of the known love of Jesus for this family. Jesus, however, makes no immediate move. As when his mother made a similar appeal (2:3), so here Jesus declines to act on the prompting of others. He will choose his own time. He will not accept the invitation to walk into a trap prepared by others, for no one takes his life from him but he lays it down of himself (10:18). The illness of Lazarus will not lead to death but will be the occasion of glory—not that Jesus will glorify himself by a miracle, but that by the death of Jesus God will be glorified in his Son (cf. 17:1-5). It is not that Jesus will be praised but that the glory of God will be manifest in the passion which is in fact that action both of the Father and of the Son, for "the glory of God is not his praise but his activity" (Barrett). From now on the theme of glory will move more and more into the foreground (e.g., 12:16, 23, 28, 41).

11:5-16

Now Jesus loved Martha and her sister and Lazarus. So when he heard that he was ill, he stayed two days longer in the place where he was. Then after this he said to the disciples, "Let us go into Judea again." The disciples said to him, "Rabbi, the Jews were but now seeking to stone you, and are you going there again?" Jesus answered, "Are there not twelve hours in the day? If any one walks in the day, he does not stumble, because he sees the light of this world. But if any one walks in the night, he stumbles, because the light is not in him." Thus he spoke, and then he said to them, "Our friend Lazarus has fallen asleep, but I go to awake him out of sleep." The disciples said to him, "Lord, if he has fallen asleep, he will recover." Now Jesus had spoken of his death, but they thought that he meant taking rest in sleep. Then Jesus told them plainly, "Lazarus is dead; and for your sake I am glad that I was not there, so that you may believe. But let us go to him." Thomas, called the Twin, said to his fellow disciples, "Let us also go, that we may die with him."

It seems probable, in view of the statement in verse 17, that we are intended to think that Lazarus was already dead at the time when the message reached Jesus. Jesus' deliberate delay would ensure that, by the time he reached the tomb, Lazarus would have passed the point at which it was believed that the soul finally leaves the body and corruption sets in. But this delay does not arise from indifference. On the contrary it is emphasized that Jesus loved Lazarus and his sisters. What will be given to them through the action of Jesus is something much more wonderful even than the granting to Lazarus of an extension of the life which terminates in death; it is the gift of a life which, beginning with the resurrection from the dead, is forever beyond the power of death to touch. Of that the raising of Lazarus will be a sign, but a sign which provides the occasion for the reality to be effected—namely, the glorification of God in the death and resurrection of Jesus. The raising of Lazarus will be the occasion of the "lifting up" of Jesus (vv. 45-53).

When Jesus does announce his intention to move from his place of retreat, he speaks of going not to Bethany but "into Judea." It is obvious that he is going into the place of greatest danger, and the disciples express their reasonable fears (cf. Mark 10:32-34). Jesus answers with a statement reminiscent of his words before the healing of the blind man. There is a time, given by the Father, in which the Son must do the Father's works. While he does so he will be secure against offenses. In going back to Judea Jesus is doing his Father's will in the time given to him. The hour which is given to the "power of darkness" will come soon enough (Luke 22:53). This is the surface meaning of the words of Jesus, but the reader is intended to remember that Jesus is himself the light of the world and that those who follow him "will not walk in darkness, but will have the light of life" (8:12).

Jesus then tells the disciples plainly what he had presumably known from the beginning, that Lazarus has died. The phrase used—"has fallen asleep"—could be misunderstood, and when the disciples do so misunderstand it, their words (in typical Johannine fashion) are an unwitting statement of the truth: natural sleep is the way to recovery; death is—in Christ—the way to life. And Lazarus is one whom Jesus counts as "friend," so his death will become the gateway to life. If Jesus had been present, Lazarus would not have died, and the disciples would not have been able to see this final sign in that series of signs by which Jesus is leading them to faith, from the true and loyal but still imperfect faith expressed by Thomas to the full faith which leads to "life in his name." The words of Thomas—so true to the character which is sketched in the Gospel—are the first recognition of the truth that to follow Jesus means to die with him. They do not yet attain to the faith that this dying is the way of life.

11:17-27

Now when Jesus came, he found that Lazarus had already been in the tomb four days. Bethany was near Jerusalem, about two miles off, and

many of the Jews had come to Martha and Mary to console them con-
cerning their brother. When Martha heard that Jesus was coming, she
went and met him, while Mary sat in the house. Martha said to Jesus,
"Lord, if you had been here, my brother would not have died. And even
now I know that whatever you ask from God, God will give you." Jesus
said to her. "Your brother will rise again." Martha said to him, "I know
that he will rise again in the resurrection at the last day." Jesus said to
her, "I am the resurrection and the life; he who believes in me, though
he die, yet shall he live, and whoever lives and believes in me shall never
die. Do you believe this?" She said to him, "Yes, Lord; I believe that
you are the Christ, the Son of God, he who is coming into the world."

Jesus is once more among the Jews, but they are there with
a godly purpose and there is no hint of hostility. From the point
of view of the unfolding of the whole narrative, however, their
presence provides the opportunity for Jesus to manifest his glory
among them so that they may believe or else refuse to believe (v.
45). The two sisters are portrayed in contrasted ways which correspond with what is suggested in Luke's description (Luke
10:38-42). Martha hurries to meet Jesus and her words imply an
appeal for his intervention even at this late stage when her brother
has been four days in the grave. She has total trust in Jesus, but
sees him as a powerful intercessor with God—like Elijah. Jesus
answers with an affirmation which she interprets as being a repetition of that belief in an ultimate resurrection with which, no
doubt, her friends from Jerusalem had sought to console her. But
the prospect of a universal resurrection on the last day is very
cold comfort. She must learn, and Jesus must now show her, that
the last day has already dawned. Jesus is himself, in his own
person, the *eschatos*, the end as he was the beginning. Resurrection
is no longer a mere doctrine: it has a living face and a name. Jesus
is himself the presence of the life which is God's gift beyond
death. To be bound to Jesus by faith is to share already now the
life which is beyond death. To one so bound, death is the gateway
to life and life is no longer bounded by death because it is the life
which is raised out of death. Jesus is the life only because he is
the resurrection, and the life which he shares with believers is not
an extension of natural life but arises out of death and therefore
does not and cannot move toward death.

Martha, whose faith in Jesus has not advanced beyond the
recognition of him as a powerful intermediary with God, is challenged to accept this stupendous affirmation. Her reply is a correct
statement of Christian belief. And yet—unlike the man born

142

blind (9:38) and unlike her sister Mary (v. 32)—she does not offer
him her total worship, and the sequel will show (vv. 39f.) that
her faith is not yet perfect. She has yet to reach the point where—
in the fullest sense—she believes. She has not yet "seen his glory."

11:28-37

*When she had said this, she went and called her sister Mary, saying
quietly, "The Teacher is here and is calling for you." And when she
heard it, she rose quickly and went to him. Now Jesus had not yet come
to the village, but was still in the place where Martha had met him.
When the Jews who were with her in the house, consoling her, saw Mary
rise quickly and go out, they followed her, supposing that she was going
to the tomb to weep there. Then Mary, when she came where Jesus was
and saw him, fell at his feet, saying to him, "Lord, if you had been here,
my brother would not have died." When Jesus saw her weeping, and the
Jews who came with her also weeping, he was deeply moved in spirit
and troubled; and he said, "Where have you laid him?" They said to
him, "Lord, come and see." Jesus wept. So the Jews said, "See how he
loved him!" But some of them said, "Could not he who opened the eyes
of the blind man have kept this man from dying?"*

The secret message to Mary brings her running not to the
place of death (as the Jews suppose) but to the one with whom
death cannot exist. Mary makes no request; she simply falls at the
feet of Jesus and pours out her tears. At this the evangelist reports
that Jesus "was deeply moved in spirit and troubled." The words
used express not only grief and perturbation but also anger. Why
was Jesus angry? The question has perplexed and divided commentators from earliest times, and perhaps there are questions
here which cannot be answered. What is clear from all the records
is that Jesus was at various times moved to the deepest emotion
in his conflict with the power of evil. His stern words to those
afflicted by illness (e.g., Mark 1:43; Matt. 9:30); his weeping at
the stubborn impenitence of Jerusalem (Luke 19:41); his agony in
the garden (Mark 14:32-42 and parallels), which John does not
record; and his perturbation in the face of treachery (13:21)—all
in different ways testify to the fact that his conflict with "the
prince of this world" (12:31) was an infinitely costly one. "In the
days of his flesh Jesus offered up prayers and supplications, with
loud cries, to him who was able to save him from death, and he
was heard for his godly fear" (Heb. 5:7). Perhaps one may dare

to say only this, that in the immediate presence of death, and of the hopeless unbelief of his friends in the face of death, Jesus was facing that power which he had come to destroy, a power which is met by the wrath of him who is the author of life, but which could only be "cast out" (12:31) when the author of life took the whole power of death upon himself.

11:38-44

Then Jesus, deeply moved again, came to the tomb; it was a cave, and a stone lay upon it. Jesus said, "Take away the stone." Martha, the sister of the dead man, said to him, "Lord, by this time there will be an odor, for he has been dead four days." Jesus said to her, "Did I not tell you that if you would believe you would see the glory of God?" So they took away the stone. And Jesus lifted up his eyes and said, "Father, I thank thee that thou hast heard me. I knew that thou hearest me always, but I have said this on account of the people standing by, that they may believe that thou didst send me." When he had said this, he cried with a loud voice, "Lazarus, come out." The dead man came out, his hands and feet bound with bandages, and his face wrapped with a cloth. Jesus said to them, "Unbind him, and let him go."

Of the first of the seven signs it was said that Jesus manifested his glory and his disciples believed on him (2:11). Now Martha, whose faith has already been expressed but clearly falls short of full commitment, is told that if she believes she will see the glory of God. In order that it may be made clear that Jesus seeks not his own glory but the glory of his Father, Jesus lifts up his eyes (cf. 17:1) and utters aloud the prayer which was always the very substance of his unbroken communion with his Father. This prayer is both petition and thanksgiving, and it is always both of these at the same time. The will of Jesus is so completely given to his Father that his whole life is both an asking and a receiving, an asking which is so confident that it can be thanksgiving while it is petition. It is into this kind of prayer that Jesus invites his disciples to enter (e.g., Matt. 7:7ff.; Mark 11:34; John 15:7; 16:23). Yet in all of this Jesus is seeking and doing not his own will but the will of him who sent him. Jesus does not come among men as one who is a wonder worker by his own power. All must know—and this is why he now utters aloud the prayer which is always binding him to the Father—that he is simply the one sent by the Father, and so come to believe.

Jesus then calls Lazarus by name and in a loud voice. The synoptics report that Jesus gave a loud cry from the cross before he gave back his spirit to the Father. In St. John's Gospel the loud cry comes here, at the point where Jesus confronts the power of death in the name of the Father who sent him. Here is a foretaste of that which he had already foretold: "The hour is coming, and now is, when the dead will hear the voice of the Son of God, and those who hear will live. For as the Father has life in himself, so he has granted the Son also to have life in himself" (5:25f.).

The supreme sign has been given, and now—therefore—is the moment at which final decisions will be made, either to believe and to behold the glory of God, or to reject and so to turn from the light of life to the darkness of death. That decision is now to be made, and by the highest tribunal of Israel.

11:45-57

Many of the Jews therefore, who had come with Mary and had seen what he did, believed in him; but some of them went to the Pharisees and told them what Jesus had done. So the chief priests and the Pharisees gathered the council, and said, "What are we to do? For this man performs many signs. If we let him go on thus, every one will believe in him, and the Romans will come and destroy both our holy place and our nation." But one of them, Caiaphas, who was high priest that year, said to them, "You know nothing at all; you do not understand that it is expedient for you that one man should die for the people, and that the whole nation should not perish." He did not say this of his own accord, but being high priest that year he prophesied that Jesus should die for the nation, and not for the nation only, but to gather into one the children of God who are scattered abroad. So from that day on they took counsel how to put him to death.

Jesus therefore no longer went about openly among the Jews, but went from there to the country near the wilderness, to a town called Ephraim; and there he stayed with the disciples.

Now the Passover of the Jews was at hand, and many went up from the country to Jerusalem before the Passover, to purify themselves. They were looking for Jesus and saying to one another as they stood in the temple, "What do you think? That he will not come to the feast?" Now the chief priests and the Pharisees had given orders that if any one knew where he was, he should let them know, so that they might arrest him.

It has already been noted that St. John's Gospel does not report a trial of Jesus before the high priest and his council (the Sanhedrin) in the way that the synoptics do, but that the elements which are brought together in the synoptic accounts of the trial are, in John, found in the earlier discussions between Jesus and the Jews. So also the synoptics do not record a formal decision of the Sanhedrin to destroy Jesus such as is found here, but all three of them open their narrative of the passion with the statement that the Jewish authorities had in fact made this decision (Mark 14:1; Luke 22:2; Matt. 25:3f.), and in Matthew's Gospel it is stated that the decision was made at a meeting of "the chief priests and elders" in the palace of Caiaphas. All agree that Jesus was—in effect—judged and condemned *in absentia*. In the synoptics the decision follows immediately upon a report of Jesus' eschatological claims; in John it follows upon the deed which was the most dramatic and inescapable enactment of these claims.

Why was Jesus condemned? The answer as John unfolds it is not simple. Both religious and political motives are involved, but in the end both of these human motives are seen to be overruled by a divine purpose which transcends them both.

The words and the deeds of Jesus are leading great numbers of Jews to believe in him. That belief, inadequate though it may be, is a genuine response of religious faith. Even the authorities are shaken, for they cannot deny the fact that the deeds of Jesus have the character of "signs." But religious questionings are quickly silenced by political fears. Weakness in the present situation will lead to popular revolutionary movements with familiar messianic overtones. The imperial authorities will conclude that the Sanhedrin is incapable of maintaining law and order. The experiment of indirect rule will be abandoned and Rome will take over. This fear is expressed in language which is typical of a certain kind of fusion between religion and politics. The place where God's glory promised to dwell is "our holy place," and the people redeemed to be God's own possession is "our nation." God's cause has become "our" political necessity.

Caiaphas, the high priest, confronts these anxieties with brutal political realism. Questions about who Jesus is, or claims to be, can be set aside. In a political crisis one must face political realities. The death of one man is a small price to pay for the survival of the whole nation. Jesus must die for the people.

The moment these words are said, the reader understands that a purpose much greater than anything in the mind of Caiaphas is at work. These small and frightened men, clothed in the robes of authority which are in fact only a covering for pitiful weakness, are the unwitting instruments of a mighty divine purpose. Like Pontius Pilate whose acts and whose failure to act at God's proper time have won him—unwitting and unwilling—a place forever in the liturgy of the universal church, so also Caiaphas, because he was the high priest in that year which was the year of God's choosing for the salvation of man, speaks and acts all unknowing as the instrument of God's purpose. The reference to "that year" does not mean that John was ignorant of the fact that the office was for life, or that this man in fact held office for nearly twenty years. It means that, as a witness of the resurrection and as a member of the new "people of God" which Jesus the good shepherd has gathered into one fold from all the nations, he knows that because it was "that year," the year of the redemption of the world, the high priest spoke and acted unknowingly as the mouthpiece and the agent of "the definite plan and foreknowledge of God" (Acts 2:22f.).

The high priest fears for the destruction of the Temple, but does not know that Jesus is himself the true temple and that though the Jews will indeed destroy that temple it will be raised up to become the place to which all the nations of the earth will come to worship God, as the prophets had foretold.

The high priest fears for the destruction of the people, but does not know that Jesus is the good shepherd promised in Ezekiel who will die for the sheep, and who will gather together into one not just the dispersed nation of Israel, but all those out of all the nations who through him are made children of God.

The high priest is the one who alone must enter the holy place once a year to make atonement for the sins of the people, "and not without taking blood which he offers for himself and for the errors of the people" (Heb. 9:7). He does not know that the whole ritual apparatus of which he is the center is but a sign pointing to the one true sacrifice which alone can taken away not only the sin of Israel but the sin of the whole world, and that the blood of Jesus which he judges to be a small price to pay for the security of his office, his Temple, and his people is in fact the blood of a new covenant freely shed for the expiation of the sin of the world.

So the decision is made—a decision in which the murderous intention of men is made to serve the redeeming love of God. The tenants to whom God entrusted his beloved vineyard have resolved to kill the son and heir so that they may secure the inheritance for themselves ("*our* holy place"). They do not know the meaning of the scripture which says: "The very stone which the builders rejected has become the head of the corner" (Mark 12:1-10). They have seen the signs of the kingdom, but these very signs have become an occasion for stumbling (Matt. 11:4-6). And yet the very stone of stumbling is also the secure foundation for a new "dwelling place of God in the Spirit" (Eph. 2:22), a "spiritual house" for people of all nations (I Pet. 2:4-8).

The decision is made, but it cannot immediately be put into effect. If there is a proper year when God's decisive act of redemption is to be wrought, there is also a proper season for it. The time of the Passover was near, the time when God's deliverance of Israel from Egypt was celebrated. That will be the proper season for the enactment of the greater deliverance of which it is a sign. Jesus, therefore, withdraws again from Judea until the proper time. His death, when it comes, will be his deed. "No one takes my life from me; I lay it down of myself." Jesus and his desciples return to the borders of the eastern desert. This time the crowds do not come to him as they did at the time of his earlier retreat (10:41). He is alone with his disciples; and while the Jews are busy with the rites of purification necessary in preparation for the Passover, Jesus is preparing his disciples for another Passover for which he will himself provide the needed cleansing (13:1-10).

Meanwhile the scene is being set in Jerusalem for the passion of Jesus and the final overthrow of the "ruler of this world." Devout pilgrims are in the Temple precincts, preparing themselves for the Passover. As at the previous Passover (7:11-13) the people are looking for Jesus in the Temple and their gossip about him is spiced with an extra element of excitement because they know that—this time—the authorities have made up their minds to put him to death. As they prepare for the ritual killing of the paschal lambs, and as they speculate about the possible fate of Jesus, they do not know that he is in fact the Lamb of God who, being slain, will take away the sin of the world and bring to its consummation and its end that ritual which they and their forefathers had cherished since Israel became a nation.

13

PRELUDE
TO THE PASSION
(12:1-50)

WE ARE NOW INTRODUCED TO THREE INCIDENTS WHICH lead to the final comment of the evangelist upon the results of the public ministry (12:37-43) and the final witness of Jesus to the nation (12:44-50). These three incidents are the anointing at Bethany, the triumphal entry into Jerusalem, and the approach of the Greek inquirers. The first two are also contained in the synoptic Gospels, though in a different order, and both of them lead to the now familiar theme of polarization between faith and unbelief.

12:1-8

Six days before the Passover, Jesus came to Bethany, where Lazarus was, whom Jesus had raised from the dead. There they made him a supper; Martha served, and Lazarus was one of those at table with him. Mary took a pound of costly ointment of pure nard and anointed the feet of Jesus and wiped his feet with her hair; and the house was filled with the fragrance of the ointment. But Judas Iscariot, one of his disciples (he who has to betray him), said, "Why was this ointment not sold for three hundred denarii and given to the poor?" This he said, not that he cared for the poor but because he was a thief, and as he had the money box he used to take what was put into it. Jesus said, "Let her alone, let her keep it for the day of my burial. The poor you always have with you, but you do not always have me."

Mark, followed by Matthew, describes the anointing of Jesus' *head* by an unnamed woman in the house of Simon the Leper at Bethany during the last week in Jerusalem. Luke describes the anointing of Jesus' *feet* by an unnamed woman in the house of

Simon the Pharisee during the Galilean ministry. John says that the *feet* of Jesus were anointed by Mary at Bethany before the entry into Jerusalem. The factual and verbal agreements and disagreements among the four accounts form a very complex pattern and make it difficult to believe that the writer of the Fourth Gospel had the first three before him in their present written form. It seems safest to conclude that John had his own access to the common stock of tradition and that, as always, he has retold this story in such a way as to further the overall purpose of his work. We must take the story as it stands.

Jesus returns from his retreat at the beginning of the week which leads to the Passover and he goes to the place—Bethany— where his mighty work of giving life to the dead has been publicly performed. A banquet is arranged in his honor. We are not told who is the host or in whose house it is held. It would be natural in view of the circumstances, and certainly natural in that society, that it should be a communal banquet organized by the whole village. Martha is one of those who serve, and Lazarus one of those who partake.

A banquet is a natural way to honor one who has indeed deserved honor and to express joy in the restoration of life to the dead. But even this is much less than an adequate recognition of the reality which is present in Jesus. The reader has already learned of Mary's utter devotion to Jesus. Now—in the midst of the banquet—she comes forward to perform a deed which is both the expression of the utmost possible humility, love, and devotion, and a sign—perhaps an unwitting sign—of that which lies before Jesus. The unnamed woman of Mark's account anoints the head of Jesus—a sign of consecration to the office of king. Mary anoints his feet, an act which can have no such meaning but which could be a symbol of the anointing of the whole body for burial— as Jesus' washing of the disciples' feet was a symbol of their total cleansing. And the shaking loose of the hair would be incomprehensible were it not the familiar sign of the deepest grief.

For behind and beneath the joyful festivity of a village banquet is the fact that Jesus is on his way to death. As he follows the way of the lamb led to the slaughter and "pours out his soul unto death" (Isa. 53:7-12), his utter devotion is, for a moment, mirrored in the devotion of Mary who pours out her precious ointment upon his feet. The love of the Savior is met and mirrored for a moment by the love of one he came to save. He sees of the travail of his soul and the whole house is filled with the fragrance. Thus shall the fragrance of the gospel eventually fill the whole world (Mark 14:9; II Cor. 2:15), for Mary is the fore-runner of the believing Church which will in time to come pour out in all the world its works of love flowing from hearts broken at the place of Jesus' sacrifice.

But this outpouring of devotion breaks the conviviality of the feast, for the coming of light cannot fail to cast shadows. The extravagant devotion of Mary cannot coexist with the mean spirit which calculates the cost of everything. The treasurer cannot help thinking of his balance sheet—the more so if he is a dishonest treasurer. The giving of alms to the poor is one of the good works commanded in the law; why throw away the opportunity for such good works by this senseless act of waste? In Mark's account the criticism is made by unnamed persons, and in Matthew's by the disciples; in both it is the occasion for Judas' decision to turn traitor. John makes Judas himself the one who criticizes, not for the stated reason but because of his own dishonest intentions.

The reply of Jesus (v. 7) is not easy to interpret; Mary cannot keep for his burial what she has already poured out. The words can have the sense "It was that she might keep it for the day of my burial," and this seems to be the meaning. Mary has not given this to the poor but has kept it for an act which is a true expression of love and devotion. As Mark has it: "She has anointed my body beforehand for burying" (Mark 4:8).

The reference to the poor in verse 8, omitted in some of the manuscripts, echoes the words of the law (Deut. 15:11) and those of Mark. To set alms to the poor over against devotion to Jesus is to miss the real motive of Christian discipleship. Devotion to Jesus and gratitude for his sacrifice will lead in fact to a service of the poor (which will always be needed) in a manner quite different from a legally required almsgiving. It will be in fact part of the fragrance of the gospel which is destined to fill the whole world.

The coming of the light creates both light and shadow. The presence of Jesus is the presence of the light, and that presence is attested with terrifying intensity in the small compass of the banquet at Bethany—in the bright light of Mary's love and the dark shadow of Judas' selfish resentment. The light shines in the darkness. We are now to see the same contrast of light and dark, faith and unbelief, love and hate in the wider context of the public festival of the Passover.

12:9-19

When the great crowd of the Jews learned that he was there, they came, not only on account of Jesus but also to see Lazarus, whom he had raised from the dead. So the chief priests planned to put Lazarus also to death, because on account of him many of the Jews were going away and believing in Jesus.

The next day a great crowd who had come to the feast heard that Jesus was coming to Jerusalem. So they took branches of palm trees and went out to meet him, crying, "Hosanna! Blessed is he who comes in the name of the Lord, even the King of Israel!" And Jesus found a young ass and sat upon it; as it is written,

"Fear not, daughter of Zion;
behold, your king is coming,
sitting on an ass's colt!"

His disciples did not understand this at first; but when Jesus was glorified, then they remembered that this had been written of him and had been done to him. The crowd that had been with him when he called Lazarus out of the tomb and raised him from the dead bore witness. The reason why the crowd went to meet him was that they heard he had done this sign. The Pharisees then said to one another, "You see that you can do nothing; look, the world has gone after him."

The fact that Jesus, as he approached the climax of his ministry, rode into Jerusalem on an ass and was welcomed by crowds gathered for the Passover is recorded by all four evangelists. The question whether John's account is dependent on that of the synoptic or whether he has a distinct source for his record is much debated. The balance of the argument seems to favor the view that John is not simply dependent on the synoptics. As he tells it, the story differs in important respects from that told by the other three evangelists. This entry is not Jesus' first arrival in Jerusalem. He is not only accompanied by crowds coming to the festival as in the synoptics, but is also met by crowds who come out from the city to acclaim him. His choice of an ass for mount is not (as in the synoptics) prearranged but seems to be made after the crowd has met him. The nature of the reception has explicit political overtones which are much less clear in the synoptic records. And finally there is the characteristic Johannine insistence that the disciples did not at the time understand what was happening, but understood only afterward. It is perhaps deliberate that John makes here an explicit link with the cleansing of the Temple which he (unlike the synoptics) has separated from the triumphal entry and placed at the beginning of the public ministry (cf. 12:16 with 2:22).

Once again we have to take the story as it stands in the development of John's master theme.

The raising of Lazarus has been the climax of all Jesus' mighty works. It leads multitudes of Jews to turn to him in faith and therefore—by contrast—leads the authorities still further along the path of violence. They will seek to destroy not only the giver of life but also the one who is a living witness to him.

Jerusalem is already full of pilgrims (11:55). They hear that Jesus is approaching and set out to welcome him. They carry in their hands the palm branches which were the widely acknowledged symbol of welcome to a king, which had been used to welcome both Simon Maccabaeus when he captured the city and Judas Maccabaeus when he purified the Temple after its pollution by Antiochus Epiphanes (I Macc. 13:51 and II Macc. 10:7), and which were used at the annual festival of the Dedication commemorating the latter event. With these symbols in their hands the crowd welcome Jesus as the king of Israel—adding this title to the words which (as in the synoptics) are quoted from the priests' greeting of the pilgrims in Psalm 118:25f. Once again, as happened after the feeding of the five thousand, the crowd hails Jesus as "the one who is to come" and interprets this to mean that he is to be the king of Israel (6:15f.).

It is at this point that Jesus finds an ass and continues his journey with the ass as his mount, deliberately (according to Matthew) fulfilling an ancient prophecy of Zechariah. Mark and Luke make no reference to the prophecy. John omits the words which Matthew quotes, "humble and mounted on an ass," and replaces the original "Rejoice greatly" with "Fear not." These last words are familiar to anyone steeped in the Old Testament and may represent only a loose use of scripture by the evangelist (cf. Mark 1:2 where words from Malachi are conflated with those from Isaiah). If we take the Zechariah passage as a whole it is clear that it is a promise of the gift of "peace to the nations" through the universal rule of Yahweh, and that the triumph of Yahweh will not be brought about by the military power of Israel. It is thus a prophetic word against the kind of political messianism represented in the popular reception which Jesus is receiving. His action in continuing his journey mounted on an ass is an acted piece of exegesis, a silent testimony from holy scripture against a false messianism. On the previous occasion when the crowds had tried to make him king he had withdrawn from them into the hills (6:15); on this occasion withdrawal is impossible and would be incompatible with the real kingship which he is about to claim and to establish (18:33-37). The familiar Palm Sunday hymn has rightly captured the meaning of the action: Jesus "rides on in majesty," but it is a majesty which is not of this world. In "lowly pomp" he rides on to die.

John tells us that "the disciples did not understand this at first." They understood only "when Jesus was glorified." No doubt there was a sense in which they understood very well what the crowds were doing. They were hailing Jesus as king. And what is wrong with that? Is not "Jesus is Lord" the fundamental Christian confession? Yes—but only if the meaning of the predicate is wholly controlled by the subject. If sovereignty is defined by human experience apart from Jesus, then the slogan "Make Jesus king" becomes a blasphemous attempt to co-opt the sovereign power of God for corrupt human ambitions. The sentence "Jesus is Lord" is a true confession only if the subject has taken total control of the predicate, only if sovereignty is defined by Calvary, only if the lordship is understood in terms of washing one another's feet. But that requires a total subversion of accepted human axioms, a total revolution which can only be the work of the sovereign Spirit himself. That is why Peter will not and cannot understand when Jesus washes his feet, but will understand afterward (13:7). And that is why it was, and could only be, after Jesus was glorified and the Spirit was given that the disciples could understand what he had done on that road from Bethany to Jerusalem.

If the disciples did not understand, the crowds certainly did not. Two crowds seem to meet and mingle in John's picture: the crowd coming in from Bethany repeats the story of the raising of Lazarus from the tomb and this further inflames the messianic enthusiasm of the Passover crowds coming out from Jerusalem. In the midst of this wild excitement the silent witness of the man on the donkey is unheard. And the authorities, looking in helpless bewilderment at the tumultuous scene in the street below, once again utter a word which is both an expression of their own despair and an unwitting statement of the truth: "The world has gone after him." Zechariah's prophecy is going to be fulfilled. Not only the Jews (as in v. 11) but the world will turn to him. "He shall command peace to the nations; his dominion shall be from sea to sea" (Zech. 9:10).

And even as they speak, this unwitting prophecy begins to find fulfilment. The vanguard of "the nations" is already at hand.

12:20-26

Now among those who went up to worship at the feast were some Greeks. So these came to Philip, who was from Bethsaida in Galilee, and said to him, "Sir, we wish to see Jesus." Philip went and told Andrew; Andrew went with Philip and they told Jesus. And Jesus answered them, "The hour has come for the Son of man to be glorified. Truly, truly, I say to you, unless a grain of wheat falls into the earth and dies, it remains alone; but if it dies, it bears much fruit. He who loves his life loses it, and he who hates his life in this world will keep it for eternal life. If any one serves me, he must follow me; and where I am, there shall my servant be also; if any one serves me, the Father will honor him."

Presumably the procession has come to its end in the outer precincts of the Temple. Caught up in this tumultuous demonstration of national-religious enthusiasm are some Gentiles—not of Jewish race, not necessarily proselytes, but "God-fearers" drawn to Jerusalem as were very many Gentiles by the attractive power of Israel's faith. Naturally they would like to have an interview with such a remarkable person as Jesus evidently is. Naturally, also, they make their contact through Philip—a man with a Greek name and coming from Gentile territory.

So at the very height of this surge of Jewish messianic excitement Jesus is told that Gentiles are coming to him. An observer might think that the "Jesus-wave" was really going to sweep from Jerusalem into the whole world. But it is not so. The saving work of God by which the "ruler of this world" is cast out and all peoples are brought to their true home in God will not be the linear extension either of Jewish religious enthusiasm or of Greek intellectual curiosity. There is no straight road from these to God and his glory. Rather there is a radical discontinuity of which the natural world provides a vivid parable. In the synoptic Gospels the seed which must fall into the ground before there can be a harvest is a parable of the kingdom of God (e.g.,

Mark 4:1-20). But it is Jesus himself who in his own person is the presence of the kingdom, and it is he himself, therefore, who must—like the grain of wheat—fall, die, and be buried. Only so can the mighty harvest of the nations be gathered. And the hour when this must happen is now present. The coming of the Gentile inquirers is a token of its presence, but their desire to see Jesus will not be fulfilled in the way they expect, just as the Jewish crowds who cry out their greetings to the "king of Israel" will find that his kingdom is utterly different from their expectation. In fact the revealing of the glory of God will be in his dying, and both Jews and Gentiles will cooperate in putting him to death. But his death will be the true glorifying of the Son of man because in it God will be glorified. That the crucifixion of a man should be the ultimate manifestation of the glory of God is as scandalous to Jewish religious messianism as it is absurd to Greek philosophy (I Cor. 1:22-24). But it is true, for the glory of God is the outpouring of love which is supremely revealed in the obedience of Jesus to death and in the action of the Father who gives his only Son for the life of the world and sustains him to the end in his obedience (17:1-5).

Because this is the true glory of God, the reflection of it is present throughout nature. The insight that new life comes through dying is embodied in myths of dying and rising gods which were widely accepted in the world for which John wrote. But nature is an endlessly rotating wheel and there is no deliverance for rational human beings in simply becoming part of the rotation. Rational man tries to understand himself as having a history, not simply as part of nature. The gospel is that there is a unique, decisive, and final action in which the one through whom all things were made, and who is the source of life, surrendered his life not of natural necessity but of freely willed and loving obedience. In that act the glory which is the flaming heart of the universe is revealed. It is both God's glorifying of his own name (v. 28) and his glorifying of the one who is truly man—the Son of man (v. 23).

Because of this act, the pattern of living through dying is no longer a necessity imposed by nature: it is a freely willed response to the love of God, and the life which is won by it is no longer merely a phase in the ever returning cycle of life and death, but "eternal life," the life of God himself, the true goal of all history, both personal and public. To the one who is willing to follow

Jesus in this freely willed love and obedience there is the promise of abiding fellowship with him and of sharing with him in the honor which the Father bestows on him. To be a servant of Jesus means to follow him on the way of the cross, and in doing so to abide in him. The full meaning of this "abiding" in Jesus and in the Father will be spelled out later in the final discourses of the Upper Room (chs. 14–16). It is briefly defined here in terms of a stark paradox which mirrors the paradox of the cross. It is a life which is not guarded and preserved but forever thrown away; yet it is a life constantly received as a fresh gift from the source of all life, in whose eternally outpoured love it has the assurance that death has lost its dominion.

12:27-36

"Now is my soul troubled. And what shall I say? 'Father, save me from this hour'? No, for this purpose I have come to this hour. Father, glorify thy name." Then a voice came from heaven, "I have glorified it, and I will glorify it again." The crowd standing by heard it and said that it had thundered. Others said, "An angel has spoken to him." Jesus answered, "This voice has come for your sake, not for mine. Now is the judgment of this world, now shall the ruler of this world be cast out; and I, when I am lifted up from the earth, will draw all men to myself." He said this to show by what death he was to die. The crowd answered him, "We have heard from the law that the Christ remains for ever. How can you say that the Son of man must be lifted up? Who is this Son of man?" Jesus said to them, "The light is with you for a little longer. Walk while you have the light, lest the darkness overtake you; he who walks in the darkness does not know where he goes. While you have the light, believe in the light, that you may become sons of light." When Jesus had said this, he departed and hid himself from them.

The death which Jesus must face is real death, and Jesus faces it with deep agony and turmoil of spirit. His attitude in the face of death is not that of the heroic pagan for whom death is simply part of nature—the other phase in the endless rhythm of life and death. Jesus belongs to Israel and his soul is troubled in the face of death, as was the soul of the saints whose prayers were so often on his lips. "My heart is in anguish within me, the terrors of death have fallen upon me. Fear and trembling come upon me, and horror overwhelms me. And I say, 'O that I had wings like a dove! I would fly away and be at rest' " (Ps. 55:4-6). The writer to the Hebrews tells us that in the days of his flesh Jesus offered up prayers and supplications, with loud cries and tears, to him who was able to save him from death (Heb. 5:7) and the three synoptics all report that, just before his arrest, Jesus was in an agony of prayer in the face of death. If we were but part of nature, death would be as "natural" as life. But if we have been awakened out of the meaningless cycle of nature to believe in and to obey and to follow one who leads us toward a new world, then death is the cruel and blind contradiction of the confidence by which we have learned to walk. Much more is it so if we face, as Jesus did, not only the fact of death, but also betrayal by his friends, rejection by his people, and the total failure of his cause. Truly he could echo the cry of another Psalm: "My tears have been my food day and night, while men say to me continually, 'Where is your God?' " (Ps. 42:3). Death is not simply a natural event, unless man is merely part of nature. Death is the visible sign and instrument of God's judgment upon all our lives and all our works, that they are not fit to endure eternally. Death is the outward form of God's judgment upon sin. Jesus, the Son of man, faces that judgment with the clear eyes which only the sinless child of God possessed. The prayer of the psalmist that he might "fly away and be at rest" trembles on his lips, but is instantly put away. He will not ask to be snatched away from this terrible hour, for it is precisely for this purpose that he has come to this hour—to bear the sin of the world, to lay down his life for the sheep both of "this fold" and of those other folds whose representatives are already waiting to be called. That was the meaning of his baptism when he took upon himself the sin of his people. That was the meaning of all his "signs." That is the meaning of his whole life—that the Father's glory may be manifested in the loving obedience of the Son. That, and that alone, shall be his prayer, displacing the prayer for deliverance which rises so easily from a heart nourished on the psalms of Israel. "Father, glorify thy name." It is the prayer which embodies the whole purpose of his life, and it is the prayer which he has taught his disciples to repeat (for the meaning is exactly the same): "Father, hallowed be thy name."

As at the baptism when he took upon himself the sin of his people, and as on the Mount of Transfiguration when (according to Luke) he communed with Moses and Elijah concerning his approaching death (Luke 9:31), so here his prayer is answered by a voice from heaven. It is not for his comfort or reassurance, for

158

he knows that every prayer of his is heard and answered. It is "the Father's public witness to the crowd of his acceptance of the obedience of the Son" (Hoskyns)—even though the crowd is incapable at that moment of understanding it. That there were disciples who understood afterward is attested by the record of the evangelist here, and by the interpretation which is given in the Johannine letter: "If we receive the testimony of men, the testimony of God is greater; for this is the testimony of God, that he has borne witness to his Son" (I John 5:9). But this understanding could come only after the mighty attestation of Easter day when Jesus was "designated Son of God in power . . . by his resurrection from the dead" (Rom. 1:4).

But now Jesus is surrounded by the incomprehension of the crowd and of his disciples, yet utterly sure of his Father. The offering up of the Son in love and obedience will consummate his ministry, a ministry which has had only one purpose—the glorifying of the Father. It is the work of the Father himself both to have manifested his glory in the ministry of Jesus and now to manifest it supremely in his death. The death of Jesus will be the judging and dethroning of "the ruler of this world." The powers that govern the life of the world will gather to sit in judgment upon Jesus. The law represented by the scribes, religion represented by the Pharisees, the established order represented by the high priests and the Sadducees, worldly *"realpolitik"* represented by the Roman governor, and popular revolutionary enthusiasm represented by the Passover crowds will all combine in a strange and unique coalition to condemn and destroy him. And by this act they will write their own doom. "The rulers of this age," as Paul calls them, did not recognize in Jesus the presence of the power and wisdom of God. "If they had, they would not have crucified the Lord of glory" (I Cor. 2:8). Having done so, they have forfeited their authority. They thought to destroy Jesus forever, nailing him and his claim to the cross and making a public exhibition of him before the world. But they did not understand what they were doing. What in fact happened was that Jesus himself nailed the old order to the cross, and in it "disarmed the principalities and powers, and made a public example of them, triumphing over them in it" (Col. 2:14-15).

These "rulers of the world," these "principalities and powers" represent, in one form or another, the attempt to organize and control human life on the basis of its own self-interest. In their attempt to control and organize they in fact divide and disrupt. They are the false shepherds who do not gather and feed the sheep but scatter and destroy them. They are supremely represented in the great imperialisms of which Babylon is the ancient type and Rome the contemporary example. In the name of human unity they create disruption (Gen. 11:1-9). Their assumed glory is a life.

But now, with the open manifesting of the true glory of God in the crucifixion of Jesus, the one true center for the unity of humankind is openly presented. Here, in an act which is the renunciation of all worldly power and all wordly wisdom, is the place to which all the scattered nations will be drawn. The "lifting up" of Jesus which is both his crucifixion and his glorifying will be the raising of the one standard to which all the families of the earth can come to find their unity—because it will be a participation in the very being of God himself (cf. 17:20-22). Here, where the Son of man is made nothing, is the place where all the children of men can be made one, because they learn to forsake their own glory and seek only the glory of the one God who is Father and Son in the unity of the Spirit. Here, as Dag Hammarskjöld in an address to the Second Assembly of the World Council of Churches (1954) said, is the one place where nations can be truly united nations.

"He said this to show by what manner of death he was to die." The evangelist later draws attention to this saying when its real meaning has become apparent (John 18:32). Jesus will not die at the hands of the Jews by stoning on the religious charge of blasphemy; he will die at the hands of the Romans by crucifixion on the political charge that he claimed to be king. He was indeed king, and by his kingship the rule of Caesar and the derived authority of Pilate are radically qualified though not denied (19:11). It is as the true king and head of the human race—Greeks and Jews alike—that he will be lifted up to die, and to reign from the tree. In him all the imperial programs by which ambitious men have sought the unification of humankind under their rule will be judged, and the rulers dethroned. Jesus alone is the true center for the unity of humankind, as he is the one in whom all things are at the end to be summed up (Eph. 1:10; Col. 2:20).

It may be that when Jesus used this language about being "lifted up," there was an echo of the strange word of Isaiah concerning the Lord's servant: "Behold, my servant shall prosper, he shall be exalted and lifted up, and shall be very high. . . . So shall he startle many nations; kings shall shut their mouths because of him; for that which has not been told them they shall see; and that which they have not heard they shall understand" (Isa. 52:13, 15). But in the minds of the crowd, filled with messianic excitement, there is the memory of other, more easily understood promises of scripture—the promise that the throne of David shall be established and sustained "for evermore" (Isa. 9:7) and that "it shall stand firm while the skies endure" (Ps. 89:37). Are these promises not to be relied on? If this is indeed the Messiah, the king of Israel (v. 13), what is the meaning of this talk of being "lifted up"? Twice previously (3:14 and 8:28) Jesus had talked of the "Son of man" being "lifted up." Now the one whom the crowds have hailed as Messiah says, "When I am lifted up from the earth." Who then is "the Son of man"? Is he the same as the Messiah? If so, what becomes of these promises? Do we doubt the promises of God, or do we doubt whether this "son of man" really is the Messiah?

The promises of God are indeed to be trusted. But they do not provide a dispensation from the necessity of recognizing and walking in the light now. The light, which is the life of God himself, has come into the world. The only proper response is to welcome it, go toward it, and walk by it. One must not use the promises of God as a shield against the actual presence of God. A proper confidence in the ancient promises of God must not become an improper and eventually fatal barrier against recognizing and rejoicing in the action of God now. Once again one must remember that while nature is cyclical and there is always another spring, another dawn, another chance, God's dealings with us are not so; there is a time to decide. The light shines, and if you do not recognize and welcome it, there is no further way by which you can be assured that it is the light. Then, inevitably, darkness overtakes you, and "he who walks in the darkness does not know where he goes." Meaninglessness is once more in control. In the dark, nothingness reigns.

This, then, is the final word in which Jesus sums up and thrusts home his word to Israel. The light *has* come into the world. You cannot postpone your recognition of it until all the theological problems have been solved. Then it will be too late. "While you have the light, believe in the light, that you may become children of light." And with these words Jesus once again withdraws.

12:37-43

Though he had done so many signs before them, yet they did not believe in him; it was that the word spoken by the prophet Isaiah might be fulfilled:
  "Lord, who has believed our report,
  and to whom has the arm of the Lord been revealed?"
Therefore they could not believe. For Isaiah again said,
  "He has blinded their eyes and hardened their heart,
  lest they should see with their eyes and perceive with their heart,
  and turn for me to heal them."
Isaiah said this because he saw his glory and spoke of him. Nevertheless many even of the authorities believed in him, but for fear of the Pharisees they did not confess it, lest they should be put out of the synagogue: for they loved the praise of men more than the praise of God.

We have reached the end of the public ministry of Jesus. From now on, until the crisis of betrayal and death, Jesus will be alone with his disciples preparing them for what lies ahead. At this point, therefore, the evangelist interjects a summary and interpretation of the nature and outcome of the public ministry. He does so by recalling words from the Old Testament which were to play a central role in the early development of the Church's understanding of the person and work of Jesus.

From the very beginning of John's record we have been repeatedly reminded of the inescapable paradoxes of revelation. How can the truth be grasped by a world whose fundamental patterns of thought are shaped by the lie? How can the glory of God be recognized by those for whom the only glory which is valued is the glory that men receive from one another? How can there be revelation without contradiction? How can one bear witness to revelation except by paradox? In the Prologue these paradoxes were stated with the utmost compression: "The world was made through him, yet the world knew him not. He came to his own house, and his own people received him not. But to all who received him . . . he gave power to become children of God" (1:10f.). The facts which these words express with extreme brevity have now been illustrated by the recounting of a carefully selected series of the deeds and words of Jesus. Now the basic facts are agains summarized. Like Moses (Deut. 29:2-4), Jesus has wrought great signs and wonders in the midst of Israel, and—like Moses—he has been met by stubborn unbelief; yet "many of the authorities believed in him." How do we understand these strange and apparently contradictory statements?

First we have to say that they are not accidental or exceptional happenings. The whole story of Israel bears witness to the contradiction of revelation. Of the servant of the Lord in Isaiah, whose "lifting up" has just been remembered (v. 32), it is complained that "the report" of him has not been believed and the mighty works ("the arm of the Lord") have not been perceived (Isa. 53:1). And—as in all the synoptic Gospels and in Paul—the terrible words spoken to Isaiah in the Temple are quoted as providing the ground and the interpretation of this unbelief: "Go, and say to this people: 'Hear and hear, but do not understand; see and see, but do not perceive.' Make the heart of this people fat, and their ears heavy, and shut their eyes; lest they see with their eyes, and hear with their ears, and understand with their hearts, and turn and be healed" (Isa. 6:9f., quoted in Mark 4:12; Matt. 13:14f.; Luke 8:10; Acts 28:26f.; cf. Rom. 10:16-23). The unbelief of Israel, which is nevertheless God's beloved and chosen people whom he can never forsake, is a major theme in almost all strands of the Old Testament literature.

Secondly, we have to face the fact that this unbelief is perceived as the work of God himself. It is he who shuts the eyes and ears of the people, as it is he who hardens the heart of Pharaoh. It is he who has "consigned all men to disobedience"—not only Israel but also the nations (Rom. 11:32).

But thirdly and immediately we have to add that we must *not* read these passages through the spectacles of a rigid and deterministic doctrine of predestination. We are forbidden to do so by the sentences which form the immediate sequels of those we have quoted. "They did not believe . . . but many even of the authorities believed." "God has consigned all men to disobedience *that he may have mercy on all*." We must understand these apparently contradictory statements in the context of the Bible as a whole and not in the context of later mataphysical arguments about predestination and free will.

It is not something marginal or accidental, but rather central and determinative for the whole witness of the Bible, that God's actual revelation of himself must be met by rejection and contradiction. The word of the cross is, and must be, scandalous to the Jew and absurd to the Greek; it cannot be co-opted by and incorporated into any of the structures by which men try to secure themselves in face of the riddle of the world. It is necessarily perceived as something subversive, whether by the righteousness of the man of religion or by the wisdom of the philosopher. If it is perceived as in truth the righteousness of God and the truth of God, that can never be an achievement of human religious insight or philosophical acuteness. It can only be an act of God. In Pauline language it is "those who are called" (I Cor. 1:24), in Johannine language "those whom the Father draws" (6:44), to whom it comes as God's righteousness and God's truth. So—even now—there are those among the authorities who do believe. Presumably they form the nucleus of that large number of priests who were later to become followers of Jesus (Acts 6:7). Now, however, they are still unable to extricate themselves from the ancient structures of wisdom and power by which a world alienated from the true glory, which is the love of God, seeks to establish and maintain its own glory. They believe, and yet they cannot escape the power of this world. They love the praise of men. The truth of God cannot be incorporated into a structure of meaning which is governed by its own self-set standards of excellence. There has to be crisis, judgment, a breaking down and a building up, a dying and a new birth. In the end it is only through a new birth that the revelation can be received. And before there can be a new birth there must be a death. The Son of man must be lifted up.

12:44-50

And Jesus cried out and said, "He who believes in me, believes not in me, but in him who sent me. And he who sees me sees him who sent me. I have come as light into the world, that whoever believes in me may not remain in darkness. If any one hears my sayings and does not keep them, I do not judge him; for I did not come to judge the world but to save the world. He who rejects me and does not receive my sayings has a judge; the word that I have spoken will be his judge on the last day. For I have not spoken on my own authority; the Father who sent me has himself given me commandment what to say and what to speak. And I know that his commandment is eternal life. What I say, therefore, I say as the Father has bidden me."

No time or place is indicated for these words. Jesus has gone into hiding (v. 36). But the evangelist concludes his account of the public ministry with this very compressed restatement of the message which Jesus has proclaimed. Its language is full of echoes both of the sayings recorded in the synoptic Gospels and of the teaching recorded by John.

Jesus is, quite simply, God's revelation of himself. It is God whom we meet when we meet Jesus. To believe in him is to believe in God, because Jesus is the perfectly obedient messenger of God.

To believe in him is to be delivered from illusion and to live in the light of truth. It is to see things as they really are and therefore to be delivered from the power of lies. But believing is not just a matter of intellectual assent; it is a matter of active obedience. It is not enough to hear the words of Jesus; one must "keep" them. It is the fool who hears and does not do (Matt. 7:26). Such a one is judged—not in the sense that Jesus condemns him, but in the sense that he has condemned himself by building on sand rather than rock, by clinging to illusion and forsaking reality. For him the rock which was offered as foundation becomes the rock of offense (Mark 12:10f.; I Pet. 2:4-8).

This is because the word of Jesus is the word of God. It is not his own invention but is the utterance of God himself, the unveiling of reality as it truly is. Both now and in the end (v. 48) it is by that reality that we must all stand or fall. The revelation is given, however, not in order to bring condemnation but to give life. For it is by the word of God that life is given, not by bread alone (Deut. 8:3). Jesus, therefore, is the giver of life because, as the utterly humble and dedicated Son of his Father, he speaks the very word of God by which alone we may have life. To believe in him and to "keep" his word is to be founded upon the rock. It is to walk in the light and so to have life.

And this message is offered to all without exception, for Jesus did not speak it in whispers, but "cried out." It is the sound of the jubilee trumpet offering redemption for the whole world.

14

THE SUPPER
(13:1-30)

13:1-11

Now before the feast of the Passover, when Jesus knew that his hour had come to depart out of this world to the Father, having loved his own who were in the world, he loved them to the end. And during supper, when the devil had already put it into the heart of Judas Iscariot, Simon's son, to betray him, Jesus, knowing that the Father had given all things into his hands, and that he had come from God and was going to God, rose from supper, laid aside his garments, and girded himself with a towel. Then he poured water into a basin, and began to wash the disciples' feet, and to wipe them with the towel with which he was girded. He came to Simon Peter; and Peter said to him, "Lord, do you wash my feet?" Jesus answered him, "What I am doing you do not know now, but afterward you will understand." Peter said to him, "You shall never wash my feet." Jesus answered him, "If I do not wash you, you have no part in me." Simon Peter said to him, "Lord, not my feet only but also my hands and my head!" Jesus said to him, "He who has bathed does not need to wash, but he is clean all over; and you are clean, but not all of you." For he knew who was to betray him; that was why he said, "You are not all clean."

The public ministry of Jesus is ended. Jesus has gathered his disciples together to share with them, as he had so often done, the evening meal. This is not, in St. John's chronology, the Passover, but the ordinary meal at the end of the day—the day before the Passover.

In the synoptic Gospels the teaching given by Jesus to his own disciples is dispersed through the account of the public ministry, although there is an especially concentrated presentation of it at the end (see Mark 13:1-14, 42). In the Fourth Gospel a sharp break is made between the public teaching which fills most of chapters 2 to 12, and the private teaching given to his own faithful community which is concentrated in chapters 13 to 16. At this point in the Gospel we move out of the streets into the quiet of a room. "The noise of the cosmos has died away: the stillness of night prevails" (Bultmann). And yet, in the quiet room, Jesus is preparing his disciples for the mission to the world on which he will send them. And the word *cosmos* occurs no less than forty times in the five chapters which begin here.

Jesus knows that his hour has come, the hour determined not by himself but by the Father. Jesus has no program of his own. He is simply the loving and obedient Son who does the will of his Father from moment to moment as it is disclosed to him in the context of the actual events. It is the hour for his departure from the world and therefore of separation from his disciples. The way he goes is the way of the cross, and though they cannot follow (or even understand) now, they will learn that he is himself the way that leads to the Father, the only way through the tangled and otherwise meaningless maze of life in this world (14:1-6).

The disciples will remain in the world. And they are the object of Jesus' love—a love which is without limit because it is the eternal love c ' the Father and which will be manifest in Jesus' obedience to the very end when he dies to take away their sin and the sin of the world.

Judas, one of those beloved disciples, has already been inwardly seduced by the evil one (cf. Luke 22:3) and the intention to betray his master has already been formed in his mind. But Jesus, in the assuredness of his unbroken communion with the Father, knows that even the treachery of Judas can only further the Father's purpose of salvation for the world, knows that this purpose has been wholly committed into his hands, and knows that it is both the source of his coming into the world and the goal of his going from the world.

That purpose can only be fulfilled through the agony, shame, and humiliation of the cross. And Jesus proceeds with the utmost deliberation to perform a prophetic action that will interpret to the disciples that terrible event which they cannot now understand. Leaving his place at their head, and putting off his clothes (and the evangelist uses words which echo the language used in ch. 10 to describe the laying down of life by the good shepherd), Jesus girds himself with the towel that a slave ties around his loins

and proceeds to the most menial of servile offices—to wash the
dirty feet of his disciples.

And so he comes to Peter. The horrified reaction of Peter is
exactly parallel to his protest recorded by the synoptics when
Jesus began to speak about his cross: "God forbid, Lord! This
shall never happen to you" (Matt. 16:22). It is the reaction of
normal human nature. That the disciple should wash his master's
feet is normal and proper. But if the master becomes a menial
slave to the disciple, then all proper order is overturned. This is
a total subversion of good order as we understand it, and as the
smooth operation of human affairs seems to require. All normal
management procedures require chains of authority. All of us
except those at the very bottom have a vested interest in keeping
it so, for as long as we duly submit to those above us we are free
to bear down on those below us. The action of Jesus subverts this
order and threatens to destabilize all society. Peter's protest is the
protest of normal human nature.

The solemn reply of Jesus shows how profound are the issues
to which his action points. This is not just an acted lesson in
humility; Peter could have understood that. But Jesus declares
that it is impossible for Peter to understand at this moment what
is being done, but that he will understand afterward. The footwashing is a sign of that ultimate subversion of all human power
and authority which took place when Jesus was crucified by the
decision of the "powers" that rule this present age. In that act the
wisdom of this world was shown to be folly, and the "powers"
of this world were disarmed (Col. 2:15). But "flesh and blood"—
ordinary human nature—is in principle incapable of understanding this. It is "to the Jew a scandal, and to the Greek folly." Only
those whom the risen Christ will call and to whom the Holy
Spirit will be given will know that this folly is the wisdom of
God and this weakness is the power of God. But this will only
be "afterward." At the moment, as the man that he is, Peter
cannot understand. The natural man makes gods in his own image, and the supreme God will be the one who stands at the
summit of the chain of command. How can the natural man
recognize the supreme God in the stooping figure of a slave, clad
only in a loincloth?

This first reply of Jesus is a call for faith and obedience even
when there is not yet—and cannot be—understanding. Peter is
asked to trust the promise: "You will understand afterward." But

Peter is too deeply shocked, and he bluntly refuses. "You shall never wash my feet." To this the answer of Jesus is almost as drastic as the synoptic "Get behind me, Satan." Without this radical subversion of the world's order you cannot be a participant in the new order of which Jesus is the head. A total conversion, a full U-turn is required if one is to follow Jesus. To accept the action of Jesus which has its consummation in the cross is to be cleansed decisively of the world's false concepts of wisdom and power. Without that acceptance there can be no place in the new order.

This drastic warning carries Peter to the other extreme. "Not my feet only, but also my hands and my head." But this shows that he still does not understand, as indeed he cannot do. The washing of the feet (and we must suppose that Peter has now accepted this) is a sign of that total overturning of the powers of this world in which the majesty of God is manifest in the menial service of a slave. To accept this is to be converted. And nothing can be added to this. If you imagine that you can add something to what is given in the cross, you delude yourself. This is the explanation of the passion with which St. Paul attacked those who thought that they could add something to baptism by circumcision (Gal. 5:4). Baptism is a sign of our being incorporated into the baptism of Jesus, which was his total self-effacement, his total identification with sinners, a baptism begun in the Jordan and to be consummated on Calvary. To try to add to it would be comparable to supposing that one could increase the efficacy of a U-turn by turning 360° instead of 180°. One would not have enhanced but negated the usefulness of the action. It is enough to have made the U-turn, to have accepted the subversion. Nothing can be added to what Jesus has done on the cross, and nothing can be added to baptism. "He who has received the washing offered by the Lord is wholly clean" (Lightfoot). This is not a matter in which one can speak of more or less: one is facing either one way or the other.

This company of Jesus' friends who have accepted (even if uncomprehending) the washing of their feet by their Lord and Master, have made the decisive turn. But among them there is one who remains in the service of the power of this age. There is treason in the very heart of the Church, and Jesus knows it and has known it from the beginning. His disciples must know it too, and be forewarned against the collapse of faith.

13:12-20

When he had washed their feet, and taken his garments, and resumed his place, he said to them, "Do you know what I have done to you? You call me Teacher and Lord; and you are right for so I am. If I then, your Lord and Teacher, have washed your feet, you also ought to wash one another's feet. For I have given you an example, that you also should do as I have done to you. Truly, truly, I say to you, a servant is not greater than his master; nor is he who is sent greater than he who sent him. If you know these things, blessed are you if you do them. I am not speaking of you all; I know whom I have chosen; it is that the scripture may be fulfilled, 'He who ate my bread has lifted his heel against me.' I tell you this now, before it takes place, that when it does take place you may believe that I am he. Truly, truly, I say to you, he who receives any one whom I send receives me; and he who receives me receives him who sent me."

With the same deliberation with which he had laid aside his garments and assumed the form of a slave, Jesus now puts on his garments and takes his place at their head—their lord and master. Both actions are described with equal care and seriousness. The master is the slave; the slave is the master. To say that is to say that all normal conceptions of power and authority are overturned. The "God" whom we fashion by projecting onto the heavens our human conceptions of power and authority is— strictly—a "vanity," a "no-god." Once again we have to learn that revelation must involve contradiction. If this slave who stoops to wash his disciples' feet is indeed master, then we must frankly declare ourselves atheists with reference to the normal use of the word "God."

But what are the implications of this? If Jesus had said: "Since I have washed your feet, you must wash my feet," then we would be fighting with one another for the privilege of being first with the basin and the towel. Then the old order of preeminence would have been restored, thinly disguised under the name of "service." The "Chief Minister" would have become the old ruler under a new name.

But Jesus says something which negates that possibility. "You ought to wash one another's feet." This is something which subverts and replaces all normal patterns of authority. It would be impossible to draw a "management chart" in which A is subject to B and B is subject to A. Yet this is what is called for. The disciples are to be—literally—"servants of one another" (Gal.

5:13). This is a kind of equality, but it must not be confused with the egalitarianism which is based upon the doctrine of the "rights of man." That, in the end, makes every man a monad fighting for his rights, because it is of the essence of our human situation that each of us tends to estimate his own rights more highly than those of his neighbor. This is a different kind of egalitarianism which is based upon the fact that the one who alone is master has proved himself the slave to us all equally. He has laid aside his life for us all. And the debt which we owe to him is to be discharged by our subjection to our neighbor in loving service. Our neighbor is the appointed agent authorized to receive what we owe to the master. We are thus bound to one another in a reciprocal obligation. But this cannot be an achievement of our own moral insight. It is, and can only be, the fruit of what Jesus has done decisively and once for all. That is why we cannot accept the view that this paragraph comes from a different source from the previous one—this one giving a "moralistic" interpretation of the footwashing and the other a "sacramental" interpretation. The one rests upon the other and is inconceivable without it.

There is one special application of this action of Jesus which touches the life of the Church at its heart. Like every human society the Church quickly developed a hierarchy, and in every version of it discernible in the New Testament the first name in the hierarchy is "apostle." The word means "one who is sent," and although St. John's Gospel uses the verbs of sending with great frequency, the only place where the famous word "*apostolos*" is used is at this point. "A servant is not greater than his master; nor is an apostle greater than the one who sent him." It is one of the many tokens of the mind of Christ in Paul that when his apostleship is questioned he replies by pointing not to his strengths and achievements, but to his participation in the humiliation of Christ so that he can even say that it is the mark of the apostles that they are "the refuse of the world, the offscouring of all things" (I Cor. 4:13). There can be no true leadership in the Church except one which has as its model the Master who does the work of a slave.

But once again we are reminded of the presence of radical disobedience in the very heart of the Church. The Church, is, and has been from the very beginning, the company chosen and called by the Lord, and yet at the same time a company in which sin is at work. This has been so from the time of the old covenant, as the word here quoted from the Psalm 41 reminds us. The disciples are warned beforehand, so that the terrible manifestation of the work of Satan in the very heart of the Church will not destroy their faith, but—on the contrary—enable them to believe that Jesus is indeed the Lord, the one who alone can say "I AM." Here is the strange paradox of the Church: it is at once holy and sinful. The Lord himself is present in its life, yet Satan is also present. This is a summons to both realism and faith. The disciple who has understood Jesus will not be shaken by sin and apostasy in the Church. He will recognize them for what they are. But these things will not shake his faith; on the contrary they will make him more sure in his confidence that Jesus reigns. When these things happen the word of the Lord in Isaiah will come true for the disciples: "You are my witnesses, and my servant whom I have chosen, that you may know and believe me and understand that I am He" (Isa. 43:10).

It follows that the disciples are the bearers of the mission of God himself. Because they have been cleansed, because—in other words—they have undergone that radical conversion which makes them a question mark against the assumptions of the world, even though sin is present in their company, they are the representatives of God's own action in the world. He has sent Jesus, and Jesus has sent them. Those who accept their witness accept the witness of God himself. The Church, sinful as it is, is the place where men and women meet not one of the "varieties of religious experience," but the living God in his actual revelation of himself.

13:21-30

When Jesus had thus spoken, he was troubled in spirit, and testified, "Truly, truly, I say to you, one of you will betray me." The disciples looked at one another, uncertain of whom he spoke. One of his disciples, whom Jesus loved, was lying close to the breast of Jesus; so Simon Peter beckoned to him and said, "Tell us who it is of whom he speaks." So lying thus, close to the breast of Jesus, he said to him, "Lord, who is it?" Jesus answered, "It is he to whom I shall give this morsel when I have dipped it." So when he had dipped the morsel, he gave it to Judas, the son of Simon Iscariot. Then after the morsel, Satan entered into him. Jesus said to him, "What you are going to do, do quickly." Now no one at the table knew why he said this to him. Some thought that, because Judas had the money box, Jesus was telling him, "Buy what we need for the feast"; or, that he should give something to the poor. So after receiving the morsel, he immediately went out; and it was night.

If the presence of sin in the Church does not destroy faith, it must yet bring agony and grief. The majestic certainties of the previous words are not incompatible with the anguish which confrontation with the powers of evil brings to Jesus here, as at the tomb of Lazarus (11:33; cf. 12:27). John records the anguish of Jesus here, rather than in the Garden of Gethsemane, and his words bring the deepest anxiety and perplexity to the disciples. If there is treason in the heart of the Church, where does it lie? Who is guilty? All four evangelists describe the agonized perplexity of the disciples. In John's account it seems that Jesus has placed Judas in the seat of honor at his left side and the "beloved disciple" on his right. All are reclining in the fashion which had been accepted by the Jews from the Graeco-Roman society, supported by the left elbow with the right hand free for eating. Thus the beloved disciple is so placed, with his head "close to the breast of Jesus," that words can be whispered between them. Peter, who must be seated at a point where he can signal to the beloved disciple across the table, makes a wordless gesture asking for an answer to the question of them all.

At this point Jesus, who has already honored Judas by placing him at his side, silently makes a further gesture of love and friendship—dipping a morsel in the dish and giving it to him. And that final act of love becomes, with a terrible immediacy, the decisive moment of judgment. At this moment we are witnessing the climax of that action of sifting, of separation, of judgment which has been the central theme in John's account of the public ministry of Jesus. "For God so loved the world that he gave his only Son, that whoever believes in him should not perish but have eternal life. For God sent the Son into the world, not to condemn the world, but that the world might be saved through him. He who believes in him is not condemned; he who does not believe is condemned already, because he has not believed in the name of the only Son of God. And this is the judgment, that the light has come into the world, and men loved darkness rather than light, because their deeds were evil" (3:16-19) So the final gesture of affection precipitates the final surrender of Judas to the power of darkness. The light shines in the darkness, and the darkness has neither understood it nor mastered it.

The secret of what has happened has been whispered to the beloved disciple; it remains closed to the others. They are left with the question "Is it I?" unanswered. Only the Lord and the beloved disciple who is in the bosom of the Lord, as Jesus is in the bosom of the Father (1:12), know the truth. Although Judas is now wholly the agent of Satan, Jesus is still in command. At his word Judas rises from the table and moves to the door. For the beloved disciple, although he knows the secret, and for the other disciples, although they do not know it, the word of Jesus is enough and there are no further questions or protests. Together, comprehending or uncomprehending, they watch a man walk of his own choice out of the light of Jesus' love into the domain of "the world rulers of this present darkness" (Eph. 6:12).

"The disciple whom Jesus loved" is here referred to by that title for the first time. The question of his identity has been exhaustively discussed down the centuries. This exposition is written in the belief that this "beloved disciple" is the one whose testimony forms the basis of this Gospel and who is referred to at its end (21:20 and 24). What is being claimed, therefore, is that we have here the true understanding of the tradition which the writer shares with the whole Church. The beloved disciple is "in the bosom of Jesus" and therefore "we know that his testimony is true."

So Judas goes out "under the Lord's protecting silence" (Temple); and it is night. The separation of light from darkness is complete and Jesus can now turn to his faithful disciples, to those who have received him (1:12) and who are the beloved children of God. With them he will now begin to unveil the things that are to come (16:12).

15

JESUS AND HIS DISCIPLES
(13:31–14:31)

13:31-35

*When he had gone out, Jesus said, "Now is the Son of man glorified,
and in him God is glorified; if God is glorified in him, God will also
glorify him in himself, and glorify him at once. Little children, yet a little
while I am with you. You will seek me; and as I said to the Jews so now
I say to you, 'Where I am going you cannot come.' A new commandment
I give to you, that you love one another; even as I have loved you, that
you also love one another. By this all men will know that you are my
disciples, if you have love for one another."*

"Now is the Son of man glorified." The moment at which
Judas, at the command of Jesus, goes out to set in motion the
events which will take Jesus to the cross, is the moment so long
expected, when God's glory is manifested in the Son of man. The
Letter to the Hebrews uses the words of Psalm 40 to interpret the
sacrifice of Jesus: "Consequently, when Christ came into the
world, he said, 'Sacrifices and offerings thou hast not desired, but
a body hast thou prepared for me; in burnt offerings and sin
offerings thou hast taken no pleasure. Then I said, 'Lo, I have
come to do thy will, O God,' as it is written of me in the roll of
the book." The writer goes on to comment: "By that will we
have been sanctified through the offering of the body of Jesus
Christ once for all" (Heb. 10:10). This act of will on the part of
Jesus is complete at the moment when Judas leaves the room.
This therefore is the moment of the manifesting of God's glory,
which is both the glorifying of the Father in the Son and of the
Son in the Father. For the glory of God is not the self-glorification
of a supreme monad; it is the glory of perfect love forever poured
out and forever received within the being of the triune God. It is

the glory of sonship (1:14) into which those who believe in Jesus are enabled to enter (17:22f.; cf. Heb. 2:10). The glory of God is manifest in the love which takes Jesus to the cross in a total offering of himself to the Father, and in the love of the Father who sustains the Son to the end in loving obedience.

"Now" is the moment of manifesting God's glory, but the "now" is pregnant with future hope. This indeed is the essential character of that "now" in which Christians are to live enabled by the work of Christ. It is a "now" which is already full of the promise of a glory to be revealed (cf. Rom. 8:16-25). The prophet Daniel had seen a vision of "one like a son of man" who comes to the Ancient of Days in the clouds of heaven and receives "dominion and glory and kingdom" (Dan. 7:13f.). Jesus, according to all the four Gospels, used for himself the mysterious title "Son of man," but insisted that "the Son of man must suffer" (Mark 8:31). John understands that the glory given to the Son of man is already manifested in his suffering. The future glory is already present, but present in the form of suffering. And the "now" in which Christians live depends upon the fact that Jesus has given himself wholly into the Father's hands. "At the moment when Judas went out, charged to execute his purpose, the passion, as the supreme act of self-sacrifice, was virtually accomplished" (Westcott).

With this "now" we are entering a wholly new situation. It is the "new covenant" of which Jeremiah had spoken and which Christians remember every time they hear the words "This cup is the new covenant in my blood." This new covenant, like the old, involves commandments—in fact, a "new commandment" which is addressed to those who, as the children of a new birth, can be called "little children" (cf. I John 2, *passim*).

The new commandment is not an arbitrary fiat of omnipotence but rests upon a new gift. It is the love of Christ which constitutes the new community. The actual presence of the love of Jesus operative in the life of a community will be what identifies it as his. This will be the one essential *nota ecclesiae*. It is this which will lead men to look to the strange figure of a crucified man as the source of life (17:23). "It is not the effect that it has on world history that legitimates the Christian faith, but its strangeness within the world" (Bultmann).

This new and strange reality must involve a sharp break with the world. There can be no smooth transition from the old to the new. There is a necessary and radical discontinuity. The new is not in any sense a development of the old. The unbelieving Jews have already been told this. The believing disciples must also be told it. Jesus must leave them behind. This—as we shall learn in a moment—is not to be for their final abandonment, but for the opening of the way that they must follow. Meanwhile there is only "a little while" in which they can enjoy the kind of fellowship they have had—a fellowship which they would gladly have prolonged forever.

The phrase "a little while," which will occur again and again in the discourse, echoes the language of the prophets (e.g., Isa. 10:25 and Jer. 51:33) and perhaps also the language of Christians groaning under the sufferings of the present age. We shall look more deeply at its meaning later (16:16-24). It is enough to say now that it expresses the sense of urgency and immediacy which must necessarily be present if we are really in the "now" of the living God.

13:36–14:7

Simon Peter said to him, "Lord, where are you going?" Jesus answered, "Where I am going you cannot follow me now; but you shall follow afterward." Peter said to him, "Lord, why cannot I follow you now? I will lay down my life for you." Jesus answered, "Will you lay down your life for me? Truly, truly, I say to you, the cock will not crow, till you have denied me three times.

Let not your hearts be troubled; believe in God, believe also in me. In my Father's house are many rooms; if it were not so, would I have told you that I go to prepare a place for you? And when I go and prepare a place for you, I will come again and will take you to myself, that where I am you may be also. And you know the way where I am going." Thomas said to him, "Lord, we do not know where you are going; how can we know the way?" Jesus said to him, "I am the way, and the truth, and the life; no one comes to the Father, but by me. If you had known me, you would have known my Father also; henceforth you know him and have seen him."

All the Gospels record the terrible fact that Peter, the leader of the apostles, denied his master at the moment of crisis. St. John, in line with the consistent teaching of his Gospel, is at pains to show that this did not arise from any moral weakness in Peter, but was one manifestation of the necessary fact that the meaning of Jesus' death can in no circumstances be grasped by human nature ("flesh and blood"), but can only be grasped from within the new dispensation of the Spirit which is inaugurated by the passion and resurrection of Jesus.

Peter had been among the first to be called by Jesus to follow him. He had followed faithfully. Why was he now to be dismissed from Jesus' company? "Lord, where are you going?" It is indeed a very human question, and the question that "flesh and blood" is bound to ask. Why does not Jesus give a straight answer to that simple question? Because the answer is the whole revelation which can only be given "afterward" when the work of Jesus is complete. All human life is lived in face of the enigma of death—our personal death, and the ultimate decay and dissolution of all our works and of the fabric of the physical world itself. We see our lives as a journey, but the way ahead—whether for our personal and private lives or for the public life which we share with others—is closed by a curtain beyond which we cannot see. Religion has been fertile in producing words to suggest what may lie beyond that curtain—"heaven," "eternal life," "the next world"—but in truth we do not and cannot see what lies beyond. This is the radical disqualification of every claim to understand the meaning of human life by the processes of observation and induction. The data needed for a valid induction are not available for observation. What is made available to us through Jesus, as we shall learn in a moment, is not a sketch of what lies beyond the curtain but a firmly marked way through the curtain, "the new and living way which he opened for us through the curtain" (Heb. 10:20) providing us "access in one Spirit to the Father" (Eph. 2:18). But that "way" is only opened through the act of Jesus in his total self-offering to the Father; it is "by the blood of Jesus" (Heb. 10:19). Therefore Peter cannot follow now. Peter is ready to "lay down his life" for Jesus, just as Jesus had said that the good shepherd lays down his life for the sheep. And Peter's word was proved true when in the darkness of the Garden of Gethsemane he drew his sword and proposed to fight single-handed against a whole company of soldiers. But that action brought only a sharp rebuke. Peter is eager to follow, but he cannot because "the way" has not yet been opened. Only Jesus can open that way, and he is going to do so. No one can follow until Jesus has done what he alone can do. Only he can "offer for all time a single sacrifice for sin" (Heb. 10:12). And even he does not do this in the time and manner of his own choosing. It is an act of loving obedience to his Father at the hour and in the manner that the Father wills. When he has done this, a way will be opened along which Peter can and will follow, along with all who "take up the cross and follow" Jesus. Peter and the other disciples will indeed be taken up into and made participants in that one sacrifice (17:19). But Peter's very human and loyal determination to follow Jesus now in the only way that he understand will mean that he will find himself lost, off the track, denying his master whom he wants to serve. "The cock will not crow till you have denied me three times."

These shattering words silence Peter, and he does not speak again. For all that company it is a moment of stunned silence. They have been told that one of their company is a traitor. They have seen Judas go out into the night. They have heard Peter warned that he will deny his master. It is therefore to a very deeply troubled group that Jesus says: "Let not your hearts be troubled."

How could they fail to be troubled? Jesus himself was "troubled in spirit" (13:21) by the presence of treachery in his company. But now he gives them a command which echoes the repeated words of the earlier Jesus (Joshua) to the children of Israel as they faced the crossing of the Jordan and the entry to the promised land: "Be strong and of a good courage" (Josh. 1:6, 7, 9, 18). The greater Joshua is about to cross a deeper and wider Jordan to open a way by which the children of God may follow. The way is the way of faith—faith in God, and faith in him who leads us through the dark waters as the "pioneer and perfecter of our faith" (Heb. 12:2). Jesus had begun his ministry by a baptism in the Jordan. Now he is to complete his baptism by a total immersion in which all the powers of darkness will roll over him.

But where is the promised land? Where is the place where we dwell with God and he with us? Is it only in another world beyond death? That is how the dominant religious experience of the human race has seen the future—escape from this world in order to have fellowship with God in that other world which is hidden from us beyond the curtain. But the promise here is different. Jesus does not leave them and go before them merely to wait for them at the end of the road. "I will come again and will take you to myself." The bridegroom comes back to meet the bride and bring her on the way to the home prepared for her. But, once again, this could be misunderstood. It could mean that there is no "abiding," no dwelling together, short of the end. It could mean that until the final consummation we are left alone to battle through wind and rain with only the hope of an "abiding place" at the end to sustain us.

In fact the truth is far more comforting than this. During the coming discourse Jesus will speak much about "abiding" with the disciples, about their "abiding" in him, and about his "abiding" in the Father. Now, at the outset and as the ground for their reassurance, he tells them that there are many "abiding places" and all of them "in my Father's house." The Father's house, as we have already learned, is not a building made with hands. Nor is it another world beyond death. It is that new dwelling place of God in the Spirit which is consituted by the resurrection of Jesus from the dead (2:19-22; cf. Eph. 2:19-22). The death and resurrection of Jesus will inaugurate a new possibility—namely, that while we are still on the way, we shall have "a place" where we can already taste the joy of journey's end, the joy of lovers' meeting, the joy of being "with the Lord" (I Thess. 4:17). It is because this is so that Jesus can assure his friends that the parting which so grieves them at the moment is only temporary. He is going to prepare a place for them where they may abide with him and he with them. But the "place" is not to be understood simply as the destination of their journey; rather there are many "abiding places" on the way, but they are all within the Father's house.

In fact the place where they are meeting is a kind of parable of these many "abiding places." The disciples—according to the synoptic tradition—had been told to follow an unknown man to an unknown destination, and there they found a room prepared for them where Jesus came to meet them and abide with them (Mark 14:13-16). At every time and place where the disciples meet to eat and drink in the name of Jesus, he is there to be with them. Like the children of Israel in their journeying they have the pillar of cloud and fire, the presence of God himself, to be with them both in their temporary encampments and on their marches (Num. 9:15-23). While still on the way, they will have already the presence of that which is promised at the end.

Peter had asked "Where are you going?", a question about the destination of the journey. Jesus does not answer the question in those terms. His answer is: "You know the way." The immediate protest of Thomas is reasonable: "If we do not know the

destination of our journey, how can we know the route?" But
that obvious protest brings us to the very heart of the matter. We
do *not* know the destination. We have no map of what lies beyond
the curtain, though theologians—and others—often use language
which suggests that we have. We do not know the limits of the
possibilites for our personal lives or for the life of the world. We
do *not* know, and cannot know, all that God has prepared for
those who love him. It is beyond the highest power of our imagination (I Cor. 2:9). We do *not* know the destination; but we do
know the way. That is the heart of the matter. The way through
the curtain is "the flesh" of Jesus (Heb. 10:20), the concrete humanity of this Jesus who lived and died and rose again. It is not
that he teaches the way, or guides us in the way: if that were so,
we could thank him for his teaching and then proceed to follow
it on our own. He himself is the way, and therefore it is only by
being made part of his humanity that we are on the way and
know that we are not lost even though we do not see the destination. Like all human beings, and like the whole human family
seen as one company of travelers, we are on a road which disappears out of sight. But when we are totally identified with
Jesus, made one through baptism and the eucharist with his dying
and his risen life, and living out our baptism and our eucharist
in daily love and obedience to the Father, though we do not
know what lies ahead, we are on a track which we can trust and
which gives us a way "through the curtain." This is discipleship
(*Nachfolge*). This is what is made possible only by the death and
resurrection of Jesus. And this is the way that Peter will follow
afterward, when he has learned the way of the cross (21:18f.).

This is the true and living way, because Jesus is both truth
and life. He is the truth in the sense that in him the faithfulness
of God is revealed and put into effect. In him God proves his
faithfulness, for "all the promises of God find their 'Yes' in him;
that is why we utter the 'Amen' through him to the glory of
God" (II Cor. 1:20). He is the life, for in him the very life of God
is poured out for man, and when we follow the way which he
is, "always carrying in the body the death of Jesus," then the life
of Jesus is manifest in our mortal body (II Cor. 4:10).

To follow this way is, in fact, the only way to the Father.
This is not to say that God has left no witness to himself in the
rest of the life of the world. We have in fact been told that Jesus
is the light that lightens *every* man. What is being said here, as

in the whole of the Gospel, is that Jesus is in fact the presence of God's truth and God's life in the world, and that to know the Father means to follow the way which Jesus is, and which he has opened through the curtain by his living, his dying, and his rising from the dead. The word "God" has had and still has an almost infinite variety of meanings. Here we are invited to accept the affirmation that there is but one way to come to the living God and to know him as Father, and that is by being made one with this meek and humble man who goes to the cross carrying the sin of the world. To know Jesus in this sense is to know the Father. We do not come to the true knowledge of God by any kind of induction from human experience, even human religious experience. In face of the fact of death that enterprise is doomed in advance. We come to the true knowledge of God by knowing Jesus, and following him along the way which he goes and which he is.

14:8-14

Philip said to him, "Lord, show us the Father, and we shall be satisfied." Jesus said to him, "Have I been with you so long, and yet you do not know me, Philip? He who has seen me has seen the Father; how can you say, 'Show us the Father'? Do you not believe that I am in the Father and the Father in me? The words that I say to you I do not speak on my own authority; but the Father who dwells in me does his works. Believe me that I am in the Father and the Father in me; or else believe me for the sake of the works themselves.

"Truly, truly, I say to you, he who believes in me will also do the works that I do; and greater works than these will he do, because I go to the Father. Whatever you ask in my name, I will do it, that the Father may be glorified in the Son; if you ask anything in my name, I will do it.

To have the vision of God is the longing of every devout soul. Moses had prayed to the Lord, "Show me thy glory," and had been granted a fleeting glimpse of that glory passing by, for "man shall not see me and live" (Ex. 33:18-23). The promise that "the glory of the LORD shall be revealed, and all flesh shall see it together" (Isa. 40:5) is one for the fulfilment of which the people of God wait with eager longing. Jesus had said to the disciples, "Henceforth you know the Father and have seen him," and it is this that prompts Philip's impetuous demand: "Show us the Fa-

ther, and we shall be satisfied." He has not yet understood the
nature of the "abiding place" which Jesus has promised. Where
Jesus abides with them the Father is also present, for the Father
abides ("dwells") in Jesus. Both the words and the works of Jesus
are the words and the works of the Father. We can know God
only by listening to the words he speaks and attending to the
works he does. These are not to be set against each other, for
God's words are deeds which accomplish what they express. It
is by the uttering of words that Jesus performed his "works,"
and the words of Jesus are still the means through which the
Father "does his works," the works of setting all people and all
creation free from their bondage to decay (Rom. 8:21). The Father
and the Son are so perfectly one in their mutual indwelling that
when we listen to the words of Jesus and attend to his works, we
are coming to see God, and it is therefore futile and irrelevant to
look elsewhere. But this "seeing" is only through believing. Personal trust in Jesus is the way by which we come to "see." We
are led to put our trust in him by his own affirmation of his
relation to the Father. His "works," those "signs" which St. John
has so carefully recorded, can be a ground of confidence for those
to whom it is given. They are of no avail in convincing unbelievers but they are signs of the glory of God to the disciples (cf.
2:11 and contrast 12:37-40). Thus, because of the "abiding" of
the Father in the Son, the disciples have already received that
vision of the glory of God which is promised for the last days.

But this is not all. The going of Jesus to the Father by the
path of suffering, death, and resurrection is the setting in motion
of a far vaster movement in which the glory of the Father will
be manifested through the works of the disciples done in the
name of the Son. The eschatological theme of the mission of the
Church to all the nations now begins to open up. The signs of
the presence of the reign of God which were given in the ministry
of Jesus carried out on the narrow stage of Galilee and Judea will
now be multiplied on a far wider stage. The glorifying of the
Father in the Son through the victory of the cross will be extended
to the whole creation through the believing words and works of
the Church, until the whole earth is filled with his glory. This
will become possible (as we shall learn in a moment) through the
coming of the Spirit. It will be the work of God himself, not—
essentially—the achievement of the Church. And therefore its
heart and center will be a ministry of intercession. The glorifying

of the Father in the mission of the Church will be the fruit of intercession offered by the Church in the name of Jesus.

This is the first introduction of the invitation to pray "in the name of Jesus." As with everything in this discourse we must remember that the immediate context is the eucharist. The efficacy of the prayer is grounded in the fact that Jesus "goes to the Father" by way of the cross. In the eucharist believers are united with this self-offering of Jesus and their intercession is that the sacrifice of Jesus may avail for the redeeming of the family of God and of the created world.

It is to be noted that here, as in the related passage in Acts 1:6-8, the world mission of the Church is introduced in terms of promise rather than of command. It is a promise that, through what Jesus has done once for all on Calvary, the mighty power of God will be made available through the works of the Church for the glorifying of the Father in the Son. And this, we are now told at once, is accomplished through the coming of the Spirit.

14:15-24

"If you love me, you will keep my commandments. And I will pray the Father, and he will give you another Counselor, to be with you for ever, even the Spirit of truth, whom the world cannot receive, because it neither sees him nor knows him; you know him, for he dwells with you, and will be in you.

"I will not leave you desolate; I will come to you. Yet a little while, and the world will see me no more, but you will see me; because I live, you will live also. In that day you will know that I am in my Father, and you in me, and I in you. He who has my commandments and keeps them, he it is who loves me; and he who loves me will be loved by my Father, and I will love him and manifest myself to him." Judas (not Iscariot) said to him, "Lord, how is it that you will manifest yourself to us, and not to the world?" Jesus answered him, "If a man loves me, he will keep my word, and my Father will love him, and we will come to him and make our home with him. He who does not love me does not keep my words; and the word which you hear is not mine but the Father's who sent me."

At the beginning of the discourse Jesus had comforted his disciples with the assurance that his departure from them was not a final bereavement, but the necessary condition for the preparation of "abiding places" where they might be with him. The development of this theme was interrupted by the necessity to clarify (in answer to Thomas) the relation between the "way" and the destination, and (in answer to Philip) the relation between knowing Jesus and knowing the Father. After these explanations, Jesus resumes the main theme, which is the comfort offered to the grieving disciples in the promise of future "abiding places."

This promise is made in a threefold form: (a) the promise of the coming of the Spirit, who is the gift of the Father, who abides now in Jesus and will abide in the disciples (vv. 15-17); (b) the promise of the coming of Jesus who abides in the Father, as the disciples will abide in him and he in them (vv. 18-20); (c) the promise that both the Father and Jesus will abide with the disciples (v. 23).

"But will God indeed dwell on the earth? Behold, heaven and the highest heaven cannot contain thee" (I Kings 8:27). The cry of King Solomon at the moment when he dedicates a building to be a house of God is answered again and again in the Old Testament by the promise that a day is coming when God will indeed dwell among his people. One of the latest of the prophets had greeted that day with a cry of joy: "Sing and rejoice, O daughter of Zion; for lo, I come and I will dwell in the midst of you, says the Lord. And many nations shall join themselves to the Lord in that day, and shall be my people; and I will dwell in the midst of you" (Zech. 2:10f.).

"In that day"! This familiar phrase of the prophets was as resonant to a devout student of scripture as was the corresponding phrase "Yet a little while" (e.g., Isa. 10:25; 26:20; Jer. 51:33). Jesus uses both these phrases, but the way in which they are used provokes yet another demand for clarification. The question of Judas is not "foolish" (so Bultmann) but reasonable on the lips of a devout Jew. "That day," the "day of the Lord," was not expected to be something secret. On the contrary it would be the day when the hidden power of God would be made manifest, when the nations would come and acknowledge that God is truly present among his people. How, then, can Jesus speak of a presence and an indwelling which "the world" will not see and cannot know? It is—once again—the same issue which is raised when— according to the Lucan tradition in Acts 1:6—the disciples ask Jesus, "Will you at this time restore the kingdom to Israel?" What does "in that day" mean if it does not mean the manifest victory of God's cause?

Jesus does, indeed, promise that he will "manifest" himself

to the disciples, using the word (and only here in St. John's Gospel) which describes God's revelation of himself to Moses (Exod. 33:13, 18). The same word is used in speaking of the appearance of the risen Jesus to his disciples, and this provides one way of entry into the complex meaning of this passage. For the disciples of Jesus the day of the Lord will no longer be something in the future. The Lord's Day is in fact the day on which Jesus, by his resurrection from the dead, made manifest the victory of God's cause. This manifestation was not to all but to those who were chosen by God as "witnesses" (Acts 10:41; cf. I Cor. 1:24). They are admitted to the "open secret" of God's abiding with his people and thus they live now in those "last days" to which the prophets had looked forward. For, in fact, the day of the Lord which when seen from afar seemed to be only a "day", is now found to be more than a single day, a whole new age which supervenes upon the old. The great rampart of the Palni Hills seen from the plains around Madurai looks like a single sharp ridge. Those who have visited and explored those lovely hills know that they are in fact a whole world of hills and valleys, forests, lakes, and streams. So when—with the resurrection of Jesus—the long desired day of the Lord dawns, those to whom its secret is given find that it is not one day, but the dawning of a new era in which God dwells in the midst of his people but in a manner which is hidden from the world. It is "the Lord's Day," and we celebrate it every week as we remember his resurrection, the victory which inaugurates the new era.

What is the manner of this indwelling? It is defined in this and the ensuing passages in terms of love and obedience. Both words are needed to set forth the manner of this "abiding," and their mutual relations are exhibited in a whole series of phrases which interpret them with cumulative effect (14:15, 21, 23, 24, 31; 15:10, 12, 14, 17). To speak of love apart from obedience would open the way to a purely emotional and sentimental interpretation of the "abiding"—a kind of amoral emotionalism into which the *bhakti* tradition in India has sometimes been tempted. To speak of obedience apart from love would open the way to the slave-mentality against which we shall be warned (15:15; cf. Rom. 8:15) and which—in spite of these warnings—has often infected Christian practice. Contemporary Christian thinking tends to avoid the category of obedience and to speak only of love. That is the way to illusion. Obedience is the test of love; love is

186

the content of obedience. In both, as we shall see, Jesus is our guide and mediator (15:9-10). (The mutual interrelatedness of love and obedience is very fully worked out in the First Letter of John—e.g., in I John 2:3-5; 3:23f.; 5:2-4.)

This dwelling of God with his people will be made possible by the coming of "another Counselor" who is the Spirit of truth and the gift of the Father. In John's understanding this gift is given to the chosen witnesses on the day of resurrection itself (20:19-23). There is the closest possible connection between Jesus' "manifesting himself" to the disciples and the imparting to them of the Spirit. John carefully records three 'manifestations" of Jesus to his disciples (21:14) with the implication that this is the end of a finite series. The other "Counselor," however, will be with the disciples "for ever." He is no stranger to them, for he dwells "with" them now and will be "in" them in the future. Who is this "Counselor"?

The Greek word *paraklētos* occurs only here in these three chapters of St. John's Gospel and nowhere else in the New Testament except in I John 2:1, where it is used of Jesus, in the classical sense of an advocate. The corresponding verb (*parakaleō*) and verbal noun (*paraklēsis*) occur, however, about 120 times, scattered through all other parts of the New Testament but (strangely) never once in any of the Johannine writings. The corresponding English words are words of calling, beseeching, entreating, comforting, consoling, exhorting. To list these words is to remind the student of the New Testament that we are talking about something which is of the very stuff of the Christian life together in the world. By using the name *Paraklētos* John is identifying the source of all this calling and comforting and exhorting and beseeching and consoling as no human achievement but as a gift from the Father, a gift whose coming is made possible by the intercession of Jesus.

Jesus is the original *Paraklētos*, the one who intercedes with the Father for the disciples (I John 2:1) and who comforts and exhorts them in their distress. This long discourse, beginning with "Let not your hearts be troubled," is the perfect model of Christian *paraklēsis*. But there is another *Paraklētos* who will never be parted from them. He is "the Spirit of truth." His *paraklēsis*, his comforting and exhorting, is the communication of the truth, and, because Jesus is the truth, this means that his work is to interpret to the disciples the words and works of Jesus (14:26 and

16:14) and to confront the world with the truth as it is in Jesus (15:18-26; 16:7-11). The Christian *paraklēsis* is the communication of truth both for the "comforting" of the Church and for the "convicting" of the world.

The *Paraklētos* is thus a personal presence which sharply distinguishes the disciples from the world. There are many "spirits" abroad in the world, but the "spiritual" may in fact be at the service not of the truth but of its opposite (I John 4:1-3). That this is so has been made manifest in the passion of Jesus. The spirits that rule this world were incapable of recognizing the truth. If they had been able to do so, "they would not have crucified the Lord of glory." But what is hidden from them is made known to the disciples through the Spirit, who is the Spirit of truth (I Cor. 2:8-10).

This Spirit dwells with them in the person of Jesus himself in whom the Spirit "abides" (1:33). He will be in them always because the risen Jesus will "breathe on them" (20:22) so that they also will have his life abiding in them. For the one in whom the Spirit "abides" is the one who baptizes with the Spirit (1:33). The ultimate meaning of this paradox of a "hidden manifestation" will, however, be made clear in the words "As the Father has sent me, even so I send you" (20:21). It is hidden in order that it may be revealed. The world does not know, but the purpose is that the world may know (17:22-26).

The occasion for and the possibility of this gift of the Spirit will be the manifestation of the risen Christ to those who have been chosen as witnesses. This is the primary reference in the second part of the threefold promise (vv. 18-21). We should probably read: "You will see me, because I live and you will live." The resurrection of Jesus means new life for Jesus and for his disciples. This life is life in the power of the Spirit. And it includes the recognition of the mutual indwelling of Jesus and the Father, and of Jesus and the disciples. Jesus is the mediator through whom God dwells with us and we abide in him. This is the fulfilment of the promise that "in that day" God will dwell with his people, but the dwelling place can be described both as "a holy temple in the Lord [Jesus]" and as a "dwelling place of God in the Spirit" (Eph. 2:21f.). And—once again—the substance of the indwelling is love made actual in obedience.

The third part of the threefold promise (v. 23f.), in reply to the question of Judas, moves the thought further in two respects.

It makes clear that the promised "abiding" is for all whose love is shown in their obedience to his word. And it makes clear that the abiding of Jesus is the abiding of the Father also. The original assurance that "in my Father's house there are many abiding places" is thus reaffirmed, the words to Philip are restated, and the ancient hope of Israel is fulfilled. God himself will dwell with them and be their God. But this divine indwelling is now understood as the indwelling of the Father and the Son through the indwelling of the Spirit. And—once again—its substance is love and obedience—obedience to the words of Jesus which are in fact the word of the Father.

14:25-31

"These things I have spoken to you, while I am still with you. But the Counselor, the Holy Spirit, whom the Father will send in my name, he will teach you all things, and bring to your remembrance all that I have said to you. Peace I leave with you; my peace I give to you; not as the world gives do I give to you. Let not your hearts be troubled, neither let them be afraid. You heard me say to you, 'I go away, and I will come to you.' If you loved me, you would have rejoiced, because I go to the Father; for the Father is greater than I. And now I have told you before it takes place, so that when it does take place, you may believe. I will no longer talk much with you, for the ruler of this world is coming. He has no power over me; but I do as the Father has commanded me, so that the world may know that I love the Father. Rise, let us go hence."

"These things I have spoken to you." This solemn phrase, seven times repeated, will remind us of the similar formula used by the prophets: "This is the word of the Lord." In this very emphatic way attention is drawn to the actual words spoken by Jesus to his disciples in the days of his flesh, "while still abiding with them." The word of the Lord has truly been spoken. There *is* a revelation of God in the words spoken in the Aramaic language to a particular group of Jews in Judea and Galilee in the time of Pontius Pilate. There is, in other words, an objective revelation which is part of the public life of the world, part of that public life which it is the business of the historian to record. It is revelation in particular concrete events which have names attached to them and which are part of the history of Palestine and not of Japan or India, of the first century and not of the tenth or twentieth. It is part of the purpose of John's Gospel to emphasize the concrete particularity, the historicity, the factuality of what he records.

But what belongs to one time and place is, by the fact, limited. It does not and cannot belong in the same way to every time and place. God is concerned with all times and places; how can his revelation be supposed to be confined to one time and place? For most of the world's religions this "scandal of particularity" has been too scandalous to tolerate. God's dealings, it has been thought, must be with all times and places and therefore with every human soul in every historical circumstance. But then religion becomes a private matter in the recesses of each human soul, and—inevitably—the public life which is the business of the historian must be seen as peripheral to the ultimate concern of religion, as a sphere—if not of illusion—of only relative and partial and ambiguous truth. To put the matter in crudely simplified terms: Is God's revelation "objective," a part of public history? If so, how can it become God's own word to me here and now? Or is God's revelation a matter of inward "subjective" experience? If so, how can I have any assurance of its truth comparable to my assurance about the public truths of science?

St. John has told the story of an "objective" revelation, of one who was both a particular Jewish man of the time of Pontius Pilate, and God's word made flesh. He is now concerned to make it clear that, in accordance with the teaching of Jesus truly understood, this "objective" revelation becomes the inward "subjective" experience of the disciples. The living God, present in the concrete individual humanity of Jesus, will also be present in a different mode in such a way as to make Jesus the living contemporary of those who come after. Because of this living presence, the words and works of Jesus will be re-presented to the disciples so that they understand their true meaning.

Revelation had to be in the "objective" form of the man whom the disciples encountered as—not their own best selves, or their own view of God—but another who called, summoned, rebuked, forgave, healed, and taught them. They encountered this "other," or rather they were encountered by him. And—as John constantly repeats—they did not understand. They did not, could not understand, not because they were stupid or wicked, but because they were human beings—"flesh and blood." In this respect they were the same as "the Jews," who also could not understand. The difference was that these had been "chosen" to be witnesses, chosen and prepared beforehand. But, since "flesh and blood" cannot know God as he truly reveals himself, they could only be made witnesses when Jesus had "gone to the Father," had "opened the way through the curtain," had—in his passion—dethroned the "rulers of this present age" who conceal the truth from human eyes. Because of this accomplished victory in which Jesus—as king—has borne witness to the truth (18:37) and unmasked the lies which rule the world (including the world of religion), God can come to men and women as the living Spirit pointing them to this once-for-all event and bearing witness in their hearts and consciences that this is the truth, that Jesus is Lord (15:26; 16:8-15; I John 2:27; I Cor. 12:3).

This is not another or a new revelation. The Spirit of whom Jesus speaks is sent by the Father who sent Jesus. And he is sent "in the name of Jesus" (v. 26). Jesus came "in the name of the Father," spoke the words of the Father, and did the works of the Father; so also the Spirit will speak to the disciples the words of Jesus and interpret to them his works. But it is the one Father who sent Jesus who also sends the Spirit in his name. The Spirit will enable the disciples to understand what they could not understand otherwise. The Spirit will take "these things"—the words and works of Jesus which belong to that particular and very limited world of first-century Judea—and by bringing them afresh to the remembrance of the disciples in every place and every time, teach them "all things," until "all things" find their true unity in Jesus as the head and king of the cosmos (Eph. 1:10; Col. 1:20).

It is because of the fulfilment of this promise that there is such a thing as the Christian faith, and that there are "Gospels" written by those who share this faith. The writing of the documents which we now have as the four Gospels is the result of the continuous process of "bringing to remembrance" the words and works of Jesus from the day of resurrection onward. This process—beginning with the preaching and mutual encouragement (*paraklēsis*) of the earliest disciples—obviously developed in different ways in the various scattered communities of Christians. The writer of the Fourth Gospel is confident that, in relying upon the testimony of the "beloved disciple," he is truly interpreting the meaning of what Jesus said and did. But this true interpretation can only be given as the Spirit who is the living presence of God dwells in the heart of the interpreter so that revelation is still going on—not in the sense of a new revelation, but in the sense that what was said and done in the particular context of first-century Judea becomes the word and deed of God in all the new situations which the believing community meets on its way to the summing up of all things in Christ. That it can and does so become is a continuous confirmation to the believing community that Jesus is indeed the word through whom all things were made and in whom they are all being made new. And the variety of testimonies to Jesus which the Church treasures, bound up in one volume in spite of all their variety, is the first evidence of the fact that the once-for-all concreteness and particularity of the "objective" revelation is not the cut-off point in God's disclosure of himself to the world, but the starting point of an action of the living Spirit of God from Judea through Samaria and into all the world until "all things" are perceived in their true unity in the word made flesh.

The community to which these promises are made is given—as Jesus' bequest—the gift of peace. Peace, *shalom*, is the essential substance of the promised blessing which is the goal of the whole human journey. It is given to the community as a sign and pledge of that long-desired consummation. But it is not the kind of peace which the world knows—only a temporary cessation of strife, a cease-fire at the end of a period of fighting. It is in fact, as will be made clear (e.g., 15:18ff.; 16:1-3, 33), something given while the battle is still going on. It is the peace which Jesus makes, the peace which he has brought about "by the blood of his cross" (Col. 1:20). It is the "peace with God through our Lord Jesus Christ" which enables us to rejoice in tribulation (Rom. 5:1ff.). And this gift of peace will stand guard over their hearts and minds (Phil. 4:7). So the encouragement (*paraklēsis*) with which the discourse began can be reaffirmed: there is no place for fear or anxiety.

It is, as we have seen, because Jesus "goes to the Father" by way of his passion, because of the victory of the cross, that this assurance can be given. The disciples should therefore have rejoiced, not only because this "going" will mean a new kind of "coming," not only because it will open the way for "greater works," not only because it will enable the Spirit to teach "all things" to them, but because it is the accomplishment of Jesus' work and his return to the glory from which he came. Jesus already sees "the joy set before him" (Heb. 12:2) and wishes his disciples to share his joy—which they should do if they love him.

The joy of the true disciple is not in his own salvation but in the victorious joy of Jesus. It was the Father who sent his beloved Son on this infinitely costly mission (3:16). Now the Son rejoices to return to the Father's house, and as he returns he gives all the glory to the Father, for "one who is sent is not greater than he who sent him" (13:16).

Once again we are reminded that the disciples cannot understand now what is being said but that afterward they will believe, for the Paraclete will interpret to them all that he has done and said. Once again, also, we are reminded of the limits that constrict the words and works of the incarnate Lord into an all-too-narrow space. There is not much more time for the Eternal to speak. Judas is already on his way. But behind Judas are the powers of law and government and religion, and behind these stands "the ruler of this world" who is blind and blinds men's eyes to the true glory (I Cor. 2:8ff.). In the trial which will follow, the ruler of this world through his representatives will declare Jesus guilty. But, as always, his supposed wisdom is self-deceived and his power is powerless. The action which is to follow is not the action of the ruler of the world; it is the action of Jesus who will disarm him and expose the foolishness and powerlessness of his claim (Col. 2:15; cf. I Cor. 1:18-25); it is the action of Jesus, an action of pure love and obedience, by which the world will be enabled to know his love for the Father. And the time for action has come. So "Up, let us go."

These words are exactly the same as those which, according to Mark, Jesus uses when he summons his sleepy disciples in the Garden of Gethsemane to get up and go to meet Judas who is advancing with his troops through the trees. Had this phrase passed into Christian usage as a sort of battle cry for timid disciples faced, as they so often were, with the need to meet the cruel power of the state? Is this another example of St. John's preference for bringing forward into the earlier part of his narrative events which the synoptic Gospels place in the context of the final trial? Or have we here the end of an earlier version of the farewell discourse which, in the final editing, has been left as it stands in spite of the fact that further discourse follows? It is probably impossible to decide between these possibilities, and it is certainly unnecessary to do so. In any case the meaning is clear. The "comfort" which Jesus gives to his disciples at this moment of parting is not cotton wool for the timid but steel for the courageous. The "calling" of the Paraclete is to "follow the Lamb" (Rev. 14:4) as he goes to meet the "prince of the world," and there is no room for "the cowardly and the faithless" (Rev. 21:8). It is the call to "take up the cross and follow." It is to those who thus follow in the way Jesus goes, which is the way he is, that the promise of "abiding" is given.

16

JESUS, THE DISCIPLES, AND THE WORLD
(15:1–16:33)

15:1-11

"I am the true vine, and my Father is the vinedresser. Every branch of mine that bears no fruit, he takes away, and every branch that does bear fruit he prunes, that it may bear more fruit. You are already made clean by the word which I have spoken to you. Abide in me, and I in you. As the branch cannot bear fruit by itself, unless it abides in the vine, neither can you, unless you abide in me. I am the vine, you are the branches. He who abides in me, and I in him, he it is that bears much fruit, for apart from me you can do nothing. If a man does not abide in me, he is cast forth as a branch and withers; and the branches are gathered, thrown into the fire and burned. If you abide in me, and my words abide in you, ask whatever you will, and it shall be done for you. By this my Father is glorified, that you bear much fruit, and so prove to be my disciples. As the Father has loved me, so have I loved you; abide in my love. If you keep my commandments, you will abide in my love, just as I have kept my Father's commandments and abide in his love. These things I have spoken to you, that my joy may be in you, and that your joy may be full."

The closing words of the previous chapter make so sharp a break in the flow of the discourse that many expositors argue either that chapters 15 to 16 (and 17) were spoken while Jesus walked from the place of the meal to the garden, or that there has been a displacement of the text. The former supposition raises insuperable difficulties. The latter leads to the following reflection. It may well be that the material ending at 14:31 originally formed a distinct unit. If that is so, the evangelist has seen fit to place it in its present position and to follow it immediately and abruptly with the passage which begins "I am the true vine." It is the business of the expositor to ask why this sequence has been adopted.

Reflection on the farewell discourse as a whole suggests an obvious answer. The whole of the first part of the discourse (13:31–14:31) has been dominated by the imminence of Jesus' separation from his disciples and by the need to comfort them with the assurance that his departure will not leave them desolate, but will rather be the means by which God's ancient promise to Israel will be fulfilled—the promise to dwell with them forever.

But that assurance does not wholly set at rest the perplexity voiced by the disciples: why is the presence of the Lord and his dwelling with his people to be known only to them and not to the whole world (14:22)? Why should there be only this partial and limited fulfilment of the hope of Israel? Was the promise not made that all the nations would come to acknowledge that the Lord does indeed dwell and reign in the midst of Israel?

Yes indeed! And Israel had constantly forgotten this. She had forgotten that the vine which the Lord had planted and tended did not exist for itself but in order to give fruit to the Gardener. The gracious indwelling of God with his people is not an invitation to settle down and forget the rest of the world: it is a summons to mission, for the Lord who dwells with his people is the one who goes before them in the pillar of fire and cloud. So the promise of his presence is clinched in the words, "Up, let us go hence." There is a mission to be fulfilled. There is a conflict to be waged with the powers of this world. There is tribulation to be endured. For Jesus who chose and called them did so not for themselves, alone, but that they should "go and bear fruit" (15:16). But he does not send them out alone: he leads the way and brings them with him. They dwell with him only as they go with him. For he is the one in whom the calling of Israel is fulfilled. He is the true vine.

It is no accident that the coins minted during the brief period of the Jewish revolt against Rome (A.D. 68-70) were stamped with the image of a vine, for this is the most prevasive of all the symbols for Israel. Israel is "a luxuriant vine" (Hos. 10:1), "a choice vine wholly of pure seed" (Jer. 2:21), a vine brought from Egypt and planted in the mountains of Israel (Ps. 80:8-11), "a vine in a vineyard . . . fruitful and full of branches" (Ezek. 19:10). The house of Israel is "the vineyard of the Lord" (Isa. 5:1-7). But the Gardener has had little joy from his vineyard. It does not yield the fruit he expects. Its fruit is only wild grapes (Isa. 5:4). The vine has turned degenerate (Jer. 2:21). The patience of the Gardener is near its end. The false vine is threatened with the axe and the fire.

But from the stump has sprung forth the branch (Isa. 11:1) who is the true vine, the real vine, the one in whom the Gardener finds the fruit he desired. There is already a pointer in this direction in the Psalm already quoted (Ps. 80) where the vine of God's planting is identified with the "son of man" who must go through tribulation but who is made strong by God for God (vv. 14-17). Jesus, the true Son of man, is also the true vine, and the disciples are the branches. They share a common life which is his life. "You will see me; because I live, you will live also" (14:19). But this shared life, this mutual indwelling of Jesus and his disciples, is not an end in itself, The point is that it results in the bearing of fruit. This fruit is not an artifact of the disciples; it is the fruit of the vine. It is the life of Jesus himself reproduced in the lives of the disciples in the midst of the life of the world. The presence of fruit is the visible evidence of the fact that the branch is part of the vine.

As the discourse proceeds we learn what the fruit is: it is love and obedience. Its presence will be the sign that the disciples belong to Jesus (13:34-35). The fruit will be recognizable as the fruit of the vine; it will be simply the life of Jesus being made visible in the midst of the life of the world. (In fact the theme of love and obedience runs continuously through the "break" at 14:31 and binds both parts of the discourse firmly into a unity.)

The production of fruit is not, directly,the responsibility of the branches. The Gardener charges himself with the responsibility. There are branches which belong to the vine but which bear no fruit. The life of the vine is not in them and they must be cut off. There are branches which bear fruit, but these must be pruned in order to be more fruitful still. (There is a play upon words in the original: some he "clears off" and some he "cleans up.") Both operations are painful. To see one of the company go out into the darkness is painful (13:30). So is it to see tendrils cut, promising beginnings "nipped in the bud." But it is the Father who is the gardener, and he does not use the pruning knife carelessly or in vain. Even Jesus himself "learned obedience through what he suffered" and so was "made perfect" (Heb. 5:8). The disciple, following him, can be relieved of anxiety about fruit-bearing. He has only one task—to "abide in the vine." The rest is the work of the Gardener. And this abiding, as we shall learn, is for them as for Jesus through love and obedience (vv. 9f.).

It is part of the paradox of our abiding in Christ that it is both something done by him "once for all" and something which needs to be reaffirmed constantly from our side. Believers "have died with Christ," and yet must constantly "put to death" the old ego (e.g., Col. 2:20–3:5). So the disciples have to be warned to "abide." When Jesus washed their feet he told them that they were clean and did not need to wash (13:10); what has been done is not to be repeated or added to. It is a cleansing by the word that Jesus has spoken. The whole revelation of God in Jesus with its focus in the cross, the whole action which was parabolically set forth in the washing of the disciples' feet, has cleansing power, for "the life" is "the light of men." But it is necessary to "abide" in Jesus, and this means a continually renewed action of the will. It is the continually renewed decision that what has been done once for all by the action of Jesus shall be the basis, the starting point, the context of all my thinking and deciding and doing. The link between verse 3 and verse 4 is brought out in another Johannine saying: "Let what you heard from the beginning abide in you. If what you heard from the beginning abides in you, then you will abide in the Son and in the Father" (I John 2:24). This "abiding" means "holding on loyally to the decision once taken, and one can only hold on to it by continually going through it again"; but "the loyalty demanded is not primarily a continual being *for*, but a being *from*; not the holding of a position but an allowing oneself to be held" (Bultmann).

The one who "holds" is Jesus himself, and therefore "abide in me" must be linked at once with "and I in you." And this mutual indwelling is the absolute condition of fruit-bearing, as the production of much fruit is the purpose of the Gardener. All life comes from God, and Jesus himself can do nothing of himself apart from the Father (5:30). But it is also true that all things were made through the word, without him was not anything made (1:3), and therefore apart from Jesus the disciples can do nothing. They may, of course, produce a number of "good works" which may even look at first like real fruit; but these will not be the real fruit of the vine, the life of Jesus reproduced in the midst of the life of the world, the pure love and obedience by which people will recognize the disciples of Jesus, the branches of the real vine.

They may bring some fleeting glory to the disciples, but they will not glorify the Father (v. 8).

There is a dark but inescapable converse to what has just been said. A barren branch cannot abide in the vine. The prophet Ezekiel had pointed out (Ezek. 15) with considerable irony that the wood of the vine is the most useless of all the woods of the forest. You cannot even make a peg from it (Ezek. 15:3). The vine considered simply as a tree is the most useless of all trees. If it does not bear fruit it is fit only for burning. "Church growth," if it does not mean "bearing fruit and growing" (Col. 1:6), is merely providing fuel for the fires of hell. For—like all the terrible words of warning which are to be found in the Gospels—these words are addressed not to the unbeliever but to the believer, not to the weeds growing around the vine but to the branches of the vine, to those who are part of the visible body of believers.

But, and we turn again to the main theme, where there is mutual abiding, where the words of Jesus form the ever fresh starting point from which discipleship begins at every moment, there four things follow—and all because the words of Jesus are the mighty acts of the Father (14:10b). The four things are: answered prayer, glory to the Father, abundant fruit, and recognition as the disciples of Jesus. And these four are closely bound together. If the words of Jesus form the foundation and context of all our doing, they will necessarily shape the prayers we offer and these will truly be prayers "through Jesus Christ our Lord" which the Father will grant (14:13). The answer to the prayers will take the form of "much fruit," and so the Gardener will be glorified in the abundant harvest. Just as the Father is glorified in the mission of Jesus (12:26; 13:31f.), so he will be glorified in the mission of the Church, of which intercession will be a central part. And because the fruit will be the genuine fruit of the true vine, it will lead people to recognize the branches as true branches. People will give glory to the Father. They will praise not the missionaries but the one who sent them.

The glory of God is the central theme of the entire discourse—from its opening words "Now is the Son of man glorified, and in him God is glorified (13:31) to the final prayer: "Father, . . . glorify thy Son that the Son may glorify thee" (17:1). We have seen that this glorifying of the Father will be continued in the mission of the Church (v. 8). But from the beginning of the discourse it has been made clear that this glorifying is through love and obedience (13:34) and this double theme—love manifested in obedience and obedience manifested in love—has been repeated over and over again. Now (vv. 9-10) we are shown how Jesus is the mediator both of God's love to us and of our obedience to him, and how it is through love and obedience that we abide in Jesus and Jesus in the Father. Jesus, we know, loved his own and loved them to the end (13:2). But this love is grounded in the love of the Father which is the very ground and stay of all his being, his speaking, and his acting. In the love of Jesus, the Father's love is present and active in the world. Just so the disciples will find the very ground and of all their being and doing in the love which Jesus has lavished upon them, and they are to do this by a continually renewed decision. It will not be something automatic. They must deliberately return again and again, each day and each moment of the day, to this one true starting point. They must "abide" in the love of Jesus as Jesus does in the love of the Father.

But love will be expressed—can only be expressed—in obedience. Jesus' "abiding" in his Father's love was expressed in his obedience. Jesus had no program of his own. He planned no career for himself. He sought no "identity" for himself, no "image." He simply responded in loving obedience to the will of his Father as it was presented to him in all the accidents, contingencies, and interruptions of daily life, among all the personal and public ambitions and fears and jealousies of that little province of the Roman Empire in the time of Herod and Pontius Pilate. Only thus did Jesus "abide" in the love of the Father. So the disciple will "abide" in the love of Jesus by following him along exactly the same road. He will not be concerned to create a character or a career for himself. He will leave that to the wise husbandry of the Gardener who alone knows what pruning, what watering and feeding, what sunshine or rain, warmth or cold is needed to produce the fruit he desires. The disciple will "learn obedience" by following Jesus in the same kind of moment-by-moment obedience to the will of the Father as it is disclosed in the contingent happenings of daily life in the place and time where God has put him. Through Jesus we know and abide in the love of the Father; through Jesus we learn and offer the obedience that we owe to the Father. He is thus, in a double sense, the mediator of our abiding in the love of God.

Through this abiding we shall share in the life of Jesus and therefore in his joy. The opening words of the discourse were the grief and perplexity of the disciples; their context was the apostasy of Judas, the predicted faithlessness of Peter, and the imminent departure of Jesus. Jesus has comforted them with the promise of a renewed presence. He has told them that his going to the Father ought to cause them joy and not gloom (14:28). Now, in the context of the parable of the Vine he assures them of the fullness of joy. For "the fruit of the vine" is celebrated in the psalms as that which God has given "to gladden the heart of man" (Ps. 104:15). Wine has always been a symbol of joyful conviviality. The wine which Jesus shared with his disciples in the Upper Room was a foretaste of the wine of the heavenly banquet (Mark 14:25). But it was also (as the immediately preceding verse in St. Mark tells us) "the blood of the new convenant poured out for many" (Mark 14:24). The whole of this discourse is placed by the evangelist "during supper" (13:2), the last meal which Jesus shared with his disciples on the night that he was betrayed. From the day of resurrection onward it had been "in the breaking of the bread" that the disciples had learned to know the "abiding" of Jesus in their midst (Luke 24:29-31). Unlike the first three evangelists St. John does not record the "words of institution" in connection with the Last Supper. He has already in chapter 6 given an elaborate discourse on Jesus as the life-giving bread, and has quoted the saying: "He who eats my flesh and drinks my blood abides in me, and I in him" (6:56). Now he has given an account of this mutual abiding in the context of the parable of the true vine. At whatever date we fix the writing of the Fourth Gospel, its writer and readers were those who were accustomed to celebrate their abiding in him and his abiding in them by sharing in the bread and wine of the eucharist. This rested upon Jesus' own words at the Supper. The fourth evangelist at this point punctuates his rendering of the words of Jesus with the solemn formula "These things I have spoken to you" and proceeds to show us that, according to the intention of Jesus, our abiding in him will mean that we share his joy to the full, the joy of total obedience and love, the joy of him who "endured the cross, despising its shame" for the sake of "the joy that was set before him" (Heb. 12:2). The cup which Jesus shares with his disciples is both the wine that makes glad the heart of man and the blood shed for the life of the world. For the perfection of surrender in love and obedience is the joy of the Lord, the very substance—

if one may dare to say so—of the Godhead. "When the burnt offering began, the song of the Lord began also, and the trumpets" (II Chron. 29:27). The eucharist which makes us sharers in the self-offering of Jesus makes us at the same time sharers in his joy.

15:12-17

"This is my commandment, that you love one another as I have loved you. Greater love has no man than this, that a man lay down his life for his friends. You are my friends if you do what I command you. No longer do I call you servants, for the servant does not know what his master is doing; but I have called you friends, for all that I have heard from my Father I have made known to you. You did not choose me, but I chose you and appointed you that you should go and bear fruit and that your fruit should abide; so that whatever you ask the Father in my name, he may give it to you. This I command you, to love one another.

Once more the double theme of love and obedience which marked the opening of the discourse and which binds it all together is restated. We have just been told (vv. 9f.) that it is by love and obedience that Jesus abides in the Father, and we in Jesus. Now we are reminded of the once-for-all deed in which Jesus was the agent of God's love. He died for those whom he made his friends, and this dying was—as we know—an act of obedience to the Father (10:18). No greater token of love can be conceived. In making this offering of his life Jesus made them his friends and made them also his missionaries (v. 16 where the word "appointed" is the same as the word "lay down" in v. 13). They will show that they are indeed his beloved, his friends, by their obedience to his command—which is the command to love one another. It is not their obedience which will make them his friends. It is Jesus who has taken the initiative and made them his friends. They are the beloved, because he loves them and lays down his life for them.

He has spoken of them as "slaves" and of himself as their master (13:12-17), and will remind them of this again (15:20). But the master has done the work of a slave for them and therefore the relationship cannot be described simply as that of master and slave. He, the master, has made them his beloved, his friends. Their obedience, therefore, will not be the uncomprehending submission of the slave. He has not only given his life for them;

he has opened to them the fullness of the Father's purpose. Therefore their obedience will be the eager, intelligent obedience of those whose master is also the one who has made them his friends. It will be the free obedience of one who is delivered from slavery by abiding in the revelation which Jesus has given of the Father (8:31f.). There is in much religion a slavish obedience which is concerned with rewards and punishments. But the obedience which Jesus asks of his friends has a quite different center of concern. Its one concern is the concern of Jesus that the Father be glorified; "Father, hallowed be thy name" will always be the prayer which controls all its desiring and doing. By their love one for another the disciples will glorify the Father, because this love is the manifestation in the life of the world of that love which binds the Father and the Son (vv. 9f.; cf. 17:22f.). It is, in fact, the fruit of the true vine.

It was in order that they might "go and bear fruit" that Jesus chose and appointed them. The initiative was his. Like the Indian guru, the Gnostic teacher of the ancient world did not seek out his disciples. The disciple must seek and find a guru who will help him on a quest which is necessarily and eternally his own enterprise. Here, by contrast, the initiative is wholly that of the master and teacher. He had (according to the synoptic tradition) chosen twelve "to be with him, and to be sent out to preach" (Mark 3:14). The first part of the discourse was, as we have seen, primarily concerned with the former of these intentions: they are to be with him and he with them. Now the emphasis is upon the latter part: they are to go and bear fruit. They are sent. The image of the vine is strained to make room for a word which expresses the apostolate, the "being sent" of the Church, but is retained in that the purpose of their being sent is defined as "to bear fruit." (There is a close similarity to the language of 12:20-24 where the future world mission of the Church is described in terms of the fruitfulness of the seed which falls into the ground and dies.) As has been pointed out, the word translated "appointed" is the same as that which is used in verse 13 for the laying down of his life by Jesus. When Jesus committed his life to his Father, he also committed to those whom he had chosen and called the mission to go and be the means by which that outpoured life, which is the unceasing outpouring of love within the being of the triune God, might be reproduced in the life of the world. They are to be fruit-bearing branches. And as they "abide" in the vine, so their fruit will "abide." Their going will not produce mere fuel for the fire, but "fruit for eternal life" (4:36).

Because their discipleship is not their own spiritual quest or their own moral program, because it is the Father who is the Gardener and whose supreme joy it is that there should be fruit, it follows that he will grant all that is asked in the name of Jesus, who is himself the vine. All that is needed for the fruitfulness of the vine, it will be the joy of the Father to give. In that confidence and freedom the disciples go forth on their mission.

Once again there is the solemn reminder ("Thus saith the Lord") that the fruit of which we are speaking, which is the very life of the vine, is love manifested in obedience, and obedience manifested in love. The initiative is wholly his. We have only to "abide" in the vine. Therein lies the source of the godly confidence and even boldness of the disciple. But it is possible for a branch to become unfruitful. When love and obedience cease we know that the branch is dead, fit only for burning. And this can happen. Therein lies the source of a proper and godly fear. Yet that very fear can be the means of a renewed and restored "abiding." There is "a godly grief which produces a repentance that leads to salvation" as there is a "worldly grief" which is the loss of belief and leads only to death (II Cor. 7:10). The confidence of the believer is that the Father is the Gardener who is glorified in the fruit-bearing vine, and who can be trusted to "work all things together for good to those who love him, who are called according to his purpose" (Rom. 8:28).

15:18-27

"If the world hates you, know that it has hated me before it hated you. If you were of the world, the world would love its own; but because you are not of the world, but I chose you out of the world, therefore the world hates you. Remember the word that I said to you, 'A servant is not greater than his master.' If they persecuted me, they will persecute you; if they kept my word, they will keep yours also. But all this they will do to you on my account, because they do not know him who sent me. If I had not come and spoken to them, they would not have sin; but now they have no excuse for their sin. He who hates me hates my Father also. If I had not done among them the works which no one else did, they would not have sin; but now they have seen and hated both me and my Father. It is to fulfil the word that is written in their law, 'They hated me without a cause.' But when the Counselor comes, whom I shall send

to you from the Father, even the Spirit of truth, who proceeds from the Father, he will bear witness to me; and you also are witnesses, because you have been with me from the beginning."

The disciples have been chosen and appointed to "go" and to "bear fruit." They are sent into the world. It is there that they are to bear fruit. But the world is the darkness in which the light shines. It contradicts, by its very nature, the mission on which they are sent. At this point, therefore, we find the Johannine version of the "mission charge" which the synoptics place earlier in the ministry (Matt. 10, esp. vv. 16-25). The love which binds Jesus to the Father and the disciples to Jesus is the total denying of the self to the point of death. It is therefore rejected totally by the world where the fullness of life is seen as something to be grasped. Self-assertion must necessarily hate and reject self-denial. Therefore the world hated and rejected Jesus, finding in the end no place for him but a cross. Inasmuch as the disciples are the beloved of Jesus whom he has chosen and made his own, they will share the same rejection. They will—in the the synoptic language—take up the cross and follow him. Therefore Christians ought not to be surprised if they are hated and rejected. Rather they should be alarmed when the world finds them very congenial, for the world loves its own (Luke 6:22 and 26). A Church which is conformed to the world will not be recognizable as the company of the friends of Jesus. The sign of the cross will be the mark by which the true friends of Jesus will be recognized.

The rejection of Jesus is in fact the rejection of the one who sent him, as the rejection of the missionaries of Jesus is the rejection of Jesus. When Saul persecutes the disciples in Damascus, it is Jesus whom he attacks (Acts 9:4). And when Jesus is attacked and rejected, it is the Father who is rejected. And this is because the world does not know the Father (17:25). Human nature seeks to affirm itself and therefore does not of itself know the Father whose glory is to give himself or the Son who reflects that glory in the total giving of himself to the Father. Glory as the world understands it is an achievement, but the glory of God is surrender. The world is therefore ignorant of the true glory, and this ignorance is not an innocent ignorance. It would be an innocent ignorance if the light had not shone into the darkness. In fact the words of Jesus (v. 22) and his works (v. 24) both—in their different ways—unveiled the true light if men had been willing to receive it. But, having heard the words and seen the works, they rejected and hated the one who spoke and acted, and in doing so rejected the one from whom he came. This constitutes their guilt. Apart from what God has done in Jesus, there is no ground for speaking of the radical sinfulness of human nature. It is because Jesus has fully revealed the love of God, and because that love has been rejected, that we know and can affirm human sinfulness. It is only in the light of the revelation that we can understand the words of the psalmist: "They hated me without a cause." When they meet this hatred, the disciples will be encouraged in their knowledge that Jesus has indeed chosen them as his friends and servants. Between those for whom the cross is shame and defeat and those for whom the cross is glory and victory there cannot be other than a total contradiction.

But exactly at this point of radical contradiction the disciple is assured that he is not left to face the world unaided. There is an Advocate who will rise up at that moment who will bring the very power and truth of God himself into the situation. He will bear witness at that moment to Jesus, penetrating the darkness of unbelief with the light which reveals Jesus as the one he truly is. Through the presence and power of the divine Advocate the words and works of the disciples will come to have the power of witnessing to Jesus, because they are the ones whom he chose at the beginning to be with him and to be sent out and because they have remained faithful to him.

The language here echoes that of the synoptic "mission charge": "You will be dragged before governors and kings for my sake, to bear testimony to them and the Gentiles. When they deliver you up, do not be anxious how you are to speak or what you are to say . . . for it is not you who speak, but the Spirit of your Father speaking through you" (Matt. 10:18f.). The hatred and rejection of the world is not to be a cause of alarm or distress. On the contrary, it is to be a ground for confidence, both because it is the confirmation of the fact that they really do belong to Jesus, and because it will be the occasion for the mighty witness of the Spirit of truth.

It is important to note what is not said. It is not said that the Spirit will help the disciple to bear witness. That would make the action of the disciples primary and that of the Spirit anxiliary. What is said is that the Spirit will bear witness and that—secondarily—the disciples are witnesses. To say (Bultmann) that "the

word *marturesai* indicates that the Spirit is the power of the proclamation in the community" is to miss the point. There is nothing
said about proclamation. The primary reference of the word *mar-
tyria* in the history of the Church is not to proclamation but to
suffering. The Gospel repeatedly affirms that it is not the work
of men but of God to bring people to the knowledge of Jesus as
he truly is. To know Jesus as Lord can never be the work of
"flesh and blood." It is always a miracle of God's grace and never
the direct result of even the most impressive "proclamation," for
no one comes to Jesus unless the Father draws him (6:44). What
is promised here is that the contradiction of "the world" which
is set up by the presence in it of a community which—in the
name of Jesus—is hated and rejected and persecuted will be the
occasion for the mighty Spirit, who is the Spirit of the Father and
the Spirit of truth, to perform his own miracle in the hearts and
consciences of people so that they are brought to recognize Jesus
as the one he is. The words, the works, and—above all—the
sufferings of the community will be the means by which the
witness is borne, but the actual agent will be the Spirit who,
because he is the Spirit of the Father, is the Spirit of truth. When
the Lord says to Israel, "You are my witnesses" (Isa. 43:10), there
is no suggestion that this is a summons to proclamation. Israel
is the witness to the majesty and glory of the Lord, not on account
of anything that Israel says or does, but on account of those
mighty works of which the Lord is the subject and Israel is the
object. It is in this sense that the disciples will be witnesses. They
were chosen and called by the Lord "from the beginning." It is
they who continued with him in his trials (Luke 22:28). He has
kept them from the power of evil (17:6-8). As his own beloved
they will bear in their own life the hatred which the world directs
against him. But the holy and life-giving Spirit of God, "the
Spirit of him who raised Jesus from the dead" (Rom. 8:11), will
be in them (14:17). Their life, their words, their deeds, their sufferings will thus be the occasion, the place, where the mighty
Spirit bears his own witness in the hearts and consciences of men
and women so that they are brought to look again at the hated,
rejected, humiliated, crucified man and confess: "Jesus is Lord."
It is the Spirit who is sovereign. The promise to the community
of the disciples is not that they will have the Spirit at their disposal
to help them in their work of proclamation. That misunderstanding has profoundly distorted the missionary action of the Church

and provided the occasion for a kind of missionary triumphalism of which we are right to be ashamed. The Spirit is not the Church's auxiliary. The promise made here is not to the Church which is powerful and "successful" in a worldly sense. It is made to the Church which shares the tribulation and the humiliation of Jesus, the tribulation which arises from faithfulness to the truth in a world which is dominated by the lie. The promise is that, exactly in this tribulation and humiliation, the mighty Spirit of God will bear his own witness to the crucified Jesus as Lord and Giver of life.

16:1-4a

"I have said all this to you to keep you from falling away. They will put you out of the synagogues; indeed, the hour is coming when whoever kills you will think he is offering service to God. And they will do this because they have not known the Father, nor me. But I have said these things to you, that when their hour comes you may remember that I told you of them."

The mission of the Church in the world must follow the pattern of him who is its author and subject. It must bear the marks of the cross. As in the synoptic Gospels the solemnly re-iterated predictions of the passion of Jesus are echoed in the "mission charge" to the disciples (e.g., Matt. 10:16-25), so here the disciples are solemnly warned ("I have said this to you") to expect rejection and hatred. As there is an "hour" for the Lord, so there will be for them (v. 4a; cf. 13:1). And it will not be the heathen and the godless who reject them, but God's own people acting in a sincere belief that they are doing God's will. Like Saul of Tarsus they will regard the rejection and excommunication of Christians as a duty owed to God (e.g., Gal. 1:13f.; Phil. 3:6; Acts 26:9). That this is so is the terrible demonstration of the fact that it is in real darkness that the light shines, that human religious zeal is in fact ignorance of God, that those who say "We see" are blind (9:40f.). The danger for the disciples is not in what the world can do to them ("Do not fear those who kill the body" [Matt. 10:28]). The danger is that they may "fall away," as in fact they will do when the crisis of the passion comes (16:32; cf. Mark 14:27). But the solemn words of Jesus which the Holy Spirit, the Advocate, will bring to their remembrance (14:26) will enable

208

them to understand that this tribulation is simply their necessary participation in the tribulation of Jesus. Once again we are at the heart of what the Church does at every eucharist when the Lord invites his disciples to eat the bread and drink the cup which make them participants in his body broken and his blood shed once for all for the life of the world.

16:4b-11

"I did not say these things to you from the beginning, because I was with you. But now I am going to him who sent me; yet none of you asks me, 'Where are you going?' But because I have said these things to you, sorrow has filled your hearts. Nevertheless I tell you the truth; it is to your advantage that I go away, for if I do not go away, the Counselor will not come to you; but if I go, I will send him to you. And when he comes, he will convict the world of sin and of righteousness and of judgment: of sin, because they do not believe in me; of righteousness, because I go to the Father, and you will see me no more; of judgment, because the ruler of this world is judged."

Jesus had "from the beginning" chosen and called certain disciples to "follow him," to be with him and to be sent out. The synoptic Gospels contain a great deal of material indicating that Jesus sought to prepare them both for his own suffering and death and for the sufferings which would necessarily come to them. In truth it was only in the light of the resurrection and by the teaching of the Spirit that they could fully understand that it is the slain lamb who reigns (Rev. 5:6) and that it is "by the blood of the lamb" that the disciples are enabled to overcome the enemy of humankind (Rev. 12:11). The first effect of the prediction of tribulation is the sorrow of the disciples. They do not yet see that the "going" of Jesus means victory; although both Peter and Thomas had earlier asked in perplexity about the "going" (13:36; 14:5) they are asking no more. They are thinking sorrowfully of their own tribulations and not inquiring eagerly (as they would do if they understood) about the goal of the journey. As is so often the case with the followers of Jesus, the words "for me" displace the words "for him"; the disciple is concerned about his own security more than he is concerned that the Lord should "see of the travail of his soul and be satisfied."

Now the real truth is triumphantly asserted. The "going" of Jesus is not a bereavement whose pain is to be eased by the promise of a return. It is the necessary condition of a greater good, of the finishing of the work for which Jesus was sent. The word was made flesh: without this there is no gospel. This man Jesus, wholly belonging to a particular time and place and therefore conditioned and limited by all the contingent factors of language and culture which belong to every particular time and place, is at the same time the presence of the eternal word of God, the word through whom all things were made, in whom all that lives has life and from whom all light comes. If the presence of the word was not given in all the contingency of a particular time and place it could not be part of human public experience. There would be no revelation. There could be, perhaps, private "revelations"—spiritual perceptions in the heart of an individual or of many individuals. But there would be no revelation of God as part of the public history of mankind, as an event whose reality could become the object of publicly shared knowledge, and the visible center of a visible community. This is what it means that the word became flesh. But if the presence remained tied to and limited by the contingencies of a time and place, it could not become part of general human experience except at second hand. What belongs to one time and place is always slipping from our grasp. It recedes farther and farther into the past, and it is therefore always surrounded by sadness, the sadness of transience, the sadness that hangs over the home of a great man where the small memorials of his particular being—his chair, his slippers, his spectacles—are lovingly and sadly cherished by generations of his disciples.

The disciples of Jesus have no need of such memorials. Their master does not belong to the past. They have with them the living Spirit who is the Spirit of the Father and who is also the Spirit of Jesus, the Spirit whose presence is the foretaste of the coming glory. Therefore they do not look back but upward and forward. But, just as the word could only be present as flesh—as concrete human being—in a manner which exposed, judged, contradicted the world's ideas, so the Spirit can only be present when that contradiction has been carried to its conclusion, when the arguments and counterarguments have been finished and judgment has been passed. The "going" of Jesus by way of the cross is that final judgment. It is judgment in a unique sense, because in it the "ruler of the world"—represented by the combined authority of law, state, religion, temple, and public opinion—passed judgment upon Jesus and yet in that act of judgment sentence was passed upon the judge. The "ruler of the world" was ejected from his seat (12:31); the "principalities and powers" were disarmed (Col. 2:15). Until this has happened, until Jesus has "finished his work" and gone back to the Father, the revelation has not been fully given, the judgment of the world has not been finally pronounced, and therefore the new relationship of God to man which the revelation establishes cannot begin. But when his work is finished, when that action is completed which is both the dying of Jesus and his glorifying, the new relation can be established, namely, the sending of the Spirit of God. He is sent by the Father in response to the prayer of the Son (14:16); he is sent by the Son from the Father (15:26); he is sent by the Son because of his going to the Father (16:7). He is the Spirit of the Father who abides in the Son (1:33), and he descended upon Jesus at his baptism (1:32) and his life is communicated by Jesus to those whom he chooses (1:33; 20:22).

And the work of the Spirit is—as we would expect—to continue the work of Jesus. It is to continue that shining of the light in the darkness which exposes and convicts the sin of the world. So the witness becomes the prosecutor. Once more we see that the Spirit is not the domesticated auxiliary of the Church; he is the powerful advocate who goes before the Church to bring the world under conviction. We have already been told that the world cannot "receive" the Spirit "because it neither sees him nor knows him" (14:17). It is therefore preferable to follow the RSV (1971) margin and read "convict" rather than "convince." What the Spirit does is the continuation of what was earlier described as the work of the Son whom the Father sent into the world not to judge it but to save it, but whose coming nevertheless brings judgment because "men loved darkness rather than light" (3:16-21). According to 3:20 the light "exposes" the deeds of evil men (the same word which is here rendered by "convict") and this is what constitutes the judgment. In the same way, the presence of the "advocate" who comes from the Father in the name of Jesus "convicts" the world in the sense that it exposes the falsity of the world's most fundamental ideas, its ideas of what is sin, what is righteousness, and what is judgment.

We are now shown in more detail what that "exposure" will mean. It will be the work of the Spirit given to the community who share the tribulation of Jesus and are witnesses of his victory to convict the world in respect of sin "because they do not believe in me." Jesus is rejected and condemned as a sinner in the name of God's law. This failure of the world to respond in faith to the coming of God in the humble person of Jesus is sin. From the beginning the Bible testifies that the root of sin is unbelief. It is man's basic unwillingness to trust God for everything that is the source and substance of sin (Gen. 3:1-5; cf. Rom. 1:18-23). "The world understands sin as revolt against its own standards and ideals, the things which give it security. But to shut oneself off from the revelation that calls all worldly security in question and opens up another security—that is real sin" (Bultmann). The revelation of the presence of God in the crucifixion—of a man condemned as a sinner—is the overthrowing of the world's idea of what sin is. The preaching of the cross by a community which—in the power of the Spirit—carries the marks of the cross will be a continually repeated exposure of the false idea of sin and a continually repeated call to accept the revelation and believe. For sin is unbelief, and the only true righteousness is that which begins and ends in faith. Thus, on the day of Pentecost, when Peter in the power of the Spirit preached to the people of Jerusalem the message of the cross, they were "cut to the heart." It was they who were convicted as sinners, not the one whom they had sought to convict.

Furthermore, the Spirit will convict the world in respect of righteousness, "because I go to the Father, and you will see me no more." As unbelief is the essence of sin so faith is the essence of righteousness, and faith means precisely that we trust where we do not see. According to the world's understanding of righteousness Jesus was found to be in the wrong by the highest judicial authorities of the Church and state. He and his disciples were discredited and scattered. The end of the story was "the curse." But in the higher tribunal of the Father he was found to be "in the right." He was "designated Son of God in power according to the Spirit of holiness by his resurrection from the dead" (Rom. 1:4). "That Jesus stands justified before the Father means that Satan stands condemned" (Brown), and Satan is the "ruler of the world." The world's "righteousness" is exposed for what it truly is and another kind of righteousness is revealed, "the righteousness of God by faith in Jesus Christ for all who believe" (Rom. 3:22). What is visible has been overcome by what is invisible, and the presence of the Spirit in the believing community will confront the world with a kind of righteousness which exposes as false the "righteousness of the law," the "righteousness" which finds its security in passing certain visible tests. The presence of the Spirit will create another kind of righteousness which finds its security only "as seeing him who is invisible" (Heb. 11:27). It will live not by sight, not by visibly verifiable achievements, but by faith and hope—hope which is "a sure and steadfast anchor of the soul . . . that enters into the inner shrine behind the curtain, where Jesus has gone as a forerunner on our behalf" (Heb. 6:19).

And finally the Spirit will convict the world in respect of judgment, "because the ruler of this world is judged." The world has its own idea about judgment which arises from its ideas about sin and righteousness. The contemporaries of Jesus were looking for the coming of the just king who would condemn sinners and vindicate the righteous. Jesus announced the presence of that kingly rule, but scandalized his contemporaries by justifying sinners and condemning the righteous. In the unforgettable conclusion of the story of the two sons (Luke 15:11-32), the sinner is in the light and joy of the Father's house and the righteous is outside in the dark. The world is proved wrong in its idea of judgment. The one who had come as the bearer of God's kingly rule, and who had told that story to interpret the manner of his kingship, was condemned as a sinner and sentenced to a death which implied not only rejection by the highest human court but the curse of God. In that act of judgment the "ruler of the world" was judged (cf. 12:31). From now on the company of those who have been chosen and called to follow Jesus in the way that he is, to abide in him in love and obedience and so to share his tribulations, will be the bearers of that kingship which overturns all the world's ideas of judgment. The Spirit who is the Spirit of the Father abiding in Jesus will abide in them, and his presence will be the presence in foretaste of the true kingship and therefore of the true judgment. The Spirit whose presence is the foretaste of the kingly rule of God, and who is therefore the primary witness to Jesus, is by the same token the one whose presence exposes as false the world's idea of judgment.

Sin, righteousness, judgment—these three related words stand for something which belongs to the universal stock of human ideas. All people everywhere have ideas of right and wrong, and all people "draw the line" somewhere to mark off and to judge

213

what has to be condemned. These lines are drawn in a marvelous variety of ways. Ethical standards are notoriously relative to time and place and culture. In fact "ethical pluralism" has become almost an article of faith in our highly mobile and differentiated modern societies. For Western man, too, though in a different way, it is "scandalous" that the judgment should have actually been pronounced at a certain time and place in the ever moving stream of history. When the Fourth Gospel was being written, the world of that time was being proved wrong in its ideas of judgment (the differing ideas of Jew and Gentile, barbarian, Scythian, slave and free man) not just by the preaching of the disciples but above all by their faithfulness unto death as they followed the *via crucis* in love and obedience to Jesus. The advocate who was with them to strengthen ("comfort") them, who was the witness to Jesus in the midst of their sufferings, was also the one who could speak with power and authority to the conscience of "the world," to overthrow its proud confidence in its own judgment, and to "bring every thought into captivity to Christ" (II Cor. 10:5). The presence of that advocate is promised to the Church which goes the way of the cross, which knows the "foolishness" and "weakness" of the message of the cross to be in fact the wisdom and the power of God (I Cor. 1:18-25). It is promised to the end, because the Spirit is the firstfruit (Rom. 8:23) and the pledge (II Cor. 1:22; Eph. 1:14) of the kingdom.

16:12-15

"I have yet many things to say to you, but you cannot bear them now. When the Spirit of truth comes, he will guide you into all the truth; for he will not speak on his own authority, but whatever he hears he will speak, and he will declare to you the things that are to come. He will glorify me, for he will take what is mine and declare it to you. All that the Father has is mine; therefore I said that he will take what is mine and declare it to you."

The shining of the true light into the darkness of the world necessarily exposes the falsity of the world's ideas. But the negative work of judgment is only the shadow cast by that which obstructs the light. The purpose of the coming of Jesus is that all should come to the light. It is not to condemn the world that he has come, but that the world might be saved through him (3:17). That which is present in the words and works of Jesus is the shining of the true light; nothing has been hidden from the disciples which they were capable of receiving (15:15). But if the light is to reach the whole world there is yet very much to be said and done which cannot be received by this group of first-century Jews around a supper table in Jerusalem. The mission of the Church is not simply to go on repeating the *ipsissima verba* of Jesus in every new situation. If that had been in fact the mission of the Church, we should have required and should have had something totally different from the New Testament as we know it. We should have had something analogous to the Qur'an—a collection of sayings in Aramaic guaranteed to be a verbatim transcript of the words of Jesus. It would have had to be understood that these were strictly untranslatable, as the Qur'an is held by Muslims to be untranslatable, since every translation is an interpretation by a fallible human being. What we have, in fact, is a varied collection of interpretations of the sayings of Jesus rendered into another language by many different interpreters, each bringing to the task his own understanding of the Gospel. We have no indubitable transcript of any word of Jesus, except perhaps the few words preserved in Aramaic, and if we relied on such a transcript the Christian faith would be something quite different from what is set forth in the New Testament.

The New Testament is, in fact, the result of the first beginnings of the fulfilment of the promises of Jesus given here. On two occasions John has said that what he is recording was not understood at the time, but only afterward (2:22; 12:16). But all the four evangelists make it clear that the disciples did not understand the words and works of Jesus at the time, and that the whole of their testimony about Jesus is given in the light of their later faith (e.g., Mark 9:31f.). Only after Jesus was glorified could the disciples receive the Spirit who would make plain to them who is "the coming one" and what is "the kingdom of our father David that is coming (Mark 11:9f.).

The whole Christian message is about "the things that are coming," with its center in "the one who is to come." It is about the final judgment of the world, about the establishment of God's reign of justice and peace, and about the one who is king, judge, and savior. The work of the Spirit of truth, who both is and imparts the truth because he is the Spirit of God, and who is promised to those who abide in him who is the truth, will be to guide them along the road which—like Israel of old—they must travel toward the fulfilment of the promise. As they travel this road they will meet wholly new situations, new peoples, new cultures, new structures which the "ruler of the world" has devised to embody his claim to power. In these new situations it will be of no avail merely to repeat the words of Jesus spoken in another situation. The Spirit of truth will show them the way to go by speaking to them the word of God (which is not other than Jesus himself) in that situation.

At an early stage of its journey the Church had a vivid confirmation of the promise when it confronted the question of the place of the Gentiles in God's purpose. The events recounted with great care in Acts 10 and 11 are often summarized as "the conversion of Cornelius," but they were equally the conversion of Peter and of the Church. It was no missionary zeal, and no native liberalism of Peter, which took him to the house of an uncircumcised Roman soldier and placed him in the position of having to tell the story of Jesus in that pagan household. It was the Spirit who put him there, and it was the Spirit who shattered all of Peter's strongest religious certainties by giving to Cornelius and his household exactly the same experience of deliverance and joy as the apostles themselves had received. In the presence of that *fait accompli* Peter, and—later—the whole Church, had simply to follow where they were led, even though it was a path for which nothing in the teaching of Jesus had mandated them. We read that when the whole assembly heard Peter's report, "They were silenced. And they glorified God, saying, 'Then to the Gentiles also God has granted repentance until life' " (Acts 11:18).

They were silenced because they had to recognize something new. Jesus had never spoken or acted to call in question the law of circumcision (as he had called in question the law of the Sabbath). The Church was entering a new way which it had not trodden before. Nor did the Church formulate a new policy in this matter by reflection upon and development of the remembered words of Jesus. It was a fresh action of the living Spirit which confronted the Church with the necessity for a new decision. "The word of Jesus is not a collection of doctrines that is in need of supplementation, nor is it a developing principle that will only be unfolded in the history of ideas; as the Spirit's proclamation it always remains the word spoken into the world from beyond" (Bultmann). But this word is the word of *Jesus*; it is not another word. The work of the Spirit does not lead past, or beyond, or away from Jesus. Cornelius and his household received the Spirit through the apostle's preaching of Jesus and they were at once baptized into the name of Jesus, confessing him as Lord. The Spirit glorifies Jesus, taking what belongs to Jesus and making it plain to the Church. In this way the Spirit guides the Church along the missionary road whose goal is that all the nations and the whole creation should be offered to him to whom it rightfully belongs.

This strict definition is not to be condemned (as in much modern writing) as arising from a narrow-minded or sectarian spirit. The Holy Spirit is not to be identified with any and every form of spiritual liveliness. John's readers were subject to the very common temptation to do just this, and needed to be on their guard. "Beloved, do not believe every spirit, but test the spirits to see whether they are of God; for many false prophets have gone out into the world. By this you know the Spirit of God: every spirit which confesses that Jesus Christ has come in the flesh is of God" (I John 4:1f.). The name of Jesus does not stand for one among the possible names in the spiritual world. Jesus is the one through whom all things were made, and therefore "all that the Father has" belongs by right to him. To deny this is to deny the truth. To confess this is not a human possibility; it is a work of the Spirit of God himself who guides the Church along its missionary road, enabling it to meet ever new and unprecedented situations, and "declaring" to it in every new situation that which belongs to Jesus because it belongs to the Father.

The pilgrim Church, the Church *in via*, does not possess all the truth. The truth in its fullness will only be known when God has completed his purpose to "unite all things in [Christ], things in heaven and things on earth" (Eph. 1:10). But, *in via*, the Church has the promise of the Spirit of truth to guide it into the "truth-as-a-whole" (v. 13), which can only be fully known at the end, when "the things that are to come" have fully come. The teaching Church can abide in the truth only if it is a learning Church, and it learns by pressing forward to share with all the nations the riches of the one who has come and is to come.

16:16-24

"A little while, and you will see me no more; again a little while, and you will see me." Some of his disciples said to one another, "What is

this that he says to us, 'A little while, and you will not see me, and again a little while, and you will see me'; and, 'because I go to the Father'?" They said, "What does he mean by 'a little while'? We do not know what he means." Jesus knew that they wanted to ask him; so he said to them, "Is this what you are asking yourselves, what I meant by saying, 'A little while, and you will not see me, and again a little while, and you will see me'? Truly, truly, I say to you, you will weep and lament, but the world will rejoice; you will be sorrowful, but your sorrow will turn into joy. When a woman is in travail she has sorrow, because her hour has come; but when she is delivered of the child, she no longer remembers the anguish, for joy that a child is born into the world. So you have sorrow now, but I will see you again and your hearts will rejoice, and no one will take your joy from you. In that day you will ask nothing of me. Truly, truly, I say to you, if you ask anything of the Father, he will give it to you in my name. Hitherto you have asked nothing in my name; ask, and you will receive, that your joy may be full."

"He will declare to you the things that are to come." But how long will they be in coming? This inescapable question is constantly heard throughout the New Testament, and it is inescapable because the fundamental message of Jesus, the "good news" which he brought, was that the reign of God has drawn near. But how far off is "near"? That question cannot but be in the minds and on the lips of those "upon whom the end of the ages has come" (I Cor. 10:11).

As the long discourse draws to a close, Jesus repeats its opening theme: "Yet a little while I am with you" (13:33), but now—resuming all the words of comfort which have followed—he adds: "Again a little while, and you will see me." Seven times in four verses the words "a little while" are repeated; nowhere else in the whole discourse is such immense emphasis laid on a single phrase. The reader is being warned that something enormously important is being said. But what, exactly, is it? What does "you will see me" mean? We have already seen how the similar promise of Jesus to "manifest himself" to the disciples evoked the perplexed question of Judas (14:21f.). Now there is a new perplexity because Jesus has said "I go to the Father, and you will see me no more" (vv. 10 and 17). What kind of "seeing" is being spoken of?

From early times interpreters have been divided. Some have understood that Jesus is speaking of his appearances to the disciples after his resurrection; others have taken it to refer to the

218

Parousia at the end of time. We saw at 14:22ff. that Jesus was promising a kind of self-manifestation which was different from the popular expectation of the Parousia in that he would be manifest to the disciples and not to the world. But at that point also the traditional language of the final coming ("in that day") was used. Here the same phrase is used (v. 23), and the eschatological emphasis is immensely strengthened by the use of a very familiar Old Testament parable—the parable of the travail of childbirth (v. 21). It was a familiar thought that as there is no birth without pain, so the joy of the new age of the Messiah must be preceded by tribulation. The tribulations of Jesus and his disciples are in fact the birth pangs of the new creation.

In other words, Jesus is speaking both of his manifestation of himself to his disciples after the resurrection, and of the full vision of God in the new age, for the one is the foretaste of the other. The ambiguity is deliberate and it conveys the essential point which is being made. "By this ambiguity John means to convey that the death and resurrection were themselves eschatological events which both prefigured and anticipated the final events" (Barrett). It is precisely in this way that the Spirit will enable the disciples to understand "the things that are to come." They will understand (and the whole New Testament bears witness to this) that the tribulations of Christ, and the share of those tribulations which comes to them as his disciples, are the birth pangs of the new age. Since they will understand this, they will not have to ask the kind of peripheral questions which they now ask (v. 23a). Rather they will have the joy of Jesus in themselves, and they will have the absolute assurance of answered petition (vv. 23b and 24) which is proper to children of a loving father. When this same theme was treated in answer to the question of Judas (14:18-24), the emphasis in describing the new life was on love and obedience. Here the emphasis is upon understanding and joy. The difference is that now we have been introduced to the work of the Spirit of truth, which is to make plain to the disciples "the things to come." These "things to come," which are the subject matter of eschatology, are seen to comprise a new and unique tension of having and hoping, of joy and patience. The disciples will be able to say of the eternal life of God, "We have seen," and at the same time, "We know that when he appears . . . we shall see him as he is" (I John 1:3 and 3:2). They will be able to speak in the same breath of rejoicing in hope and rejoicing in tribulation (Rom. 5:2f.) because they have received the Spirit as the first-fruit of the new creation (Rom. 8:18-25).

This does not mean that "the evangelist has used the primitive Christian ideas and hopes to describe the stages through which the life of the believer has to pass" (Bultmann). The Bible is concerned with the public history of the world; this reductionist conversion of it into religions psychology is a product of the contemporary Western culture which accepts another public "myth" and privatizes the gospel. There are really "things which are to come," but "he who is to come" has come. The birth pangs of the new world have begun in his passion, and those who follow him share them. But the joy of the new creation has also begun in his resurrection, and those who follow the way of the cross also share the joy of the new world. For them, the sufferings of this present age are but "a little while" compared to the glory that is already dawning (Rom. 8:18-39).

16:25-28

"I have said this to you in figures; the hour is coming when I shall no longer speak to you in figures but tell you plainly of the Father. In that day you will ask in my name; and I do not say to you that I shall pray the Father for you; for the Father himself loves you, because you have loved me and have believed that I came from the Father. I came from the Father and have come into the world; again, I am leaving the world and going to the Father."

St. John has twice explicitly stated that the disciples did not understand the words of Jesus until after his resurrection. The synoptic Gospels also make it clear that the teaching of Jesus was "riddles" except to those to whom the secret was given (Mark 4:11f.). It was not that the teachings of Jesus were complicated; they were—in one sense—extremely clear and simple so that even a child can easily remember and retell his words. It is rather that because they embody God's revelation of himself which overturns all human wisdom, they can only be understood by those who have been "born from above" by the power of the Spirit (3:1-5). But "the hour" of this new dispensation has not yet come. It is "coming," and when it comes Jesus will speak to them "plainly of the Father." The word translated "plainly" (*parrhēsia*) is very often used in the New Testament to describe the "boldness" with which believers make both their prayers to God and their public witness to the world. It is a characteristic mark of the presence of the Spirit, who assures us that we are not slaves but children of God and so enables us to pray boldly, "Abba, Father" (Rom. 8:15-17). As it will be the work of the Spirit to take what belongs to Jesus and make it plain to the disciples (16:14), so Jesus himself will speak to them as he did to John on Patmos when he was "in the Spirit on the Lord's day" (Rev. 1:10). This boldness in the Spirit will enable believers to "draw near with confidence (*parrhēsia*) to the throne of grace" (Heb. 4:16), because they come in the name of Jesus and are united with him in love and faith (v. 27). Jesus will no longer be—so to speak—a separate mediator standing between them and the Father. They will come in Jesus' name, as those whose life is his life, who can say "Abba" with the same freedom as his, and who are beloved by the Father as he is.

These disciples have truly believed that Jesus "came from the Father" (vv. 27b and 30). But this half of the full truth is not enough to secure their full loyalty when the crisis comes. As the sequel will show, they have not yet understood what is meant when Jesus says: "I am leaving the world and going to the Father" (v. 28b). This hiddenness of the revelation which they have received, and the consequent "scattering" (v. 32) and "falling away" (Mark 14:27) of the disciples, is something which they cannot yet understand or accept. Even the words of comfort which he has spoken to them will not be understood until "the hour" comes when the Spirit is given.

16:29-33

His disciples said, "Ah, now you are speaking plainly, not in any figure! Now we know that you know all things, and need none to question you; by this we believe that you came from God." Jesus answered them, "Do you now believe? The hour is coming, indeed it has come, when you will be scattered, every man to his home, and will leave me alone; yet I am not alone, for the Father is with me. I have said this to you, that in me you may have peace. In the world you have tribulation; but be of good cheer, I have overcome the world."

The disciples are confident that they do understand. As at the end of the long discourse on the bread of life they are sure that they "have believed, and have come to know" (6:69), so it is now. Jesus has answered all their questions even before they have been able to ask (vv. 16-19). He knows the secrets of all men's hearts. They are convinced that he is indeed the one sent from God. But even Nicodemus could say as much (3:2). They have not yet understood the second part of what he said: "I am leaving the world and going to the Father." They have not understood the necessity for the passion of Jesus, for his going on before them, and for his new mode of presence with them in the Spirit. Consequently the hour is at hand when they will be scattered. This "hour" is not in the future but "now." The "hour" of which Jesus had so often spoken, the eschatological hour of revelation and judgment, will be—first of all—an hour of dismay and unbelief for the disciples. Jesus will be alone. The terrible prophecy of the day of judgment will be fulfilled: "Alone I have trodden the wine press, and from the peoples no one was with me" (Isa. 63:3). In the final confrontation between the reign of God and the ruler of this world, Jesus will be left alone. The whole world will be on the other side in the final battle. The disciples will have been scattered to their own homes, taking refuge in the supposed securities of the old order, part of the unbelieving world.

Yet Jesus is not alone, for the Father himself is present in his confrontation with the ruler of this world. The cross is, in fact, the victory of God in which the ruler of this world is judged and cast out. And these disciples whom Jesus has chosen and bound to himself in love and obedience will, by their union with him, share in the victory even as they share in the tribulation which he has endured for their sake. The victory is wholly his. At the end, the triumph song of the Church will not be "We have overcome" but "Worthy is the Lamb who was slain" (Rev. 5:12). Meanwhile the Church will have peace in the midst of tribulation, the peace which is God's gift in Jesus Christ. The life of the Church will thus be a strange paradox—the peace which is the mark of God's victorious reign enjoyed here and now in the midst of the battle with the powers of this world. Precisely these tribulations, the mark of the final conflict between the kingdom of God and the powers of the world, will be the mark of those who already enjoy in foretaste the peace of God's victory.

So the long discourse which began with the double theme of glory and separation (13:31-33) ends with a restatement of the same theme in reverse order: the scattering of the disciples and the victory of their Lord.

THE CONSECRATION
(17:1-26)

WHEN A MAN IS GOING ON A LONG JOURNEY HE WILL FIND time on the eve of departure for quiet talk with his family, and—if he is a man of God—will end by commending to God not only himself and his journey, but also the family whom he leaves behind. Very surely will this be so if his journey is the last journey. Moses, at the end of his long farewell discourse to the family of Israel, turns his eyes to heaven to invoke the blessing of the Lord (Deut. 32–33). So Jesus, at the end of his long farewell discourse, lifts his eyes to heaven and prays for himself and for his disciples. (The proposal of Bultmann to place this prayer before the discourse must surely be accounted "a blunder against good literary sense" [Brown].) The prayer leads us into the very heart of the ministry and message of Jesus, and no exposition can hope to do more than suggest some aspects of its meaning.

The whole discourse was set in motion by the abrupt departure of Judas on the errand that was to bring Jesus to the cross. It is a concentrated setting forth of the source, nature, and end of that new kind of existence which will be made possible for the disciples by the dying of Jesus. It falls, as we have seen, into two parts. In the first the main emphasis is on the fact that the disciples will participate in the realization of the eschatological promise of the dwelling of God with his people; in the second part the emphasis is on the mission of the disciples to continue in the world the mission for which Jesus came from the Father. Now all is drawn together in a prayer in which Jesus solemnly consecrates himself to the Father and consecrates his disciples to be sent into the world as the means by which the world may come to believe.

All four Gospels make reference to the prayers of Jesus, both

223

alone and in the presence of the disciples. In no other place do we have such a long and carefully composed record of his prayer. The setting—let us again remember—is the last supper of Jesus with his disciples. The synoptic Gospels do not refer to a prayer of Jesus at the supper; they lay great emphasis upon his prayer in the garden immediately before the betrayal and arrest. But they also record the mysterious words, for which we have also the earlier authority of St. Paul, spoken as he gave to the disciples the bread and the wine: "Take, eat; this is my body." "Drink of it, all of you; for this is my blood of the covenant, which is poured out for many for the forgiveness of sins" (Matt. 26:26f.). We know that from earliest times the Church was accustomed to meet regularly to eat and drink bread and wine with the repetition of these words, and that the action was preceded by the reading and exposition of the words of Jesus and of the apostles and by prayer. The evangelist (so it would appear), confident of his true understanding of the mind of Jesus, and no doubt knowing that Jesus did in fact pray in this way during the supper, has given us this rendering of his prayer in words which express in con-centrated form his understanding of the mysterious words and actions of the Lord on that night when his disciples were still unable to grasp his intention. He can do this because the promise of Jesus has been fulfilled that the Holy Spirit "will bring to your remembrance all that I have said to you" (14:26). The prayer is not a free invention of the evangelist; nor is it a tape recording of the words of Jesus. It is a representation of what Jesus was doing when he prayed in the presence of his disciples during the supper, a re-presentation which rests upon the authority of the beloved disciple guided by the Holy Spirit in and through the continuous experience of the community which gathers week by week to rehearse again the words and action of Jesus on that night when he was betrayed.

The words with which the whole long discourse began were: "Now is the Son of man glorified," and glory is the central theme of the prayer. To interpret the word "glory" is to interpret the whole Gospel, and although we have met the word many times in earlier chapters it is here that the fullest exposition is called for. By way of introduction let it be simply noted that the first two evangelists do not speak of glory in relation to the earthly min-istry of Jesus, but only in relation to the future appearing of the Son of man. St. Luke refers also to the manifestation of glory in the transfiguration of Jesus on the mountain. St. John, as we have seen, affirms that Jesus manifested his glory to the disciples during his earthly ministry but concentrates his references to the theme of glory primarily upon the passion. The central theme, therefore, of the consecration prayer is the theme of glory.

17:1-5

When Jesus had spoken these words, he lifted up his eyes to heaven and said, "Father, the hour has come; glorify thy Son that the Son may glorify thee, since thou hast given him power over all flesh, to give eternal life to all whom thou hast given him. And this is eternal life, that they know thee the only true God, and Jesus Christ whom thou hast sent. I glorified thee on earth, having accomplished the work which thou gavest me to do; and now, Father, glorify thou me in thy own presence with the glory which I had with thee before the world was made."

Jesus had "spoken these words." They are truly the word of the Lord, as he has repeatedly emphasized, and they have been given to the disciples. Now he "lifted his eyes to heaven." He did what the publican did not dare to do (Luke 18:13). The synoptic Gospels all tell us that Jesus "looked up" when he prayed. For the Lord is also the child, the Son, who looks up in the freedom of love and obedience to the Father. "Abba," that tender and intimate word, contains in itself all the substance of the new relationship to God which the death of Jesus was to make possible for sinful human beings (Gal. 4:4-7). It is the Father who has brought Jesus to this hour, the hour whose imminence has been the horizon of the whole ministry.

"Glorify thy Son that the Son may glorify thee." This terse petition contains the essential substance of the whole. "Glory" is plainly one of the fundamental words of the Bible. It expresses that which is—so to speak—constitutive of God's being and nature, and at the same time it denotes the honor which ought to be paid to God. But—and this is what the whole Gospel tells us—these two meanings are mutually bound together because the glory of God as it is revealed in Jesus is seen not in seeking honor but in giving honor. The word "God" does not mean a monad seeking honor for itself. At the very outset of the Gospel, where the evangelist says of Jesus, "We beheld his glory," he at once adds: "glory as of the only Son from the Father" (1:14). Jesus does not seek to be honored but honors the Father: in that he manifests the divine glory. But he can only do this as the Father gives him the power to do so. In the decisive hour, when the honoring of his Father must be accomplished at the cost of the agony and shame of the passion, he prays that the Father may honor him so that he may be enabled by the offering of perfect love and obedience to honor the Father. The glory of God is a reciprocal relationship: it is something forever freely given.

The purpose of this manifestation in the midst of history ("on earth") of the eternal glory of God in heaven is—as we shall see—the communication of this glory to those who believe, making them partakers of the divine glory (vv. 22f.). It is "to bring many sons to glory" (Heb. 2:10). For this purpose Jesus is the bearer of the universal authority of God over the whole creation. All authority in heaven and on earth is given to him (cf. Matt. 28:18). He is therefore able to give "to all who received him, who believe in his name" (1:12) the authority to become—through him—children of God and so to share in his eternal life. But to believe in him is, as we have been repeatedly told, no human possibility. It is the gift of God, for no one can come to Jesus unless the Father draws him (6:44). Here the disciples are seen as a single gift of the Father to the Son, one body to be consecrated and sent into the world to continue the mission of the Son (vv. 18f.). They are a very small company but they have a universal mission because Jesus is the bearer of universal authority.

They are the Father's gift to Jesus, and his gift to them is "eternal life," which is defined as the knowledge of the Father and the Son. The Old Testament speaks of "knowing the LORD" as the supreme blessing available to men, and when Jesus was challenged by the Sadducees on the belief in resurrection he replied by quoting the passage in which God is described as the God of Abraham, of Isaac, and of Jacob. These patriarchs "knew the LORD," and the Lord acknowledged them. They therefore belong to him, and it is inconceivable that God should be a god of the dead. Knowing the Lord is not merely intellectual apprehension: it is sharing in the life of God which is beyond the ravages of time. But how is God to be known? Jesus had said— according to a saying preserved in the first and third Gospels— "No one knows the Son except the Father, and no one knows the Father except the Son and any one to whom the Son chooses to reveal him" (Matt. 11:27 and Luke 10:22). True knowledge of God is to be enabled through Jesus in every situation, in face of every disaster, and in the hour of death itself to look up and say, "Father." To be able to do that is the gift which Jesus has authority to give. It is not a purely intellectual but supremely a practical knowledge. It is following "the way" (14:6) which leads to the Father. It is already a participation in the eternal life of God in which the transience of human experience is redeemed by the presence of its unchanging source and goal. It is life in the Spirit through whom we are able to cry "Abba, Father," who assures us that we are children of God and whose presence is the foretaste of glory for those who are willing to suffer with Jesus (Rom. 8:15-17).

Jesus has manifested God's glory on earth by a life of total love and obedience to be consummated in the cross (cf. 19:30: "It is accomplished"). In this way he has given honor to the Father. Now, as he approaches the consummation he prays that the Father may honor him, enabling him to offer the perfect sacrifice of love and thus to manifest on earth the perfect glory which is the life of heaven—the eternal love of God in whom Father and Son are one in an unceasing life of self-giving. It is by treading the road to the cross in utter faithfulness to the end that Jesus manifests the glory of God and so makes it possible for those whom the Father has given to share in this glory. "It was fitting that he, for whom and by whom all things exist, in bringing many sons to glory, should make the pioneer of their salvation perfect through suffering" (Heb. 2:10). And thus those who follow the way of the cross can say: "We all, with unveiled faces, beholding the glory of the Lord, are being changed into his likeness from one degree of glory to another" (II Cor. 3:19). Thus the intention of God "before the world was made" is fulfilled, for all things exist for God's glory, and a man who has lost the capacity for worship, who does not know how to "look up," has lost the clue to his humanity.

17:6-19

"I have manifested thy name to the men whom thou gavest me out of the world; thine they were, and thou gavest them to me, and they have kept thy word. Now they know that everything that thou hast given me is from thee; for I have given them the words which thou gavest me, and they have received them and know in truth that I came from thee; and they have believed that thou didst send me. I am praying for them; I am

not praying for the world but for those whom thou hast given me, for they are thine; all mine are thine, and thine are mine, and I am glorified in them. And now I am no more in the world, but they are in the world, and I am coming to thee. Holy Father, keep them in thy name, which thou hast given me, that they may be one, even as we are one. While I was with them, I kept them in thy name, which thou hast given me; I have guarded them, and none of them is lost but the son of perdition, that the scripture might be fulfilled. But now I am coming to thee; and these things I speak in the world, that they may have my joy fulfilled in themselves. I have given them thy word; and the world has hated them because they are not of the world, even as I am not of the world. I do not pray that thou shouldst take them out of the world, but that thou shouldst keep them from the evil one. They are not of the world, even as I am not of the world. Sanctify them in the truth; thy word is truth. As thou didst send me into the world, so I have sent them into the world. And for their sake I consecrate myself, that they also may be consecrated in truth."

The work of Jesus is the communication of the name of God to a community. He does not bequeath to posterity a body of teaching preserved in a book—like the Qur'an. He does not leave behind an ideal or a program. He leaves behind a community—the Church.

This community exists not because of decisions which its members have made. It is not constituted by the faith, insight, or moral excellence of its members. It exists because God has called its members out of the world by his own action and given them to Jesus. They are those whom God had chosen "before the foundation of the world" (Eph. 1:4).

Jesus has manifested to this God-given community the "name of God." Without that they cannot be sent on their mission, as Moses could not be sent on his mission to liberate Israel from bondage unless he was entrusted with the name of the one who sent him (Ex. 3:13-14). That mysterious name "I am" was revealed to Moses at the burning bush. For centuries it had been held in such reverence that it could not be pronounced in public. But Jesus has spoken it and in so doing has communicated not merely the sound of the name but the real presence of the one who alone can say, "I am." These disciples have received and have believed this communication of the name. There are many things that they have not understood, many things they have misunderstood. Consequently at the crucial moment they will be put to shame (16:29-32). But this they have received and believed, that Jesus is the one whom the Father has sent; and that the words of Jesus are the words of God. And it is through them that the world will come to believe the same (vv. 21 and 23). Through them, therefore, the ancient word of the Lord will be fulfilled: "To me every knee shall bow, every tongue shall swear" (Isa. 45:23), but the fulfilment will come "at the name of Jesus . . . to the glory of God the Father" (Phil. 2:10f.), for it is Jesus who has manifested the name of God—not by claiming glory for himself but by giving glory to the Father in a life and death of perfect love and obedience.

This the disciples have come to know and believe, and upon their faithful witness to what they have heard and seen and touched and handled (I John 1:1) the fulfilment of Jesus' mission depends. Therefore, before he sends them on their mission he prays for them. His purpose is that the world should be saved (3:17), but he does not pray directly for the world because he is not carrying out this purpose otherwise than through the community which is the Father's gift. The name of Jesus is not to be represented in the world by a series of doctrines, moral ideals, principles, or programs. It is to be represented by a community which—with all its misunderstandings, sins, and betrayals—believes and knows that Jesus is the apostle of God and that his words are the word of God.

This community is one among the many communities of which human society is made up. It is not distinguished by any special graces or virtues or powers. It might be described as a collection of "nobodies" (I Cor. 1:26-28). But—offensive as it may be to a certain kind of rationality—it is to this community that the name of the God of heaven and earth is revealed, for Jesus is not the head of a sect but the king and head of the human race (Eph. 1:22f.). All that belongs to Jesus belongs to God. But also all that belongs to God belongs to Jesus. The pronouns have moved from personal to neuter, emphasizing the cosmic universality of Christ's person and work, but in the last phrase—"I am glorified in them"—we are reminded that it is in those (persons) who have been given by the Father to Jesus that the glory of God is shown forth and Jesus is honored. They are the firstfruit and sign of the new creation in which all things in heaven and earth will be brought into a unity with Jesus as their head (Eph. 1:10; cf. Col. 1:18-20).

But this bringing of the whole creation into a unity is not and cannot be a smooth evolutionary process in which the powers inherent in the world move toward their consummation. There is no straight line to the "Omega point." For the world, which God made and loves, has fallen under a hostile power and the way to unity can only be by way of conflict and separation. That conflict took place in the passion of Jesus. The way Jesus goes, the way the disciples must follow, is the way of the cross. This means separation. These friends of Jesus, the nucleus of the new creation which had been the gift of the Father to Jesus, must suffer abrupt separation from him who had hitherto guarded them in the power of the name of God. The God whose name is "I am" and who had chosen Israel to be the bearer of that name, had said, "Consecrate yourselves therefore, and be holy, for I am holy" (Lev. 11:44). Jesus now uses the phrase "Holy Father" as he prays that the reconstituted Israel may be kept in the name which the Father had given to Jesus and he had given to them, for "the name of the LORD is a strong tower; the righteous man runs into it and is safe" (Prov. 18:10). To be kept in this name is to be holy, for holiness is the quality of that which belongs wholly to God. It is also to be one, for God is one. Holiness and unity are therefore not alternative options for the Church. If the disciples are kept in the name which Jesus has received from the Father, they will be one.

This unity is threatened by the power of the devil, the evil one whose characteristic work is to divide, to undermine faith, to sow suspicion and strife. This work of the devil has always threatened the company of disciples. Even at the supper there had been strife as to who was the greatest (Luke 22:24ff.). But Jesus had mastered the evil one, breaking down his stronghold and plundering his goods (Mark 2:27). Therefore he had been able to keep the disciples from becoming captives again to the devil, and to ensure that when they were scattered and dispersed they would be brought together again (Luke 22:31f.).

Yet the devil has his secret agent in the very heart of that company (13:2 and 27). It is by his deed that the final conflict will be precipitated, the conflict in which the power of the devil will be finally unmasked and broken. Therefore the treachery of Judas is taken up into the divine strategy of salvation even as it had been already anticipated in many passages of scripture (e.g., Ps. 41:9). It is in fact this act of Judas which provides the occasion for Jesus to "come to the Father," making that decisive separation which is the necessary condition for the gathering up of all things

into a unity in the name of Jesus. This means also a separation
for the disciples. They will no longer be under his immediate
protection as they have been; they will be separated from the
world because it will direct against them the hatred which it has
directed against Jesus. But they will have the joy of Jesus fulfilled
in themselves, the joy of total surrender to the Father. Thus they
will be blessed when the world reviles and persecutes them (Matt.
5:11). Affliction will be the occasion of joy in the Holy Spirit
(I Thess. 1:6). They will know that their share in Christ's sufferings will be the pledge of their share in his glory (Rom. 8:17).

When the Church is kept in the holy name of God it has a
final commitment which is outside the comprehension of the
world. Without this radical otherworldliness the Church has no
serious business with the world. Archimedes said: "Give me a
point outside the world for a fulcrum and I will move the world
with a lever." If the Church does not rest on a point outside the
world it has no leverage with the world. All its tugging and
straining is but a minor disturbance within the life of the world,
and therefore it is still under the power of the evil one. The
Church is marked off from the world by the fact that it has
received and must witness to the word of God which is the truth
and which thereby calls in question all the so-called axioms, ab-
solutes, and self-evident propositions which are the stock-in-trade
of the world's life. It has to bear witness to the weakness and
folly of a crucified messiah as the power and wisdom by which
the world exists, is sustained, and will be judged. To accept this
means to accept the overturning of the accepted wisdom of the
world. It is therefore not a human possibility; it is a gift of God,
a miracle, a new birth from above. Between the Church and the
world, therefore, lies the boundary line which is called "conversion," and if the Church seeks a relation with the world which
ignores this, it falls into the power of the evil one. Jesus prays—
and this is the unceasing prayer of the glorified Christ (Heb.
7:25)—that they may be kept as the absolute possession of the
holy Father in the truth which is his word spoken in the Son. He
prays the prayer which they must daily pray: "Deliver us from
the evil one."

But this does not mean that they are to find their safety in
separation from the world. That kind of otherworldliness is forbidden. They are not to inhabit a ghetto but to go forth on a
mission. They are sent, as Jesus was sent. At this point the word

"mission" cannot be replaced by the word "presence." The second person of the Holy Trinity has been present in the world from its beginning. "He was in the world, and the world was made by him" (1:10). But—and this is the mystery of the power of the evil one—"the world knew him not," and therefore it was necessary that he should "come to his own" (1:11), that the Father should send him—send him who was always present. The recognition that Jesus is the one whom the Father sent is the essence of the Christian faith, and its corollary in that Jesus has sent his disciples into the world in the same manner and for the same purpose for which he himself was sent by the Father.

It was the Father who consecrated Jesus and sent him into the world (10:36), and now Jesus prays to the Father that he will likewise consecrate the disciples so that they may be sent into the world. But these two consecrations are not parallel actions. Their consecration depends absolutely on his. They will be consecrated in the truth which is God's self-revelation only because he consecrates himself. No priest in the old covenant could say, "I consecrate myself." The priest is consecrated by God, and in turn consecrates to God an offering which must be without blemish (e.g., Lev. 22:20). Jesus alone is without blemish and therefore he alone, both priest and victim, can say: "I consecrate myself." The writer to the Hebrews takes the words of Psalm 40 to interpret the action to which the words of Jesus refer. "Sacrifice and offering thou hast not desired, but a body hast thou prepared for me; in burnt offerings and sin offerings thou hast taken no pleasure. Then I said: 'Lo, I have come to do thy will, O God' " (Heb. 10:5f.; see Ps. 40:6-8). This perfect act of love and obedience to the Father is that act in which all sacrifice is consummated and ended. No further sacrifice can be added to this. But it would be a terrible misunderstanding if we left the matter there—as evangelical Christianity sometimes has done. The self-consecration of Jesus in that one "full, perfect, and sufficient sacrifice" is "for their sake, that they also may be consecrated in the truth." The purpose is that in and through the sacrifice of Jesus the disciples also may become a consecrated offering to the Father in the truth which is God's word. The writer to the Hebrews expresses the same thing in another way when he says: "By that will we have been sanctified through the offering of the body of Jesus Christ once for all."

In thus interpreting the prayer of Jesus at the supper, the

beloved disciple is expounding the true meaning of the mysterious words which Jesus had spoken when he shared bread and wine with the disciples, told them that he was giving them his broken body and his shed blood, and commanded them both to eat and drink now, and to continue doing so in the future as an act of recall. The meaning of these words and actions, and of this command which the disciples had obeyed even when they did not understand, was that his dying was to be no isolated event which might be remembered or forgotten in the vast jumble of historical happenings. Rather it was to be the means by which they themselves would be taken up into his perfect consecration to the Father and sent into the world to continue, not only by verbal proclamation but also by a common life which embodied the same consecration, his total consecration in love and obedience to the Father. The Church is sent into the world to challenge the false pretensions of the prince of the world, not in any power or wisdom or greatness of its own. It is sent in the power of his consecration. Its victory is the paradoxical victory of the cross. It is sent "bearing about in the body the dying of Jesus, that the life of Jesus may also be manifested in the body" (II Cor. 4:10). The mission of the Church is effected only through its participation in the passion of Jesus as he challenges and masters the power of the evil one. And, conversely, there is no participation in Christ without participation in this passion and this conflict.

17:20-26

"I do not pray for these only, but also for those who believe in me through their word, that they may all be one; even as thou, Father, art in me and I in thee, that they also may be in us, so that the world may believe that thou hast sent me. The glory which thou hast given me I have given to them, that they may be one even as we are one, I in them and thou in me, that they may become perfectly one, so that the world may know that thou hast sent me and hast loved them even as thou hast loved me. Father, I desire that they also, whom thou hast given me, may be with me where I am, to behold my glory which thou hast given me in thy love for me before the foundation of the world. O righteous Father, the world has not know thee, but I have known thee; and these know that thou hast sent me. I made known to them thy name, and I will make it known, that the love with which thou hast loved me may be in them, and I in them."

The sending of the disciples into the world is not an empty gesture. They are chosen and sent in order to "go and bear fruit" (15:16). And so the prayer of Jesus extends beyond the first disciples to include all who will come to believe "through their word." The disciples are to be present in the world, not withdrawn from it. But presence is not enough; they must also speak, for faith comes by hearing. There can be no believing that Jesus is the messenger of God unless the name of Jesus is spoken.

To those who thus believe there is given that same glory which the Father has given to Jesus. They also will be taken up into that mutual honoring which is a participation in the being of God. They will learn to look up and say, "Abba, Father." They will come to be children of God and therefore share in the unique "glory as of the only Son from the Father" (1:14). In them, therefore, Jesus will be glorified (v. 10). As they learn to look up "with unveiled faces" they will be changed "from one degree of glory to another" (II Cor. 3:10). Even the agents of the churches engaged in the humble task of collecting charitable gifts will be "the glory of Christ" (II Cor. 8:23). And the sufferings of one for the sake of the gospel will be the glory of all (Eph. 3:13).

The corollary is that those who receive this glory will be one. Children of one Father should live together as one family. Therefore, as Jesus prays that his disciples may be kept one in the name of God, so he prays that all who believe may be one, living in one household, for "God has no grandchildren." This manifest unity in the one name will challenge the world to recognize that the name of Jesus is not the name of "one of the prophets" (Matt. 16:14) but the name of the one sent by the Father to whom all that belongs to the Father has been given (v. 10).

The unity for which Jesus prays is therefore a spiritual unity—a gift of the Spirit by whose supernatural working alone it is possible to confess that Jesus is Lord. Therefore it is a unity which not merely reflects but actually participates in the unity of God—the unity of love and obedience which binds the Son to the Father (cf. 15:9-10). As they grow into this unity they are made "perfectly one" and they advance from "glory to glory" because the glory of God is nothing other than the eternal self-giving of the Father who loves and honors the Son and the Son who loves and honors the Father.

The unity of believers thus has its invisible source in the

work of the Spirit, but it is a visible reality which challenges "the world" to recognize that Jesus is not what "flesh and blood" supposes (Matt. 16:17). Expositors anxious to legitimize the fragmentation of Christendom affirm that "the actual division of the Church . . . does not necessarily frustrate the unity of the proclamation" (Barrett and Bultmann in identical words). But a proclamation which is contradicted by the practice of those who proclaim it is not what Jesus here prays for. This attempt to justify the fragmentations of Protestantism is not a legitimate exposition of the text. Jesus is praying for visible unity among those who believe. "If we walk in the light, as he is in the light, we have fellowship one with another" (I John 1:7). The prayer of Jesus is for a unity which is a real participation of believers in the love and obedience which unites Jesus with the Father, a participation which is as invisible as the flow of sap which unites the branches with the vine, and which is at the same time as visible as the unity of branch and vine—as visible as the love and obedience of Jesus. It is this visible unity which will bring the world to believe (v. 21) and know (v. 23) what otherwise it does not and cannot know (v. 25), namely, God himself in his revelation as the Father of Jesus. Moreover, this unity will enable the world to know the love of God not just as an idea or a doctrine but as a palpable reality experienced in the supernatural love which holds believers together in spite of all their human diversities. "By this all men will know that you are my disciples, if you have love one for another" (13:35).

But now (v. 24) the prayer of Jesus looks toward the end of all things. The element of "realized eschatology" in the Johannine interpretation of the teaching of Jesus never excludes a real future to which he looks forward and to which the Church also is bidden to look forward. According to the synoptic Gospels, Jesus had seen this last supper with his disciples as a foretaste of the heavenly banquet when the disciples would feast with him in the kingdom of God (Mark 14:25; Luke 22:29). According to John, Jesus prayed also that all who should believe, seen as a single gift to him from the Father, should share in the final vision of his glory. That glory is the glory which Jesus shared eternally with the Father as the only Son of the Father (1:14) who was "with God" (1:1) before the world was. Those who believe, who are already made children of God, will then share his glory, for they will see him as he is (I John 3:2). And this is possible because Jesus will come again and take them to himself (14:3). And yet this "coming again" is not only at the end but also along the way, for Jesus is himself the way (14:6) and those who have seen Jesus have seen the Father and have received the manifestation of glory. To have the full fruition of that glory is the goal to which the Church presses forward, for it is the true end for which all things exist as it is the source from which they come. No other goal is worthy of man and no other end can satisfy him, for "man's chief end is to glorify God and to enjoy him forever."

But the prayer does not close with this vision of glory. There is also a dark shadow cast by the splendor of that light. "The world has not known thee." He has prayed "that the world may know" through the unity of the believing disciples. But the world has not known. He does not pray for the judgment of the world. His coming was not for judgment, but that the world might believe and be saved. The unbelieving world is left in the hands of the righteous Father. The contrast is simply left to stand:

The world has not known thee.

I have known thee.

These have known that thou didst send me.

So far as our world is concerned, the line between light and darkness is drawn there. To know that Jesus is the apostle of God is to be in the light. Not to know that is to be in darkness.

But the light shines in the darkness, and the darkness does not overcome it. "I have made known thy name, and I will make it known." The mission of the Church goes on. Through its mission the name and the nature of God are made known. There is an area of light in the midst of darkness. There is a place where men can walk without wandering, and have fellowship one with another because the name and the nature of God have been revealed. That is the place where Jesus dwells and therefore where the love of God dwells. In the Old Testament the presence of the glory of the Lord in the midst of his people is associated with the tabernacle and the ark of the covenant. When John first uses the word "glory" he speaks of the word (*logos*) "tabernacling" among us. Now in the final words of the consecration prayer, he leaves us with the picture of Jesus dwelling in the midst of believers as the bearer of the love of God which the world does not know and by which the world is to be saved.

236

18

THE VICTORIOUS PASSION
(18:1–19:42)

IN WHAT IS PROBABLY OUR EARLIEST RECORDED STATE-
ment of the essential Christian tradition, Paul writes: "I delivered
to you as of first importance what I also received, that Christ
died for our sins according to the scriptures" (I Cor. 15:3). The
synoptic Gospels record the events of the passion with a fullness
of detail absent from the earlier part of the story of Jesus. St. John
also makes it clear from the beginning of his work that everything
leads up to and is consummated in the passion. And all the earliest
sources we have—Christian, Jewish, and Roman—whatever the
differences between them, agree on this: "Jesus of Nazareth was
sentenced by a Roman prefect to be crucified on the political
charge that he claimed to be 'the King of the Jews' " (Brown).

However, it is obvious that there are many differences of
detail, some substantial, between the accounts of the passion in
the four Gospels, and that the fourth has certain elements and
emphases which distinguish it from the first three. (Westcott gives
a very full and precise list of the identities and differences.) Leaving aside matters of detail, the main distinctive features of the
Johannine presentation could be summarized as follows:

1. The theological intention of the writer (as stated in 20:31)
is emphasized at every point.

2. Throughout the events described Jesus is portrayed not
as the passive victim but as the majestic and sovereign initiator
and master of all that takes place. It is made clear that in the
judgment passed on Jesus it is the judges who are being judged.

3. There is no detailed account of an examination and condemnation by the Sanhedrin. Their judgment has been previously
recorded (11:47-53). Similarly the Jewish charge of blasphemy,

237

in which the Romans were not interested, and on which according to the synoptics Jesus was condemned by the Sanhedrin (Mark 14:64 and parallels), has been fully developed in the earlier part of John's record (10:31–33) and is omitted here.

4. The great emphasis in John's account is placed upon the confrontation with the power of Rome. Roman soldiers take part in the arrest, and the examination before Pilate occupies four times the space given to that before the high priest. The real issue, in other words, is the issue of sovereignty, of the nature of the kingship of God. The ultimate adversary of Jesus is "the ruler of this world," and therefore in the final conflict Jewish religion plays only an ancillary role. Jesus does not die by stoning on a charge of blasphemy but by crucifixion on the charge that he claimed kingship. His death was not by being crushed but by being "lifted up" where all could see and where his title as king could be proclaimed to all the world (cf. 12:32 and 19:20).

This listing of the distinctive "notes" of the Johannine account necessarily prompts the question of historical reliability. Is John, as has sometimes been suggested, simply bending the historical record) presumably as embodied in the synoptics) to his own theological purpose? That view is improbable in the light of research. It is virtually certain that John is drawing upon early tradition similar to but distinct from that upon which the first three evangelists relied. It is by no means certain that John had the Marcan material before him, and the evidence seems to point the other way. The conclusion of Brown seems to have good grounds "that John does not draw to any extent on the existing synoptic Gospels or on their sources as reconstructed by scholars" (p. 791).

Whatever be our conclusions on these debatable matters, our task here is to expound the text before us as it stands.

18:1–11

When Jesus had spoken these words, he went forth with his disciples across the Kidron valley, where there was a garden, which he and his disciples entered. Now Judas, who betrayed him, also knew the place; for Jesus often met there with his disciples. So Judas, procuring a band of soldiers and some officers from the chief priests and the Pharisees, went there with lanterns and torches and weapons. Then Jesus, knowing all that was to befall him, came forward and said to them, "Whom do you seek?" They answered him, "Jesus of Nazareth." Jesus said to them,

"I am he." Judas, who betrayed him, was standing with them. When he said to them, "I am he," they drew back and fell to the ground. Again he asked them, "Whom do you seek?" And they said, "Jesus of Naza-reth." Jesus answered, "I told you that I am he; so, if you seek me, let these men go." This was to fulfil the word which he had spoken, "Of those whom thou gavest me I lost not one." Then Simon Peter, having a sword, drew it and struck the high priest's slave and cut off his right ear. The slave's name was Malchus. Jesus said to Peter, "Put your sword into its sheath; shall I not drink the cup which the Father has given me?"

The Kidron Valley divides the city from the Mount of Ol-ives, and ancient olive trees still grow in that quiet spot at its foot. The garden is not named, but it is described as a favorite resort of Jesus and his disciples—perhaps as a place of quiet retreat away from city crowds. No mention is made of the prayer and agony of Jesus, for this has already been recorded (12:27f.). Why, then, did Jesus lead his disciples down the long flight of steps from the city and across the Kidron?

In John's understanding the escape of the disciples was not an ignominious flight (as in Mark 14:50), but a free departure ordered and demanded by Jesus as the condition of his surrender of himself into the hands of the authorities (v. 8). We may con-clude that Jesus led his disciples out of the city and into the se-cluded garden in order that they might be enabled to go free.

But because the place was known to Judas it was easy for him to guess where Jesus had gone. That he should have been able to bring not only Jewish police (cf. 7:32) but also Roman soldiers from the garrison which was kept in the Antonia Tower overlooking the Temple under the control of the prefect is not very surprising in view of the evidence of good relations between Caiaphas and Pilate (Brown, p. 798) and in view of constant Ro-man anxiety about outbreaks of violence at the great festivals.

They come armed with weapons and furnished with lan-terns. Judas had gone out into the darkness (13:30). Now he returns with the agents of the power of darkness, who must carry lanterns because they belong to the world of darkness (cf. Luke 22:53).

Jesus does not wait to be seized. Leaving his disciples in the safety of the garden, he comes out to meet Judas and his troop. When the wolves come the good shepherd does not flee, but goes forth to lay down his life so that the sheep may be safe. That is his purpose now. He, not the disciples, must face the powers of darkness. So the officers are challenged by the one whom they have come to challenge: "Whom do you seek?"

"Jesus of Nazareth"—a man whose name and address are as accessible to public investigation as any other. But the one being investigated has another name. Jesus repeats the mysterious words "I am" three times. They could be a routine acknowledgment of identity (cf. 9:9). But the threefold repetition warns the reader to recognize again the utterance of the name of supreme majesty, the "I am" of the divine self-manifestation. Before that manifestation the assembled police and soldiers withdraw and prostrate themselves in awe and fear.

Jesus alone is in command of the situation. He will give himself up according to the Father's will, but on condition that those whom the Father has given him are kept safe (10:17f.; 17:12). As he had told them, he must go to meet the ruler of this world alone, and they cannot follow now (13:36). But—once again—Simon Peter is unwilling to accept the Lord's warning. He will join in his own way in the fight against the powers of evil on behalf of the kingdom of God. He will also have his passion. Single-handed he will take on a whole cohort.

All this heroism adds up to a futile and humiliating gesture which achieves nothing except a sharp rebuke. Once again Peter is the agent of "flesh and blood" to tempt the Lord from doing his Father's will (cf. Mark 8:31-33). But Jesus cannot be turned aside. The conflict which lies before him is the cup which the Father has prepared for him. As the psalmists and prophets had said many times, "in the hand of the Lord there is a cup . . . and all the wicked of the earth shall drain it down to the dregs" (Ps. 75:8, cf. Isa. 51:17; Jer. 25:15f.; Heb. 2:16). In the strange mercy of God the cup of his righteous wrath against the sin of the world is given into the hands, not of his enemies, but of his beloved Son. And he will drink it down to the dregs until the moment comes when "I thirst" gives place to "It is finished" (19:28-30).

18:12-27

So the band of soldiers and their captain and the officers of the Jews seized Jesus and bound him. First they led him to Annas; for he was the father-in-law of Caiaphas, who was high priest that year. It was Caiaphas who had given counsel to the Jews that it was expedient that one man should die for the people.

240

Simon Peter followed Jesus, and so did another disciple. As this disciple was known to the high priest, he entered the court of the high priest along with Jesus, while Peter stood outside at the door. So the other disciple, who was known to the high priest, went out and spoke to the maid who kept the door, and brought Peter in. The maid who kept the door said to Peter, "Are not you also one of this man's disciples?" He said, "I am not." Now the servants and officers had made a charcoal fire, because it was cold, and they were standing and warming themselves; Peter also was with them, standing and warming himself.

The high priest then questioned Jesus about his disciples and his teaching. Jesus answered him, "I have spoken openly to the world; I have always taught in synagogues and in the temple, where all Jews come together; I have said nothing secretly. Why do you ask me? Ask those who have heard me, what I said to them; they know what I said." When he had said this, one of the officers standing by struck Jesus with his hand, saying, "Is that how you answer the high priest?" Jesus answered him, "If I have spoken wrongly, bear witness to the wrong; but if I have spoken rightly, why do you strike me?" Annas then sent him bound to Caiaphas the high priest.

Now Simon Peter was standing and warming himself. They said to him, "Are not you also one of his disciples?" He denied it and said, "I am not." One of the servants of the high priest, a kinsman of the man whose ear Peter had cut off, asked, "Did I not see you in the garden with him?" Peter again denied it; and at once the cock crowed.

The narrative as it stands appears incoherent. Annas is introduced as the father-in-law of the high priest. The interrogation is conducted by the high priest, who is apparently Annas and not Caiaphas, and at the end Annas sends the prisoner to Caiaphas. Who was and who was not high priest? From Josephus we know that Annas was high priest from A.D. 6 to 15, that he was deposed by the Romans, and that he was succeeded by five of his sons and by Caiaphas—here identified as his son-in-law. It seems clear that for the period extending up to A.D. 26 Annas was the "power behind the throne," and it seems plausible to guess that, since in Jewish eyes the pagan occupying power had no authority either to appoint or to depose a high priest, Annas might continue to be referred to as "the high priest." In fact Luke writes as if Annas and Caiaphas were both "high priests" (Luke 3:2) and as if the high priesthood was a family affair ("Annas the high priest and Caiaphas and John and Alexander and all who were of the high-priestly family" [Acts 4:6]). We may safely conclude that according to John's understanding the "high priest" who conducted the interrogation (vv. 19-24) was Annas.

This midnight encounter is not a formal trial with charges made and witnesses brought to prove them. It is in no way comparable with the trial before the Sanhedrin recorded in Mark 14:53-65. It is a preliminary interrogation in order to frame charges. Jesus, to use the current euphemism, is "helping the police with their inquiries." He refuses this procedure and demands a proper trial with witnesses. When he is insultingly struck by one of the police, he responds with a quiet and dignified reminder to the agents of the law that they are also under the law. He invokes the law against those who use legal authority to transgress the law. He has at no time been a purveyor of esoteric secrets or of clandestine propaganda. The words of Paul accurately echo the language of his master: "We refuse to practise cunning . . . but by the open statement of the truth, we would commend ourselves to every man's conscience in the sight of God" (II Cor. 4:2). The light has never been put under a bushel; it has shone out clearly, and only those who fear the light have hidden themselves from it. It follows that Jesus will not bear witness for himself. There are witnesses—those who have heard and received his word. They are the ones to be interrogated. He declines to embody his teaching in a definitive statement of his own. He is himself the word, and the revelation of the word is given into the hands of human witnesses. The whole work of Jesus is entrusted to them.

But while this interrogation proceeds there is another interrogation going on outside the high priest's residence. One of those who should have been a witness for Jesus is being questioned, and we are again reminded that "flesh and blood" is of itself unable to bear witness to Jesus: only the Spirit of truth can do that. So, while Jesus has protected his disciples from danger with the thrice-repeated words "I am," the disciple is betraying his master with the thrice-repeated denial "I am not."

Why does Peter deny Jesus? Not from cowardice; that Peter was no coward has been demonstrated by his readiness to draw his sword alone in defense of his master against a cohort of Roman soldiers. Peter is simply a human being—"flesh and blood." And flesh and blood cannot bear witness to Jesus. Peter has been told, "You cannot follow me now" (13:36ff.). But Peter has insisted on following—and so he has lost the way, for "the way" is Jesus himself in his unique consecration to the Father in the death of the cross. Peter's way has ended in humiliation and defeat, and so when the sharp question comes, "Are you not his disciple?" the answer is: "No—not any more." Peter is in the dark. He has lost the way.

And then the cock crew—the first sign that the night is passing and the day is at hand. It is the eloquent reminder that Jesus had warned Peter, and that Peter had not heeded the warning. Peter is just a human being—"flesh." Since all flesh is grass, it falls, but the word of the Lord stands.

After the interrogation before Annas, Jesus is sent to Caiaphas, but no formal trial and sentence are recorded. We have noted that the charges against Jesus in the Sanhedrin court which are recounted in the synoptic narrative (referring to his alleged words about the Temple and the alleged messianic claim) have all been described earlier in John's narrative (e.g., 1:51; 2:19; 10:24f., 33, 36) and that the decision of the Sanhedrin that he was to be put to death has been recorded (11:47-53). It is probably impossible to determine which of the versions—synoptic or Johannine—corresponds most closely to the actual course of events. Against the assertion of Barrett that "no reliance can be placed on [John's] version of the story" of the interrogation we may place Dodd's belief that "his account of the interrogation is drawn from some source, almost certainly oral, which was well informed about the situation at the time and had contact with the Jewish tradition about the trial and condemnation of Jesus," and against Barrett ("John is altering Mark where necessary in the interests of his theology") we may set Bultmann ("It is plain that John has not utilised the synoptics but a source in which the same tradition was differently formed"). It would seem a perverse scepticism to deny the probability that the unnamed disciple of verses 15 and 16, for whose anonymous appearance no theological reason can be alleged, had something to do with the tradition on which John relied. The debate on these points will continue, but John hurries us on to the scene which is for him central to the story—the meeting between the King of kings and the representative of the ruler of this world.

The following passage (18:28–19:16) is an intensely dramatic account of the trial of Jesus before the Roman court. It is very much more detailed than the accounts in the synoptic Gospels. Seven scenes, alternately outside and inside the Governor's palace, show us the steps by which Pilate was persuaded to condemn a man he believed to be innocent. What confidence can be placed in the historical accuracy of this account?

It is beyond question that Jesus died by crucifixion, a form of execution which only a Roman court could have decreed. It is also clear that the pressure for condemnation came from the Jewish authorities, and all the Gospels indicate that Pilate acted reluctantly. Clearly also the two parties had different interests— the one primarily religious, the other political. St. John's account gives by far the fullest explanation of the interaction between these two interests and between the parties representing them. The effect of this presentation of the story is to move the question of kingship into the center of attention. In the synoptic Gospels the kingdom of God is at the very center of Jesus' teaching, and it becomes clear that it is the presence of Jesus himself which makes the kingdom present. In the Fourth Gospel Jesus himself is explicitly the center of the teaching, but now—at the climax of the story—John makes it clear that it is as king that Jesus is condemned and as king that he dies. Certainly we can have here no verbatim record of the private conversations between Jesus and the Governor. As always we are dealing with an interpretation of what took place. But there are solid grounds for accepting the conclusion of Dodd that this record rests upon early and independent tradition which "in some respects seems to be better informed than the tradition behind the synoptics, whose confused account it clarifies" (*Tradition*, p. 120).

18:28-32

Then they led Jesus from the house of Caiaphas to the praetorium. It was early. They themselves did not enter the praetorium, so that they might not be defiled, but might eat the passover. So Pilate went out to them and said, "What accusation do you bring against this man?" They answered him, "If this man were not an evildoer, we would not have handed him over." Pilate said to them, "Take him yourselves and judge him by your own law." The Jews said to him, "It is not lawful for us to put any man to death." This was to fulfil the word which Jesus had spoken to show by what death he was to die.

Jesus is taken from the high priest's house to the Governor's palace—perhaps the Antonia fortress near the Temple or, more probably, the Herodian palace on the West Hill overlooking the city. It is not—as in Mark—the day of the Passover but the day of Preparation. Fidelity to the letter of the law prevents the Jews from entering a building which would not have been cleansed. They stand outside, and so the scene is set for the series of confrontations in which Jesus faces alternately the religious leaders outside and the political authority inside the building. In a larger perspective, the scene is set for the slaying of the true paschal lamb for the sin, not just of Israel, but of the world.

If the Roman authority had already provided troops for the arrest of Jesus during the night (18:3), it is understandable that the Governor was prepared at an early hour to deal with the man arrested. But he must know what is the charge before there can be any trial (v. 29). The reply of the Jews is simply that he is an evildoer whom they want to hand over to the Romans. The reply rests on the assumption that Pilate had already been "tipped off" when he authorized the provision of troops. If it suggests "extraordinary and almost incredible impudence" (Barrett), it is in keeping with the style in which the Jewish leaders deal with the Governor throughout the whole scene.

Pilate's answer is in an equally surly vein. He has provided the troops. They have got their man. Now let them get on with it and deal with him themselves. The assumption is that it is a minor domestic affair which they themselves can attend to. The reply of the Jews alerts Pilate to their real intention: Jesus—as the Sanhedrin had already decided (11:47-53)—must be destroyed. And Pilate is to be the instrument (willing or unwilling) of their purpose. The Jews had twice attempted to put Jesus to death by stoning (8:59; 9:31). This was the penalty prescribed in the law for blasphemy. Whether the Jews had or had not the power to inflict this punishment at this period of the Roman rule is a point on which there is some conflict of evidence. For the evangelist, however, the overruling purpose of God in all these events is clear. Jesus will die, not by being crushed to the ground under a heap of stones, but by being "lifted up" for all to see, like the brazen serpent in the wilderness, so that he may draw all people to himself (12:32). Therefore it is by the hand of the Romans that he must die. His death will be not a provincial but a world event.

18:33-38a

Pilate entered the praetorium again and called Jesus, and said to him, "Are you the King of the Jews?" Jesus answered, "Do you say this of

your own accord, or did others say it to you about me?" Pilate answered,
"Am I a Jew? Your own nation and the chief priests have handed you
over to me; what have you done?" Jesus answered, "My kingship is not
of this world; if my kingship were of this world, my servants would fight,
that I might not be handed over to the Jews; but my kingship is not from
the world." Pilate said to him, "So you are a king?" Jesus answered,
"You say that I am a king. For this I was born, and for this I have come
into the world, to bear witness to the truth. Every one who is of the truth
hears my voice." Pilate said to him, "What is truth?"

The scene shifts to the inside of the palace. The Jews remain
outside. Jesus and Pilate are face to face. The trial begins.

But what is the charge? John starts his account abruptly with
the question to Jesus, but only Luke explains it by reporting that
the Jews explicitly alleged against Jesus that he claimed to be
"Christ a king" (Luke 23:2). A Roman official was not interested
in allegations of blasphemy against the god of the Jews, but talk
about "the kingdom of God" could be subversive. We are to
assume that the Jews have presented it as a political case.

The tone of the question is probably contemptuous: "So you
are the 'king of the Jews,' are you?" The answer of Jesus is that
of the one who has come as light into the world, and whose
coming must necessarily bring judgment. It is Pilate who is on
trial and must be questioned. Has he begun to "see" the kingship
of God, or is he merely repeating hostile allegations? Pilate's
scornful reply shows no trace of understanding. He only wants
to know whether this "king of the Jews" is a real political danger
or not.

Jesus will not deny kingship nor will he accept Pilate's idea
of kingship. If he were a king in Pilate's sense, he too would have
troops to defend him against Pilate's (the same word as in v. 3).
The kingship of Jesus has its source and therefore its nature from
elsewhere. It is in fact none other than the kingship of God.

Pilate thinks he sees the way to a verdict. The prisoner has
admitted that he claims to be a king. That could settle the matter.
Once again Jesus, accepting the word that Pilate has used, gives
his own definition of it. The birth of Jesus, his coming into this
world from the Father, was and is in order that there may be in
this world a witness to the reality which is otherwise hidden from
this world. Jesus is himself the truth—that is to say, the actual
presence of God who alone is true—and both his words and his
works bear witness to that reality. This is what "the kingdom of

God" means. Jesus has come into the world "to make God's reality effective over against the world in the great trial between God and the world" (Bultmann). "He who comes from heaven is above all. . . . He bears witness to what he has seen and heard, yet no one receives his testimony; he who receives his testimony sets his seal to this, that God is true" (3:31-33).

"Truth?" asks Pilate. "What is that?" The prisoner is talking a language which is not the language of politics. Pilate is not one of those to whom it is given to receive the testimony of Jesus. But he recognizes that there is no ground for a verdict of sedition, and he decides accordingly. Jesus is not guilty of the charge.

18:38b-40

After he had said this, he went out to the Jews again, and told them, "I find no crime in him. But you have a custom that I should release one man for you at the Passover; will you have me release for you the King of the Jews?" They cried out again, "Not this man, but Barabbas!" Now Barabbas was a robber.

The scene shifts again to the crowd outside which is waiting for the verdict. Pilate announces his finding, but then attempts a stratagem to defuse the situation. The incident of Barabbas, common to all four Gospels, is an integral part of the tradition, though we have no independent evidence of the custom referred to. Pilate hopes to satisfy the crowd without actually putting to death a man he knows to be innocent. Because he is not of the truth he cannot face the hatred of the world which the truth always arouses (cf. 7:7). Therefore he is trapped by his own stratagem, for when the Jews shout for Barabbas it is no longer possible for him to set Jesus free. So, having arrested and handed over an innocent man as though he were a bandit (18:3), they now shout for the release of a bandit and for the death of the innocent. The pretense of zeal for national security is cynically exposed. Pilate can have no excuse for being deceived by it. But the Governor is trapped. Having failed to acknowledge the truth, he is in the power of the lie.

19:1-3

Then Pilate took Jesus and scourged him. And the soldiers plaited a crown of thorns, and put it on his head, and arrayed him in a purple

247

*robe; they came up to him, saying, "Hail, King of the Jews!" and struck
him with their hands.*

Jesus is innocent. He ought not to be put to death. He cannot
be freed. Perhaps the crowd will be satisfied by a compromise,
something less than actual execution. Pilate retreats again into the
palace and orders the scourging which was a frequent preliminary
to crucifixion. The Roman soldiers, delighted no doubt to have
an opportunity of venting their contempt for the natives and their
nationalist pretensions, stage a mock coronation for the "king of
the Jews." The savage and cruel scene is described in words which
remind the reader of the suffering servant of the Lord (e.g., Isa.
50:6; 53:5). Throughout the terrible scene Jesus is silent; "like a
sheep that before its shearers is dumb, so he opened not his
mouth" (Isa. 53:7). The paschal lamb is being prepared for
slaughter.

19:4-8

*Pilate went out again, and said to them, "Behold, I am bringing him out
to you, that you may know that I find no crime in him." So Jesus came
out, wearing the crown of thorns and the purple robe. Pilate said to them,
"Here is the man!" When the chief priests and the officers saw him, they
cried out, "Crucify him, crucify him!" Pilate said to them, "Take him
yourselves and crucify him, for I find no crime in him." The Jews answered him, "We have a law, and by that law he ought to die, because
he has made himself the Son of God." When Pilate heard these words,
he was the more afraid.*

Pilate again brings the prisoner out to the waiting crowds.
Perhaps, when they see the battered and wounded body of Jesus,
they will be satisfied. But Jesus is wearing the insignia of a king.
The stricken lamb is also the king (cf. Rev. 5:5f.). Jesus has been
mockingly acknowledged, crowned, and invested with the robes
of royalty. Now—in the final act of a mock coronation—he is
presented to his people. The double meaning of the whole proceeding is embodied in the words of Pilate: "Here is the man!"
At one level it is part of Pilate's impotent protest: "Here is the
fellow who is supposed to be your king; do you really want me
to execute him?" At another level the evangelist is reminding us
that here is indeed the "Son of man" of whom Jesus had said,
"When you have lifted up the Son of man, then you will know

that I am he" (8:28). "The man" is both the humiliated and wounded victim of the world's hatred and the one who is to rule over all. Here the central affirmation of the Gospel that the word was made flesh "has become visible in its extremest consequence" (Bultmann).

Pilate's plan fails totally but God's plan moves forward with majestic certainty. The shout of the crowd for crucifixion destroys Pilate's hope for a compromise, but fulfils God's purpose that the Son of man shall be "lifted up."

Pilate is reduced to angry bluster. When he says "Crucify him yourselves" he knows that they never can, and never will, do what he is trying to avoid doing. But he is already on a slippery slope on which he cannot halt. He will not act freely, but he can be forced. The crowd knows its power. Pilate is vulnerable to complaints to the Emperor that he fails to respect local religious feeling. Blasphemy may not interest a Roman governor but it is a capital offense among the people he has to rule, and he cannot with impunity outrage native law and custom. The implicit threat is barbed with a shrewd appeal to Pilate's pagan susceptibilities. "Son of a god" is the phrase they use, not the title "Son of God" which Christians use of Jesus. It is enough to awaken superstitious fears in the heathen heart of Pilate. Who is this strange man? Is he possessed of divine power? Is it, then, dangerous to lay hands on him? Pilate is afraid, and resolves to retreat again into his palace and inquire further.

19:9-12

He entered the praetorium again and said to Jesus, "Where are you from?" But Jesus gave no answer. Pilate therefore said to him, "You will not speak to me? Do you not know that I have power to release you, and power to crucify you?" Jesus answered him, "You would have no power over me unless it had been given you from above; therefore he who delivered me to you has the greater sin." Upon this Pilate sought to release him, but the Jews cried out, "If you release this man, you are not Caesar's friend; every one who makes himself a king sets himself against Caesar."

So, once again, Jesus is face to face with Pilate while the crowd demonstrates outside. The earlier conversation is about kingship; this one is about authority. In both the outward form

249

is a trial of Jesus by Pilate, but in both it becomes clear that the reality is the trial of Pilate by the truth.

Pilate's first question arises directly from the fear that Jesus is some sort of supernatural being: "Where are you from?" It is a question which Jesus will not answer in the context of this encounter. "The silence of Jesus provokes Pilate, who desires to release him. By provoking the next question the silence continues the conversation as effectively as a reply" (Barrett). Pilate's impotence in face of the Jews prompts him to remind Jesus that at least he has total power to order the life or death of Jesus. In reply Jesus must bear witness to the truth. Pilate has authority over Jesus only because the Father has given Jesus over into his hands. It is by "the definite plan and foreknowledge of God that Jesus has been 'delivered up' to be 'crucified and killed by men outside the law' " (Acts 2:23). Pilate's authority is not his own. It has been given to him, and therefore he is responsible to the one who gave it. The guilt rests upon those—the religious leaders—who are using the authority of the state to condemn the innocent.

Pilate is trying to find a way to release Jesus. Jesus is bearing witness to the truth by which both Pilate and the Jews are judged. It is Pilate who is facing judgment. Because he is not of the truth, he is still helplessly caught between his desires and his fears. He makes one more appeal to the Jews, and it fails. "Friend of Caesar" was a title of honor conferred by the Emperor, and it could be withdrawn. Pilate's standing at the imperial court was not such that he could afford to shrug off the threatened blackmail. He gives up the struggle. Because he is not "of the truth" and has not come to the light, he becomes—in spite of his good intentions—an instrument of the power of darkness.

19:13-16

When Pilate heard these words, he brought Jesus out and sat down on the judgment seat at a place called The Pavement, and in Hebrew, Gabbatha. Now it was the day of Preparation of the Passover; it was about the sixth hour. He said to the Jews, "Here is your King!" They cried out, "Away with him, away with him, crucify him!" Pilate said to them, "Shall I crucify your King?" The chief priests answered, "We have no king but Caesar." Then he handed him over to them to be crucified.

Pilate comes out again and takes his seat on the bench. He will give judgment. Or will he? Who is the judge? The Greek can be rendered "He brought Jesus out and set him on the judgment seat." Perhaps John intends the ambiguity, for—as we shall see—the whole scene makes clear that the true judgment is given by him who is the truth and by none other.

With solemn precision John states the details of place, day, and hour. The place is a paved space in front of the palace, of which he gives the name both in Greek and in Aramaic. The hour is noon on the day called "preparation," the day on which the lambs to be eaten that night were to be slain. The law (Ex. 12:6) required that the lamb be slain in the evening, but in the time of Jesus, on account of the huge numbers of pilgrims gathered in Jerusalem for the festival, the slaughtering was done by the priests in the Temple from noon onward. The reader understands that the true paschal lamb is being presented for slaughter.

But it is as "your king" that Pilate presents Jesus to the Jews. Humiliated but impotent, Pilate tries to mock the Jews and their passionate nationalism by offering them the battered and blood-stained figure as their king. Yet, like the cynical realism of Caiaphas, the impotent contempt of Pilate is made the vehicle of God's truth, for it is God's purpose which is being fulfilled in these events. Pilate, against himself, witnesses to the truth that Jesus is king, just as Caiaphas had testified that Jesus must die for Israel and for all the children of God (11:51f.).

This attempted ridicule only increases the fury of the crowd. So far from accepting this man as king, they demand his immediate death. Pilate, determined to carry his mockery to the limit, asks whether the proud Jewish nation is really asking the hated pagan imperialist to crucify their leader. The answer is a formal act of apostasy spoken through the lips of the chief priests: "We have no king but Caesar." By denying the kingship of Jesus they place themselves in a position where they have finally denied the kingship of God. Pilate's mockery has achieved nothing. There is no way out for him but to abandon the innocent prisoner to the fury of the people. No formal sentence is passed. Pilate, in effect, abandons his duty as judge and surrenders to the forces of which he is afraid.

Thus, with an appalling abruptness, the trial ends. The central faith by which Israel lives—that Yahweh alone is Lord—has been publicly denied by the official spokesmen of the nation. The central purpose for which the political order exists—namely, to defend the good and punish the evildoer—has been publicly abandoned by the representative of the imperial power. And all this is because the one who had been presented before them as king is in fact the presence of the light shining in the darkness and his coming into the world necessarily means judgment for the world. The claims of religion and of statecraft to authority over human affairs have been unmasked. The "powers" have been disarmed (Col. 2:15). Only one claim remains, which can never be withdrawn: that Jesus, the slain lamb, is king. That is the gospel, the gospel of the kingdom of God.

19:17-22

So they took Jesus, and he went out, bearing his own cross, to the place called the place of a skull, which is called in Hebrew Golgotha. There they crucified him, and with him two others, one on either side, and Jesus between them. Pilate also wrote a title and put it on the cross; it read, "Jesus of Nazareth, the King of the Jews." Many of the Jews read this title, for the place where Jesus was crucified was near the city; and it was written in Hebrew, in Latin, and in Greek. The chief priests of the Jews then said to Pilate, "Do not write, 'The King of the Jews,' but, 'This man said, I am King of the Jews.' " Pilate answered, "What I have written I have written."

A prisoner condemned to crucifixion was required to carry the cross-beam to the place of execution, where it was fixed on top of the upright stake which always remained in place. Jesus goes out from the place of trial bearing the cross-beam. Only he can do this. No mention is made of Simon of Cyrene, for whose role in these events there is, however, extremely strong evidence (cf. Mark 15:21 and 16:13). Is John deliberately omitting this element in the story for theological reasons? Or is Mark adding to the earlier tradition an episode which had special interest for his Roman readers? Mark's narrative indicates that the conscription of Simon was an emergency operation. It was not the normal procedure. "That Jesus went out (from the Lithostraton) carrying his own cross, but later had to be relieved of it, is a perfectly reasonable interpretation of the evidence" (Dodd, *Tradition*, p. 125).

John omits any details which might suggest pity for the victim. On the contrary, the crucifixion is described as an enthronement in which the king gives the gifts of his bounty to his people. The title on the cross, about which all four Gospels are substantially agreed, is a proclamation not only to Israel but to the whole world that Jesus is king. The writing of the title in the three languages makes the enthronement an international event. John brings out the immense seriousness of the title on the cross by his report of the argument between Pilate and the Jews. Does Pilate, driven against his will to condemn an innocent man, wish to carry his public mockery of the Jews still further? Or does he wish to assert his own belief that Jesus is, in some sense, a king? Perhaps both motives are present. For the Jewish leaders the title is an intolerable affront. "If they accepted it, it was tantamount to an admission of sedition; and . . . to suggest that a powerless, condemned and dying outcast was the king of their nation was a studied insult" (Barrett). They demand that the title be amended to make clear that the claim to kingship is not acknowledged.

But at this point Pilate, who has been driven to such helpless vacillation between the prisoner and his accusers, suddenly becomes firm. He refuses absolutely to alter the title, and the reader knows that what he has written will stand, not because Pilate is stubborn, but because he is the unwitting witness of the truth. On the cross, Jesus reigns.

19:23-25a

When the soldiers had crucified Jesus they took his garments and made four parts, one for each soldier; also his tunic. But the tunic was without seam, woven from top to bottom; so they said to one another, "Let us not tear it, but cast lots for it to see whose it shall be." This was to fulfil the scripture, "They parted my garments among them, and for my clothing they cast lots." So the soldiers did this.

The clothes of an executed prisoner were a perquisite of the executioner's job. The first three evangelists simply record the fact that the soldiers tossed for the clothes. Psalm 22 (a very frequent text for early Christian interpretations of the passion) is in mind but they do not quote directly. John quotes the Greek text of the Psalm verbatim and states that the doubled complaint of the psalmist was exactly fulfilled in the events of the passion. Modern scholars know that this doubling ("they divide my garments among them" / "for my raiment they cast lots") is simply a form of Hebrew poetry. The evangelist understands it as an account of two distinct events: the outer garments of Jesus were distributed among the soldiers, but the inner tunic, being a single seamless piece of weaving, was disposed of by lot. The solemnly reiterated phrase "The soldiers did this" indicates that the reader is to pause and note carefully what happened, but its significance is not explained. Two lines of interpretation have been followed by John's Christian readers, and he may well have had both of them in mind. The Greek of Psalm 22:18 uses the word *himatismos* in the second half of the verse, but John uses the word *chiton* for the tunic of Jesus. This is the word used in the Old Testament for the coat of the high priest, and according to Josephus this coat was "without seam." This seamless coat of the high priest was the focus of a good deal of Jewish theological interpretation, and it may well be that John wants us to understand that Jesus died not only as king but also as priest.

The other line of interpretation begins from the fact that, while the outer garments were divided, the inner garment which immediately clothed the body of the Lord could not be divided. The presence of Jesus had repeatedly precipitated division among the Jews (e.g., 7:43; 9:16; 10:19), but those who are Jesus' own cannot be so divided (e.g., 10:16; 15:1ff.; 17:20-23). There is a long tradition which has seen in the seamless garment of Jesus a symbol of the Church, and this, too, may have been in the mind of the evangelist when he gave us this interpretation of what the Roman soldiers were doing at the foot of the cross while Jesus died. "Since we have a great high priest over the house of God, let us draw near with a true heart in full assurance of faith . . . not neglecting to meet together as is the habit of some. . . ." (Heb. 10:19-25).

19:25b-27

But standing by the cross of Jesus were his mother, and his mother's sister, Mary the wife of Clopas, and Mary Magdalene. When Jesus saw his mother, and the disciple whom he loved standing near, he said to his mother, "Woman, behold, your son!" Then he said to the disciple, "Behold, your mother!" And from that hour the disciple took her to his own home.

Women had been among the faithful disciples of Jesus from the beginning, and at the end it is they who remain with him at his death and who are the first witnesses of his resurrection. Mark, perhaps influenced by the language of Psalm 38:11, has them standing at a distance, yet records words which could only have been heard by those close by. John's independent tradition has them standing by the cross, and includes the mother of Jesus along with others. Efforts to determine the relation between the lists in Mark and John do not yield conclusive results, but it seems probable that in John's tradition there are four women—perhaps corresponding to four soldiers dividing up his clothes.

Only once before has John referred to the mother of Jesus. At the marriage in Cana, when she sought to play a role in Jesus' ministry, she was rebuked with the words "My hour has not yet come" (2:4). Now, as the reader knows, the "hour" is present. It is the hour of the travail of the new creation. "When a woman is in travail she has sorrow, because her hour has come; but when she is delivered of the child, she no longer remembers the anguish, for joy that a man is born into the world" (16:21). That hour of the new birth has come. At the hour of his passion a new family begins. Mary loses her son according to the flesh, but there is given to her a new family born out of the passion of Jesus who, "having loved his own who were in the world, loved them to the end" (13:1). The beloved disciple, like the mother of Jesus, is not named. He appears alone, uniquely at this point without the companionship of Peter who has denied his Lord and has (for a time) disappeared from the story. "From that hour," the hour of the completed sacrifice, the mother of Jesus and his beloved disciple are one family—a home which is indeed home for the whole family of God. The ancient promise to Zion is at last to be fulfilled: "The children born in your bereavement will say in your ears: 'The place is too narrow for me; make room for me to dwell in it' " (Isa. 49:20). The work of Jesus is finished (v. 28). He has manifested the name of God to those who were given to him (17:6). A new family has come into being, "born not of the will of man but of God" (1:12). Mary is the mother of that family (and the very understandable reaction against a deformed Mariology must not be allowed to exclude the recognition of the place of Mary which has been and is so important a part of Christian piety from the beginning). The beloved disciple is the representative of all the great company of those who will be with Jesus in his lonely passion, and will be the witnesses of his victory over death. Jesus has finished his work. The new community is born. (Since "that hour" is to be understood in the sense which

255

it always has in John's Gospel, there is no justification for the contention of some pedantic commentators that the witness in v. 35 cannot be the beloved disciple because he had left the scene at this moment.)

19:28-30

After this Jesus, knowing that all was now finished, said (to fulfil the scripture), "I thirst." A bowl full of vinegar stood there; so they put a sponge full of the vinegar on hyssop and held it to his mouth. When Jesus had received the vinegar, he said, "It is finished"; and he bowed his head and gave up his spirit.

The death of Jesus is his own act of love and obedience to the Father. It is the "finishing" of the work he has been sent to do (4:34). At the well of Sychar Jesus had asked for a drink, yet made it clear that he was the giver of "living water" and that he had food to eat of which his disciples were not yet aware (4:7, 10, 32). On the cross he cries "I thirst," and yet it is in his own power and of his own will that he will drink the cup the Father has given him (18:11). Now he thirsts to drink it to the bottom. The terrible physical thirst of a man hanging on a cross in the fierce heat of the afternoon disappears into the thirst of the Son to complete the work for which he has come. In the synoptic Gospels it is recorded that the soldiers offered him a taste of their own wine by soaking a sponge and lifting it up on a reed. In John the reed has become a hyssop—surely a plant not rigid enough for the purpose but expressing the fact that this is the true Passover in which hyssop played a necessary part (Ex. 12:22). Psalm 69 has already twice provided the background for understanding the mission of Jesus (cf. 2:17 and Ps. 69:9; 15:25 and Ps. 69:4), and its prophetic words are again fulfilled (Ps. 69:21: "For my thirst they gave me vinegar to drink").

And now the mighty work of Jesus is done. The sacrifice is complete. "Christ, our paschal lamb, has been sacrificed" (I Cor. 5:7). His death is not defeat but victory. It is his voluntary act to the end. The final action is that he bows his head and "delivers" his spirit. Till then his head is erect—as in the early portrayals of the crucifixion. It is his act. "Christ loved us and gave himself up for us, a fragrant offering and sacrifice to God" (Eph. 5:2). This is the witness of the beloved disciple and of all who have followed him. The final word of Jesus is a cry of victory: "It is finished."

19:31-37

Since it was the day of Preparation, in order to prevent the bodies from remaining on the cross on the sabbath (for that sabbath was a high day), the Jews asked Pilate that their legs might be broken, and that they might be taken away. So the soldiers came and broke the legs of the first, and of the other who had been crucified with him; but when they came to Jesus and saw that he was already dead, they did not break his legs. But one of the soldiers pierced his side with a spear, and at once there came out blood and water. He who saw it was borne witness—his testimony is true, and he knows that he tells the truth—that you also may believe. For these things took place that the scripture might be fulfilled, "Not a bone of him shall be broken." And again another scripture says, "They shall look on him whom they have pierced."

Jewish law required that the bodies be taken down before nightfall (Deut. 21:22f.). On the eve of a great festival it was especially important that this be done, "for a hanged man is accursed before God" (Deut. 21:22f.). Breaking the legs of the victim was a way of hastening death. Surprisingly (cf. Mark 15:44) Jesus is apparently already dead. To make sure of the matter one of the soldiers casually and brutally jabs his side with his spear. What followed is something which the evangelist believes to be of immense importance to faith. For the first and only time in his narrative he inserts a statement that the fact he is reporting rests upon the evidence of an eyewitness and that it is reported in order to bring the reader to faith. The close parallel with 21:24 suggests that the verse is the work of the author of that chapter. He is asserting three things: that what he reports really happened; that it is truth, reality—and in the Fourth Gospel this means that it is the truth of God; and that the witness to the reality is intended to create faith. There is no adequate ground for doubting that the eyewitness referred to is the beloved disciple of verse 26. What is it that he saw and why is it so important for faith?

The fact is described with extreme economy of language: "At once there came out blood and water." There appears to be no ground for declaring that what is described here is impossible on the ground of medical science. Why is it significant? At the simplest level it is the evidence that Jesus really died, and that his death was the death of a human being of flesh and blood. The many attempts from earliest times until today to declare on theological grounds that Jesus did not die, are excluded on grounds of fact. The thoughtless action of a Roman soldier was the oc-

257

casion of a happening which points to the deepest truth. Jesus is dead. That is established. But this death is itself the source of life. The dying of Jesus is the means by which the life-giving and cleansing power of God is released into the life of the world. The first witness to Jesus, John the Baptizer, had sharply distinguished his baptism in water from the baptism with the Spirit which Jesus would give (1:33)—Jesus who is the paschal lamb (1:36). And when the evangelist reports the words of Jesus, "He who believes in me . . . out of his heart shall flow rivers of living water," he adds: "This he said about the Spirit, which those who believed in him were to receive; for the Spirit had not yet been given, because Jesus was not yet glorified" (7:38f.). The Spirit will only be joined to the water of baptism when Jesus has been "lifted up" and his blood has been shed (3:5-15). Now Jesus has been glorified by his death, and therefore the Spirit will be given (20:22). The effusion of blood and water is a sign that this will come to pass. The baptism of water has to be completed by the baptism of blood; only then can the Spirit be given—the Spirit who is himself the witness (15:26f. and 16:7f.) and who makes it possible for the beloved disciple to testify and for the readers of his testimony to believe. The full meaning of what is here recorded is brought out in a passage of the First Epistle of John: "This is he who came by water and blood, Jesus Christ, not with the water only, but with the water and the blood. And the Spirit is the witness, because the Spirit is the truth. There are three witnesses, the Spirit, the water, and the blood; and these three agree" (I John 5:6-8). Water is a symbol both of cleansing and of giving life. The Christian reader knows that "the blood of Jesus cleanses us from all sin" (I John 1:7), and that it is by drinking the blood of Jesus that he receives the gift of life (6:53-55). He also knows that it is necessary both to share the baptism of Jesus and to drink his blood if he is to share his kingly rule (Mark 10:35-40). "The water had to be mingled with Jesus' blood before the Spirit could give testimony" (Brown). But because of the real death of Jesus, the beloved disciple can and does give this testimony and therefore makes it possible for the new community formed at the foot of the cross to believe and in turn to give their witness. "The soldier's lance-thrust was meant to demonstrate that Jesus was dead; but this affirmation of death is paradoxically the beginning of life" (Brown). The outflow of blood and water is the sign and pledge that it will be so.

The immense and eternal significance of these apparently trivial incidents in the brutal narrative of a Roman execution is emphasized by two quotations from holy scripture. "Not a bone of him shall be broken" evokes immediately the injunctions for the killing of the paschal lamb (Ex. 12:10; Num. 9:12), as well as the promise to the righteous sufferers of Psalm 34. Both were probably in the mind of the evangelist both reach their true exposition in this scene on the hill of Calvary.

"They shall look on him whom they have pierced" is a Greek rendering of the Hebrew text of Zechariah 12:10, a rendering which does not follow the Septuagint interpretation. We have already noted how frequently the prophecy of Zechariah provides the background for interpreting the events of Jesus' life and death. The "mourning" in Zechariah is associated with repentance leading to cleansing. "I will pour out on the house of David and the inhabitants of Jerusalem a spirit of compassion and supplication, so that, when they look on him whom they have pierced, they shall mourn for him, as one mourns for an only child, and weep bitterly over him, as one weeps over a first-born. . . . On that day there shall be a fountain opened for the house of David and the inhabitants of Jerusalem to cleanse them from sin and uncleanness" (Zech. 12:10–13:1). The passage is quoted in Matthew 24:30 and Revelation 1:7 in the context of the threat of coming judgment, and perhaps the same passage is in mind in Luke's account of Jesus' words to the weeping women of Jerusalem (Luke 23:27-31). Who—in John's mind—are "they" who will look on the one they have pierced? Is this a threat of impending judgment on those who have killed Jesus, or does it have in it the notes of repentance and hope which mark the original text? The evangelist does not give any hint, and perhaps it is wise to conclude that neither interpretation is to be excluded. "The dead Jesus remains the focal point of judgment as did the living Jesus: at the foot of the cross there stand those who reject the light as well as those who are attracted to it (3:18-21). The former look upon the pierced Jesus to be condemned; the latter look upon him to be saved" (Brown).

19:38–42

After this Joseph of Arimathea, who was a disciple of Jesus, but secretly, for fear of the Jews, asked Pilate that he might take away the body of Jesus, and Pilate gave him leave. So he came and took away his body.

Nicodemus also, who had at first come to him by night, came bringing a mixture of myrrh and aloes, about a hundred pounds' weight. They took the body of Jesus, and bound it in linen cloths with the spices, as is the burial custom of the Jews. Now in the place where he was crucified there was a garden, and in the garden a new tomb where no one had ever been laid. So because of the Jewish day of Preparation, as the tomb was close at hand, they laid Jesus there.

After the savage cruelties of the preceding scene we are suddenly in an atmosphere of calm and sad reverence. Two of the secret believers whose existence among the "establishment" has already been noted (12:42) come forward to honor in death the man they had not been brave enough to acknowledge openly when he was alive. Pilate's surly spirit has changed to complacence. The two men are permitted to give Jesus an honorable burial according to Jewish custom, and they spare no expense but bring for his embalming a vast quantity of spices sufficient for the burial of a king (cf. II Chron. 16:14). The place of his burial is in a garden close to the place of crucifixion. There is good evidence for thinking that the present Church of the Holy Sepulchre marks the authentic place. The fact that the death and burial of Jesus took place in a garden has furnished the Christian imagination with much material for relating this to the events in the Garden of Eden, but there is no evidence that this was in the mind of the writer. John's record is severely factual, resting on traditions different from those underlying the synoptics. Jesus is dead, and those who perform the last rites do so in the belief that the story is finished. It is dangerous to follow a living prophet, but safe and pious to honor a dead one (Matt. 23:29ff.). The good work must be done before the Sabbath begins.

They do not know that it will be the last sabbath of the old creation and that on the first day of the week a new creation will begin. The word through whom all things were made cannot be consigned to the past and cannot become merely the object of pious reverence but will be the living subject who rises from the dead to become the author of life to all who believe. Reverence for a dead prophet is part of the old creation. Joseph, Nicodemus, and the costly materials of their devotion still belong to the world which is passing away. That chapter comes to an end on the Sabbath when Jesus lies in the tomb. A new creation will come forth from the tomb, and then the only fitting attitude to him who is its author will be "My Lord and my God!" (20:28).

19

REUNION IN JERUSALEM
(20:1-31)

St. John's account of what happened "on the third day" after the death of Jesus has a markedly different atmosphere from those of the first three evangelists. Whereas they speak of dazzling apparitions, of an earthquake, and of fear and amazement among the witnesses, the Johannine account is calm and unspectacular. The emphasis is upon the restoration of the personal relationship broken by the events of Friday, upon the way in which Mary of Magdala, the disciples, and Thomas are brought into a new and deeply intimate relationship with Jesus. Because John sees the lifting up of Jesus on the cross as the supreme manifestation of the divine glory, he sees the resurrection not as the reversal of the passion, not as the bringing of glory out of defeat, but rather as the enabling of the disciples to believe and so to be brought into a relationship with him whom death cannot destroy—in other words, to have "life in his name." The promises of chapter 14 are here fulfilled: "I will not leave you desolate; I will come to you" (14:18).

There are many evidences to suggest that the material of verses 1 to 18 has been drawn from different strands of tradition the relations of which to the synoptic records are difficult to unravel. It seems probable that we have to recognize (following Brown, Lindars, and Barrett) three traditions going back to the earliest times:

(1) The story of the women who found the tomb empty, were deeply disturbed, and reported it to the apostles.
(2) The story that several disciples, including Peter, visited the tomb after hearing the women's story, and were puzzled.

(3) The story of an appearance of Jesus to Mary.
If these stories come to the evangelist as originally distinct elements in the tradition, some of the difficulties in interpreting the present narrative would be understandable.

20:1-10

Now on the first day of the week Mary Magdalene came to the tomb early, while it was still dark, and saw that the stone had been taken away from the tomb. So she ran, and went to Simon Peter and the other disciple, the one whom Jesus loved, and said to them, "They have taken the Lord out of the tomb, and we do not know where they have laid him." Peter then came out with the other disciple, and they went toward the tomb. They both ran, but the other disciple outran Peter and reached the tomb first; and stooping to look in, he saw the linen cloths lying there, but he did not go in. Then Simon Peter came, following him, and went into the tomb; he saw the linen cloths lying, and the napkin, which had been on his head, not lying with the linen cloths but rolled up in a place by itself. Then the other disciple, who reached the tomb first, also went in, and he saw and believed; for as yet they did not know the scripture, that he must rise from the dead. Then the disciples went back to their homes.

It is a striking fact that, while the accounts of the appearances of the risen Jesus to his disciples vary very widely, the four Gospels are unanimous in affirming as the first fact in the story they tell that women came to the tomb early on Sunday morning and found it empty. All four name Mary Magdalene first; John names her alone but implies (by the "we" of v. 2) that others were with her. The empty tomb is the first and fundamental witness from which the good news begins. (And it is notable that this is clearly implied in the earliest account of all—that of Paul in I Cor. 15. In reciting the basic tradition he does not say, "Jesus died and subsequently appeared to his disciples"; he says that Jesus died, was buried, was raised on the third day, and appeared to the disciples.) That Jesus was buried in the tomb of Joseph of Arimathea and that on the following Sunday morning the tomb was empty—these affirmations belong to the central core of the testimony of the New Testament writers. And no anti-Christian writer of the first two centuries seems to have denied that the tomb was empty.

Why did Mary go to the tomb? Not—as in the synoptics—to anoint the body, for that had already been done. She went, one must assume, to mourn the dead—for in cultures which do not try to pretend that death does not exist that is the human and proper thing to do. She will do the duty of the nearest and dearest—sit by the body and weep.

But the body is not there; it must have been stolen—for tomb-robbing was a sufficiently common crime to provoke an imperial edict against it. So Mary's mourning has to be broken off in horror as she runs to Peter and the beloved disciple, who have gone each to his own home (16:32), to give them the shocking news. Both run to the tomb. To see into the open cave in the side of the hill one must stoop; in Luke 24:12 Peter is described as doing this. Here the other disciple does so, but does not venture to go in. Peter—slower in the running but more impetuous in his determination to know the facts—enters the tomb and the beloved disciple follows.

What they see makes the theory of tomb-robbing impossible. All is calm and orderly. The wrappings of a corpse are left behind in their places, but they no longer enclose the body of Jesus. Lazarus came forth from the tomb still bound by the wrappings, and he will die again. "Christ, being raised from the dead, will never die again; death has no more dominion over him" (Rom. 6:9). The grave clothes are left behind.

The evidence is before the eyes of both disciples. They are not yet believers in the full Christian sense, understanding that the death and resurrection of Jesus constitute the fulfilment of the hope of Israel. That evening the disciples will be meeting behind closed doors—still dominated by fear and not by joy. But the beloved disciple, the one who is closest to the Lord and·who most fully shares his purpose, though he has not seen the risen Jesus, yet having seen the traces—so to speak—of his resurrection, becomes the first believer. It is possible to see and not to believe. It is possible to believe without having seen (20:29). But such faith rests upon the testimony of those who have seen and believed. Of such, the beloved disciple, is the first, and it is upon his testimony that the whole Gospel is based (21:24).

Why does John tell us about the relative running speeds of the two disciples? Not—one may believe—in order to enter proleptically into debates about the limits of papal authority or even about the relations of Jewish and Gentile Christianity. It is simpler to believe that it is so recorded because it so happened. The whole style of John's narrative is—one may think—designed to be as simple and factual as possible. The evangelist does not wish the reader to forget "that the Christian religion is one of divine incarnation, and that its truth must be found to prevail in the realm of flesh and blood, subject as these are to space and time" (Lightfoot). He is narrating real history. The resurrection of Jesus from the dead happened, and theologians can only deny its historical character by defining "history" in such a way as to exclude it. That this definition has been common in all ages is natural, for if "history" has a source and goal other than Jesus Christ, the resurrection cannot be an event in history. St. John's Gospel is written in the faith that Jesus is indeed the word through whom all things were made, and in whom all truth is to be made manifest (16:12-15). The resurrection cannot be part of any history unless it is the center and turning point. St. John's narrative is history written in the faith that it is. That is the Christian faith and the Christian understanding of history.

20:11-18

But Mary stood weeping outside the tomb, and as she wept she stooped to look into the tomb; and she saw two angels in white, sitting where the body of Jesus had lain, one at the head and one at the feet. They said to her, "Woman, why are you weeping?" She said to them, "Because they have taken away my Lord, and I do not know where they laid him." Saying this, she turned round and saw Jesus standing, but she did not know that it was Jesus. Jesus said to her, "Woman, why are you weeping? Whom do you seek?" Supposing him to be the gardener, she said to him, "Sir, if you have carried him away, tell me where you have laid him, and I will take him away." Jesus said to her, "Mary." She turned and said to him in Hebrew, "Rabboni!" (which means Teacher). Jesus said to her, "Do not hold me, for I have not yet ascended to the Father; but go to my brethren and say to them, I am ascending to my Father and your Father, to my God and your God." Mary Magdalene went and said to the disciples, "I have seen the Lord"; and she told them that he had said these things to her.

We are to assume, though we are not told, that Mary has followed the two disciples back to the tomb. (She also was capable of running, as both John [v. 2] and Matthew [28:8] tell us.) But why does she now stand weeping? Why did the beloved disciple not at once console her with his new-found faith? Is this the result of imperfect editoral joining of distinct traditions? It may be so, for this exquisite account of the meeting between

Jesus and Mary has no parallel in the synoptic Gospels, and it is hard to believe that it is not an authentic memory preserved and handed on by Mary herself. "It has something indefinably first-hand about it. It stands in any case alone. There is nothing quite like it in the Gospels. Is there anything quite like it in all ancient literature?" (Dodd, *Tradition*, p. 148). But if this is indeed a piece of very ancient tradition, has the evangelist failed to link it convincingly with what precedes? I think not. In its present place it leads the reader from the empty tomb to that which is the real meaning of the resurrection—the creation of a new relationship between Jesus and those who believe in him. The faith of a Christian has not been fully described if it falls short of a direct personal relationship of love and trust between the Christian and his Lord. But—as this narrative shows—the relationship is of a new kind, different from that of Jesus and his disciples in the days of his flesh. This new relationship will be mediated by the Spirit whose coming depends upon the completion of Jesus' journey to the Father (7:39; 16:7). This is what is now to be made clear.

As in the synoptic account, Mary finds that there are supernatural visitors to the tomb. But here there is no suggestion of alarm or amazement—only an unquenchable longing for the Lord himself. He is, in fact, standing behind her, but—like the disciples on the Emmaus road—she does not recognize him. But the good shepherd calls his own by name, for he knows them and they know him (10:3, 14). The name spoken is enough to create instant recognition. The beloved teacher has come back from the dead. Mary's grief is banished and in joy she clings to him. Had he not said: "I will not leave you desolate; I will come to you" (14:18)? The promise has been kept, and Mary is filled with joy.

But once again—for the last time in the Gospel—the words "Not yet" have to be spoken. Mary is the first of the disciples to meet and recognize the risen Lord, but she has not yet understood what the new relationship is to be. It will not be the old relationship of teacher and disciple, of *guru* and *sishya*. Therefore Mary must relinquish the old relationship. Jesus is—even now—on his way to his Father. He had always spoken of "going to the Father," of "being lifted up," and of "ascending." Both passion and resurrection are moments in that "ascension." It is not yet complete. It will be complete only when the Spirit is given by whom those who belong to Jesus will be made sons and daughters of God and will live in a relationship of love and obedience to

265

Jesus which nothing can destroy. Both the empty tomb and the appearance of the risen Lord to the disciples are signs to lead them into this full experience of communion. Thomas will later be invited to test the reality of the signs, but Mary is warned that she must not cling to the sign but prepare herself and the other disciples for that to which the signs point.

So the message with which she is sent to the other disciples is not—as in Matthew—that Jesus is risen and will meet them in Galilee (Matt. 28:7), but that he is on the way to that exaltation at the right hand of God which—by the giving of the Spirit— will make them the Father's children and his brothers and sisters. The warning of Jesus to Mary "has nothing to do with the ethereal nature of his body, but is concerned with establishing the proper relationship which must exist from now on" (Lindars).

Jesus had always spoken of "my Father" and had spoken much of "going to the Father." Now he is near the end of that journey. He had told them that the Father's house to which he was going had many abiding places and that he was going to prepare a place there for them (14:1-3). Now the promise is on the point of fulfilment. By the completion of his journey he will "bring many sons to glory" (Heb. 2:10) and become "the firstborn among many brethren" (Rom. 8:29). Now he can speak not only of "my Father," but also, for the first time, of "your Father." "Through his departure the Father of Jesus has become the Father of those who belong to him. For this reason he also says 'Go off to my brothers'. Thus the situation has come about that the love of God is directed to those who belong to Jesus just as it is directed to Jesus himself" (Bultmann).

With immediate obedience Mary leaves Jesus and goes to carry out his command. Her witness to the disciples is that she has seen the risen Lord, and at the same time that he has told her of the new reality of which his risen presence is the sign.

20:19-23

On the evening of that day, the first day of the week, the doors being shut where the disciples were, for fear of the Jews, Jesus came and stood among them and said to them, "Peace be with you." When he had said this, he showed them his hands and his side. Then the disciples were glad when they say the Lord. Jesus said to them again, "Peace be with you. As the Father has sent me, even so I send you." And when he had said this, he breathed on them, and said to them, "Receive the Holy Spirit. If you forgive the sins of any, they are forgiven; if you retain the sins of any, they are retained."

All of the witnesses speak of an appearance of Jesus in the presence of the company of disciples gathered in one place (Matt. 28:6-18; Luke 24:30-49; I Cor. 15:5; Mark 16:14). There are, however, discrepancies among the accounts as to whether the appearance was in Galilee or in Jerusalem; Matthew places it in Galilee, Luke in Jerusalem. John's 21st chapter, clearly added to the record which originally ended at 20:31, speaks in great detail of an appearance by the lakeside in Galilee. As we shall see in discussing that chapter, the balance of probability is in favor of the view that the Galilean appearances were before those in Jerusalem. However, John's Gospel in its original design (apart from ch. 21) moves immediately from the empty tomb and the meeting with Mary to a meeting with the company of disciples assembled, we must suppose, in Jerusalem. While this account of the meeting has close affinities with that in Luke 24:30ff., there are good grounds for thinking that it represents an earlier form of the tradition.

The opening reference to "that day" (v. 19) deliberately echoes the same phrase used in the farewell discourse (14:20, etc.). It is, indeed, the long-promised day of the Lord, and John's readers know that by the resurrection of Jesus and the coming of the Spirit the first day of the week has now become exactly that—the Lord's Day. But the frightened disciples have not yet come to know this—even if (which is not here suggested) they have heard of the empty tomb and the message of Mary. Fear of what the authorities may yet do to obliterate the memory of Jesus still dominates them, and so they have locked the doors in self-protection.

And then—as he had promised to even two or three gathered in his name—he is there in their midst (v. 20). There is no suggestion that he has passed through closed doors to reach them—he does not need to do that. He is already the victorious and ascended Lord. But he is also the same Jesus who was crucified, and the scars of his passion are the marks by which they can know who he is and rejoice that he is with them again and they with him. His promise is fulfilled. Their sorrow is turned to joy (16:22) and his peace is theirs even in the midst of the tribulation of which those wounds are the visible sign (16:33).

Peace (*shalom*), his gift to them, is that which belongs to the new age which God has promised (v. 21). It is because Jesus bears the wounds of his decisive battle with evil that he has that peace in his gift. He has "made peace by the blood of his cross" (Col. 1:20). But the gift of peace is not for them alone. On the contrary he has chosen and appointed them to be the bearers of *shalom* into the life of the world. Forty times in this Gospel Jesus is described as the one sent by the Father; now he sends them to continue and to complete his mission. This mission wholly defines the nature of the Church as a body of men and women sent into the public life of the world to be the bearer of that peace which Christ has wrought "by the blood of his cross." They will participate in his mission as they participate in his passion. The authentic marks of apostolicity will be the marks of tribulation (e.g., I Cor. 4:9-13; II Cor. 6:3-10; 11:22-29). It will be as they "carry in the body the death of Jesus" that "the life also of Jesus will be manifest" in them (II Cor. 4:10). Jesus consecrated himself to the sacrifice of the cross in order that these, the ones given him by God, might be consecrated and sent into the world (17:18f.). Now that his sacrifice is complete the moment has come to send them forth into the world.

This sending, however, is not simply the commissioning of a company of people by a man (v. 22). It is as those "consecrated in the truth" that they are to be sent (17:19). Only the Spirit of him who is the truth can so consecrate them. At the first creation God himself breathed his own breath into the creature he had formed, "and man became a living being" (Gen. 2:7). He who came as the "last Adam" (I Cor. 15:45-49), the beginning of the new creation, was anointed and empowered by the Holy Spirit of God at the moment when by baptism he took upon himself the sin of the world in order to take it away. It is he, therefore, who—having completed on Calvary that baptism which was begun in the Jordan—can bestow upon his company that same Holy Spirit. "The Lamb of God, who takes away the sin of the world," upon whom the Spirit "descended and remained," is he who "baptizes with Holy Spirit" (1:29-33 and Mark 1:8). Jesus has completed his journey to the Father; he has judged and cast out the ruler of this world (12:31); therefore he can now fulfil the promise that he had made—the promise of a Paraclete who would continue the work of manifesting the divine righteousness (16:7-11). Jesus has been glorified and therefore the Spirit is now given (7:39). The disciples are sent out on their mission not as the representatives of an absent master, but "sanctified in the truth" because bearing in their life the life of God himself, continuing the mission of Jesus in the power of that same Spirit who abides eternally in him and in them through him.

Central to the mission of Jesus was the forgiveness of sin (v. 23). He is the Lamb of God who takes away the sin of the world. He was sent "not to condemn the world, but that the world might be saved through him" (3:17). Therefore his coming necessarily brought judgment in that those who love what is evil will refuse the gift and seek refuge in darkness (3:19). To such he has to say: "Your guilt remains" (9:41). In his words of promise regarding the Paraclete who is the Spirit of truth Jesus had told his disciples that the Paraclete would "convict the world in respect of sin, of righteousness, and of judgment," thus continuing that work of exposure which the coming of light into darkness necessarily involves. For the coming of the Spirit is the foretaste of the end, when all things must be brought into the light of God's presence (e.g., Mark 4:22 and parallels). As Jesus now sends out his disciples, consecrated in the power of the Spirit who is the truth, he solemnly authorizes them to continue his mission as the one who takes away the sin of the world. The responsibility given to them is effective, not merely declaratory—for the remission of guilt has to be an effective action by one who has authority from the injured party. God has in Christ taken away the sin of the world. The Church, consecrated in the truth by the promise of the Spirit, is sent into the whole world to be the bearer of that effective action. It will be so insofar as it manifests in its corporate life the marks of Christ's passion. And as the effective presence of the light it will also bear the dread responsibility of being the occasion of judgment upon those who prefer the darkness to the light. So Jesus addresses his disciples in words which echo the word of the Lord to the one whom he will set over the household of Israel in place of the false steward who has used his position for his own glory: "I will place on his shoulder the key of the house of David; he shall open, and none shall shut; and he shall shut, and none shall open" (Isa. 22:22).

In the synoptic passage which is closest to the Johannine record we read that "repentance and forgiveness of sins should be preached in [Jesus'] name to all the nations" (Luke 24:47), but there are obvious parallels with the passages in Matthew where

269

the power of the keys is promised to Peter (Matt. 16:19) and—in somewhat different words—to the Church as a whole (Matt. 18:18). To whom is this authority given? John describes those gathered in the locked room as "the disciples" and does not give further specification. The reference to "the twelve" in verse 24 may or may not imply that only "the ten" were present on the previous Sunday. Who, then, are "the disciples" who are the recipients of the commission given here, as of the whole of the teaching embodied in chapters 13 to 17? Much debate concerning the doctrine of the ministry has revolved around this question. In a famous work *The Christian Ecclesia* (1914) F. J. A. Hort argued that those present—whether the ten or a larger number—"represented the whole Ecclesia of the future," and this is the view which is generally accepted. "It is not an ordination to a position of authority within the Church for an internal ministry, though this is not excluded. The disciples, and the whole Church following them, carry on the mission of Christ which he received from the Father" (Lindars). In fact the argument rests on a false premise. There can be no dichotomy between the priestly authority of the ministry and the priestly authority of the Church as a whole in its mission to the world. The former is for the sake of the latter, and it is only when the missionary character of the Church is forgotten that the dichotomy appears.

It has become clear in our exposition that John does not separate resurrection, ascension, and the giving of the Spirit in the way that Luke does. He understands them as—in some sense—a single event. Jesus "goes to the Father" by way of the cross and resurrection, and because he is already glorified in his death he can bestow the Spirit upon his disciples. The empty tomb and the appearances to the disciples are but signs to lead them to the new reality, which is an abiding in him as he forever abides in the Father through the presence of the Spirit. It may well be that in this respect the Johannine version represents a more primitive understanding of the victory of Jesus, and that the Lucan version represents a later development.

20:24-29

Now Thomas, one of the twelve, called the Twin, was not with them when Jesus came. So the other disciples told him, "We have seen the Lord." But he said to them, "Unless I see in his hands the print of the

270

*nails, and place my finger in the mark of the nails, and place my hand
in his side, I will not believe."*

*Eight days later, his disciples were again in the house, and Thomas
was with them. The doors were shut, but Jesus came and stood among
them, and said, "Peace be with you." Then he said to Thomas, "Put
your finger here, and see my hands, and put out your hand, and place
it in my side; do not be faithless, but believing." Thomas answered him,
"My Lord and my God!" Jesus said to him, "Have you believed because
you have seen me? Blessed are those who have not seen and yet believe."*

The other three Gospels speak at several points of the slowness of the disciples to believe in the resurrection (Matt. 28:17; Luke 24:11, 25, 28, 41; Mark 16:10, 13, 14). John now introduces this theme and identifies as the "unbeliever" (v. 27) that doggedly loyal but sceptical disciple Thomas. Although the other disciples "kept on telling him" that they had seen the risen Lord, he insisted stubbornly on physical proof of the reality of the resurrection.

The risen and ascended Lord knows his unbelief, and when the company are gathered on the following Lord's day he is again in their midst with the gift of his peace. Thomas is invited to make exactly the crude physical experiment which he had demanded and is challenged to show himself not an unbeliever but a believer. It is implied that he ought to have believed the testimony of his fellow disciples. They had seen and believed and had given their testimony to him, but he was still unbelieving. Now the gracious Lord gives him the same vision of himself that he had given them, and the unbelief of Thomas is instantly converted into an adoring faith: "My Lord and my God!" From the mouth of the sceptic thus comes the final christological affirmation of the Gospel. Jesus is not only "My master" (v. 16); he is the one of whom John has been speaking "from the beginning," the one who was with God and who was God (1:1). The prayer of Jesus is fulfilled; he has now from the Father the glory which he had with him before the world was (17:5), and his disciples are with him to behold and to acknowledge that glory (17:24). He had said to the Jews, "When you have lifted up the Son of man, then you will know that I AM" (8:28). Now that word is fulfilled. The name which belongs to God alone belongs to Jesus, the "name which is above every name," the name at which in the end "every knee shall bow" (Phil. 2:9-11). And if that was also the name blasphemously assumed by an earthly emperor ("*Dominus et Deus noster*"), there will be a great company of those who are ready to pay the price of refusing that blasphemy. They are truly blessed because, unlike Thomas, they are willing to believe on the word of the eyewitnesses without having seen the risen Lord themselves. Thomas has been given the privilege of being enlisted as the last of the eyewitnesses. Like the others, he has seen and believed and his faith is the true faith which gives life (v. 31). But he and they stand on the boundary line of the new age, the age of the Spirit, when Jesus will dwell with his believing people and they with him not by their seeing but by their believing through the word of the apostles (17:20).

This does not mean that seeing is irrelevant. It does not mean that "fundamentally it ought not to be the sight of the Risen Lord that first moves the disciples to believe 'the Word that Jesus spoke' (2:22), for the word alone should have had the power to convince them" (Bultmann). This is to eliminate the incarnation in favor of a purely cerebral experience. That "the Word was made flesh," that he wrought signs in the sight of the people and of his disciples, and that in his risen body he manifestly appeared to his disciples—all this belongs to the core of the gospel. The faith of Thomas, like that of the others before him, is true faith and is not to be disqualified because it rests upon "that which we have seen with our eyes, which we have looked upon and touched with our hands" (I John 1:1). But Thomas and his fellow apostles have no superiority over those who are to come after; they are only eyewitnesses in order that they may become "servants of the word" (Luke 1:2) to that great company who, not having seen, will believe. The fullness of blessing belongs truly to them.

20:30-31

Now Jesus did many other signs in the presence of the disciples, which are not written in this book; but these are written that you may believe that Jesus is the Christ, the Son of God, and that believing you may have life in his name.

The evangelist has come to the end of his story. There is a vast body of tradition treasured in the far-flung Christian family concerning the words and deeds of Jesus. What he has recorded is a small selection chosen with a purpose. He has recorded the "signs" which Jesus wrought in the presence of the whole nation of Israel and has summarized the result at the end of the first half of his story: "Though he had done so many signs before them, yet they did not believe him" (12:37). The end of that part of the story is unbelief. But these signs had also been wrought in the presence of the chosen disciples whom the Father had given him, and in their case they had been the means of coming to faith (2:11; 5:20). In the second part of his record John has shown how, both by his words and by the actual manifestation of his glory, these disciples have been led to the fullness of true faith—a faith finally confessed in the words of Thomas.

The purpose for which he has made this record, selected from the vast abundance of material, is that his readers may be brought to that same faith. What it means to use of Jesus the ancient titles "Messiah" and "Son of God" has been unfolded as the story has been told. These old titles, which could have narrowly limited meanings, have acquired in the person of Jesus a fullness which can only be expressed in the adoring words of Thomas with which the story closes. To have the faith which is expressed in these words is to have life "in his name"—the life which is truly his life given to the believer, so that it can no longer be identified by any other name than that of Jesus. It is the life which has been described with classic simplicity by St. Paul: "It is no longer I who live, but Christ who lives in me; and the life I now live in the flesh I live by faith in the Son of God, who loved me and gave himself for me" (Gal. 2:20).

John has made his record so that the reader may share that life.

20

REUNION IN GALILEE
(21:1-25)

THE EXPOSITION OF THE LAST CHAPTER, WHICH HAS OFTEN
been described as an epilogue, presents difficult problems. The
end of chapter 20 is clearly written as a conclusion to the whole
record; why add a further series of events? And how is it that
Peter and the other disciples, after the solemn commission of
20:19-23, have gone back to their old life and are apparently unable to recognize Jesus? Clearly there is a discontinuity to be
explained. On the other hand there is no evidence whatever that
the Gospel of John was ever in circulation without this chapter;
the style and matter are very Johannine and the chapter is explicitly linked to the previous chapter by verse 14.

How are these unities and discontinuities to be explained?
Scholars are far from agreement on this question, but the following is perhaps a reasonable way of interpreting the evidence. We
know that the material of the Gospel has been drawn from the
great reservoir of memory treasured in the early Church and
presumably existing in many varied units of both written and
oral tradition. Among these were memories of Jesus appearing
to his disciples both in Galilee and in Jerusalem. Mark's selection
implies the former (16:7), and Matthew's affirms it (28:16-20).
Matthew records an appearance in Jerusalem to the women but
none to "the disciples." Luke, on the other hand, selects only the
traditions of appearances in and around Jerusalem. Possibly these
different memories were treasured in different communities and
had never been fully integrated. John has recorded only appearances in Jerusalem, but his concluding paragraph reminds the
reader that what he has recorded is only a selection from a great
reservoir of memories (20:30), and that the selection was made

for a theological purpose. We must suppose that at a point in time
after the work which concludes with chapter 20 had been done,
the evangelist himself, or a member of his community, thought
it necessary to include also material from the Galilean tradition
in order to bring out more clearly the underlying meaning of the
commission given in 20:19-23, and to explain the special roles of
Peter and the beloved disciple in the Christian fellowship. As
chapters 20 and 21 now stand there is a continuity of theological
theme in that the mission of the Church to all the nations is
envisaged more explicitly in chapter 21 than in chapter 20, but
this has been achieved at the cost of an awkward discontinuity in
the historical record—for it is impossible to believe that the disciples who had received the commission of 20:21-23 could have
forgotten it so quickly. As in the case of the similar "break" at
the end of chapter 14, we may believe that the author of the
Gospel in its final form has—in arranging the units of tradition
which came to his hand—given a higher priority to continuity
of theological development than to preserving the order of events
as they happened. We conclude (recognizing that other opinions
are possible) that chapter 21 records meetings which took place
before the meetings of 20:19-29.

21:1-14

*After this Jesus revealed himself again to the disciples by the Sea of
Tiberias; and he revealed himself in this way. Simon Peter, Thomas
called the Twin, Nathanael of Cana in Galilee, the sons of Zebedee, and
two others of his disciples were together. Simon Peter said to them, "I
am going fishing." They said to him, "We will go with you." They
went out and got into the boat; but that night they caught nothing.*

*Just as day was breaking, Jesus stood on the beach; yet the disciples
did not know that it was Jesus. Jesus said to them, "Children, have you
any fish?" They answered him, "No." He said to them, "Cast the net
on the right side of the boat, and you will find some." So they cast it,
and now they were not able to haul it in, for the quantity of fish. That
disciple whom Jesus loved said to Peter, "It is the Lord!" When Simon
Peter heard that it was the Lord, he put on his clothes, for he was stripped
for work, and sprang into the sea. But the other disciples came in the
boat, dragging the net full of fish, for they were not far from the land,
but about a hundred yards off.*

*When they got out on land, they saw a charcoal fire there, with fish
laying on it, and bread. Jesus said to them, "Bring some of the fish that
you have just caught." So Simon Peter went aboard and hauled the net*

ashore, full of large fish, a hundred and fifty-three of them; and although there were so many, the net was not torn. Jesus said to them, "Come and have breakfast." Now none of the disciples dared to ask him, "Who are you?" They knew it was the Lord. Jesus came and took the bread and gave it to them, and so with the fish. This was now the third time that Jesus was revealed to the disciples after he was raised from the dead.

When we examine the internal structure of this passage, and compare it with similar material elsewhere in the Gospels, it seems clear that we have here the conflation of two distinct memories—of a miraculous draft of fish, which leads to the repentance and commissioning of Peter, and of a meal given by Jesus in which he is recognized by his disciples.

The first of these has also been preserved by Luke (5:1-11), who—however—places it early in the ministry where Mark has the calling of Peter and Andrew and the promise "I will make you become fishers of men" (Mark 1:17; cf. Luke 5:10). While it is impossible to be certain, there are good reasons for thinking that this was rightly received by John as the memory of an appearance of the risen Jesus, and that it is Luke who has placed it at the earlier point in the story, because he has no record of such appearances except in Jerusalem.

The second memory is of a meal of bread and fish given by Jesus to the disciples. This inevitably reminds us not only of the feeding of the 5,000 (with which there are several verbal parallels) but also of the appearances recorded by Luke to the disciples at Emmaus and to the "eleven" in Jerusalem where fish was part of the meal (Luke 24:30-43).

The two stories are linked by the shared theme of fish, but, as we shall see, this complicates matters because the fish which are caught are not eaten. We are suddenly introduced to Peter and a group of disciples again in Galilee. They are fishermen—a fact which is nowhere else hinted at in the Fourth Gospel. They have—we must suppose—fled from Jerusalem, scattered to their own homes as Jesus had foretold (16:32). The list of disciples includes those in whom John has shown a special interest as well as the sons of Zebedee, who have not been previously mentioned in the Gospel. In the synoptic Gospels they are very prominent, but here they are the last named. There are two unnamed disciples and there is "the disciple whom Jesus loved," and his identity is—as always—shrouded in complete anonymity.

Led by Peter they have apparently turned their backs on the

traumatic events in Jerusalem to return to their old craft. But in this they meet total failure. A profitless night draws to its end, and they have yet to learn the truth of Jesus' words: "Apart from me you can do nothing."

A figure dimly perceived standing on the shore calls to them: "Lads, you haven't caught anything to eat, have you?" "No," they answer. "Cast your net to the right of the boat, and you'll find something," comes the reply. When they obey the unknown stranger, their nets are filled with a mighty catch.

Who is he? Once again it is the unnamed beloved disciple whose insight pierces through ignorance to the truth. And once again it is Peter who acts instantly on the insight of his friend. The fisherman is stripped for his work, but greeting a stranger is a religious act which must be done with the modesty which proper clothing denotes.

Peter starts first; we are not told whether he reached the shore first or—as on a previous occasion (20:4)—was overtaken. However it may have been, all the seven disembark and find that there is a meal of bread and fish already prepared for them. The food which they will eat will be his gift, not theirs. Jesus calls them to the meal and, in language which awakes memories of the desert feeding and of the eucharist, takes and gives them bread and fish. In awestruck silence they eat. They dare not ask, "Who are you?", for the answer could only be: "I AM." So they eat what the Lord gives them and the sharing in the meal is the unveiling of the presence (v. 14).

But what about the vast catch of fish? It was so great that the disciples on their own were not able to "haul it in," but Peter, on the command of the Lord, does exactly that. The verb which is used is the one used earlier of drawing people to Jesus as Savior (6:44; 12:32). The promise "I will make you become fishers of men" is being fulfilled in an acted parable. Much ingenuity has been expended over many centuries in seeking to interpret the figure 153, and there is no certainty about the result except that it signifies a vast number. In the Matthean form of the tradition those fishermen will go and "make disciples of all nations." And— a distinctively Johannine theme—this vast multitude will be held together in unity. There will be no "schism" in the net (the same word that is used in 7:43, 9:16, and 10:19). This is possible only because Peter acts in implicit obedience to the Lord.

The commission to Peter will now be expounded in terms

of another parable: the shepherd replaces the fishermen. But the writer who is responsible for including this episode in his story identifies it as the third appearance of Jesus to his disciples. He thus—like St. Paul in I Corinthians 15—omits the appearances to Mary and refers only to those meetings with the assembled disciples which he has recorded in the previous chapter.

21:15-19

When they had finished breakfast, Jesus said to Simon Peter, "Simon, son of John, do you love me more than these?" He said to him, "Yes, Lord; you know that I love you." He said to him, "Feed my lambs." A second time he said to him, "Simon, son of John, do you love me?" He said to him, "Yes, Lord; you know that I love you." He said to him, "Tend my sheep." He said to him the third time, "Simon, son of John, do you love me?" Peter was grieved because he said to him the third time, "Do you love me?" And he said to him, "Lord, you know everything; you know that I love you." Jesus said to him, "Feed my sheep. Truly, truly, I say to you, when you were young, you girded yourself and walked where you would; but when you are old, you will stretch out your hands, and another will gird you and carry you where you do not wish to go." (This he said to show by what death he was to glorify God.) And after this he said to him, "Follow me."

Among all the disciples, Peter was the one who had protested his devotion to Jesus most vehemently, promising to follow him even to death (13:37). But he had three times denied his Lord, and it was he—apparently—who had led the flight from Jerusalem back to the old life of fishing (21:1). Now he is face to face with the friend he has denied and abandoned. Once again, as on that night of threefold apostasy, Jesus looks at him across "a charcoal fire" (18:18 and 21:9). Three times Jesus presses the simple yet painfully searching question "Do you love me?" The question is addressed not to "Peter," for the rock has proved an unstable quicksand. The disciple is addressed by his old name, the name he had before Jesus met and called him by the same lakeside: "Simon, son of John, do you love me more than these [do]?"

Three times Peter answers with an affirmation of his love— but an affirmation which rests its confidence not on the strength of his own love but on the sureness of Jesus' knowledge. "You know everything; you know that I love you." And three times

Jesus solemnly gives to the grieved and humbled disciple the commission to be the shepherd, guiding, guarding, and nourishing the flock which belongs to Jesus.

We have learned that the good shepherd is one who "lays down his life from the sheep" (10:11). Peter has protested his readiness to lay down his life for Jesus, and had demanded on this basis the right to follow. Jesus had told him, "You cannot follow me now; but you shall follow afterward" (13:36f.). Now Peter has learned what following means. In the past he had "followed" according to his own desires and in his own strength. Now he will learn that following Jesus means going the way of the cross (vv. 18-19). And so because he now knows what "following" means he can hear again from the lips of Jesus the word that he desired and was not given earlier: "Follow me."

This "following" along the way of the cross will glorify God, for just as Jesus manifested the glory of God in his death (12:27f.; 13:31f.; 17:1-5), so the same glory will be manifested in the disciples whom he sends into the world (17:10, 22f.).

The threefold denial is wiped out and forgiven in the threefold commissioning. Yet the record is one more reminder that the flock which belongs to Jesus consists not of the righteous but of sinners called to repentance. If Peter has a primacy among the apostles, it is because he has primacy as a forgiven sinner. "You are Peter" is said to the one to whom in the next breath Jesus will say, "Get behind me, Satan" (Matt. 16:18, 23). It is to the fisherman overwhelmed by the realization of his sinfulness that Jesus says, "Do not be afraid; henceforth you will be catching men" (Luke 5:8-10). It is to the disciple who will fall away that Jesus says, "When you have turned again, strengthen your brethren" (Luke 22:31f.).

Peter is to be both a fisher of men and a shepherd. He can be both of them only as he is first a disciple. The key word in the paragraph is "Follow me." Leadership in the Church has to be both missionary and pastoral. The separation of these from one another is always a distortion of churchmanship. They are one insofar as they are rooted in something still more fundamental, in discipleship, in following Jesus along the way of the cross in such a way that those whom he calls may be enabled to follow too, and that so God may be glorified in them (17:20-23).

21:20-25

Peter turned and saw following them the disciple whom Jesus loved, who had lain close to his breast at the supper and had said, "Lord, who is it that is going to betray you?" When Peter saw him, he said to Jesus, "Lord, what about this man?" Jesus said to him, "If it is my will that he remain until I come, what is that to you? Follow me!" The saying spread abroad among the brethren that this disciple was not to die; yet Jesus did not say to him that he was not to die, but, "If it is my will that he remain until I come, what is that to you?"

This is the disciple who is bearing witness to these things, and who has written these things; and we know that his testimony is true.

But there are also many other things which Jesus did; were every one of them to be written, I suppose that the world itself could not contain the books that would be written.

To "follow Jesus" is what it means to be a disciple. The Gospel has shown us what is involved in "following." At the very outset we read that as Jesus was walking he turned, and saw two disciples of John following, and asked them, "What are you looking for?" (1:38) One of these two was Andrew; the other is unnamed. In the intervening period Peter has learned that "following" will mean for him the way of the cross. Now he turns, sees the other disciple, and asks: "What about this man? Is it to be the same road for him too?"

The answer of Jesus is a sharp rebuke. Peter must not turn to look over his shoulder (cf. Luke 9:62). Discipleship means a single-minded following of Jesus, and there is no place for speculation about the discipleship of others. If the Lord wants the other to remain alive while he calls Peter to die, that is not Peter's concern. He has only one responsibility: to follow Jesus.

There is abundant evidence to show that the early Church looked expectantly for the victorious return of Christ within the lifetime of many of its members, even though this eager hope was controlled by the many reminders that no one except the Father knows when that day will be. Did this word of Jesus mean that the unnamed disciple would live to see that day? This, we must suppose, had become an anxious question in the community in which the Gospel was written. Perhaps the unnamed disciple has died and yet the end has not come. Or perhaps he has reached such a great age that—if the Lord did make this promise—the end of all things must be very near. Whichever be the case, the writer wishes to assure his readers that Jesus made no promise that the beloved disciple would remain alive till his coming.

We are left with the picture of two disciples. Both follow Jesus. One of them will glorify God by his death, and to him is entrusted the pastoral care of Christ's flock. The other, the un-named one, is no less a follower of Jesus but he bears witness in a different way. For it is he who was closest to his master and who could discern the true meaning of his master's deeds and words. He is, in fact, the one whose witness is embodied in the book which lies before us. "And we know that his testimony is true." In the Prologue to the Gospel we heard the words of the Church which is the custodian and bearer of this testimony: "We have beheld his glory" (1:14). Now at the end the Church which has treasured the witness of the beloved disciple identifies itself with this witness and affirms that it is true. It is from the same community of faith that we have the opening words of the first Johannine letter affirming that their testimony is of "that which we have seen with our eyes, which we have looked upon and touched with our hands" (I John 1:1). The witness of the beloved disciple comes not as a disembodied word, but as the witness of a community which has found and still finds in that word the power of everlasting life (cf. 20:31 and I John 1:1).

And, once again, we are reminded that what has been re-corded is only a small selection of the immeasurably rich store-house of the memory of Jesus' deeds which has been entrusted to the keeping of those who obey the call which comes from Jesus as his final word to all his disciples: "Follow me."